Scotland's Radicals

Ron Culley
www.ronculley.com
author@ronculley.com

Edited by John McManus

Grosvenor House
Publishing Limited

This book is published by
Grosvenor House Publishing Ltd
Link House
140 The Broadway, Tolworth, Surrey, KT6 7HT.
www.grosvenorhousepublishing.co.uk

A CIP record for this book
is available from the British Library

Paperback ISBN 978-1-83615-493-8
Hardback ISBN 978-1-83615-602-4
eBook ISBN 978-1-83615-494-5

Previous books by Ron Culley

The New Guards/The Kaibab Resolution.
Kennedy & Boyd 2010.
I Belong To Glasgow (foreword by Sir Alex Ferguson)
The Grimsay Press, 2011.
A Confusion of Mandarins Grosvenor House. 2011.
Glasgow Belongs To Me Grosvenor House
(electronic media only) 2012.
The Patriot Game. Grosvenor House 2013.
Shoeshine Man A one-act play. SCDA. 2014.
One Year. Grosvenor House 2015.
Alba: Who Shot Willie McRae? Grosvenor House 2016.
The Last Colony Grosvenor House 2017.
The Never Ending Story (Editor) Downie Allison Downie 2018.
Odyssey Grosvenor House 2018.
The Bootlace Saga (Editor) Downie Allison Downie 2019.
Rebellious Scots To Crush Grosvenor House 2020.
The Odyssean Companion Downie Allison Downie 2021.
Dalriada Grosvenor House 2022.
Firebrand Grosvenor House 2022.
For As Long As But A Hundred Of Us Remain Alive
Grosvenor House 2024.

Web address
www.ronculley.com

Dedicated to my wee brother, Campbell Culley (1953 – 2025), the least radical guy I knew.

Gum biodh fois shìorraidh aige na anam

Photographs

Every biography is covered by a photograph of the individual represented. In almost every case the image was taken from public realm or open source origins to avoid difficulties with copyright. In consequence, because of copyright restrictions and early photographs of some antiquity, certain images are of poorer quality than I would have liked. Throughout I used Wikimedia Commons which provides free to use images. Exceptions to images available in the public domain are that of Ivor Cutler, George MacLeod, Ian Hamilton, David Stirling, Tommy MacPherson and Bud Neil: as follows,

A photograph of the surrealist poet and humourist Ivor Cutler taken by his friend Roger Kohn, at Ivor's flat in Gospel Oak, North London (1973).

© Ron Ferguson of George MacLeod, published by Wild Goose Publications, 4th Floor, Savoy House, 140 Sauchiehall Street, Glasgow G2 3DH, UK.

Ian Hamilton via Scottish Legal News, Scotland's leading independent legal portal serving the entire Scottish legal community.

Major David Stirling. WW2 Productions by Geoffrey John Keating, War Office official photographer.

Colonel Sir Tommy MacPherson. Commando Veterans Archive.

Bud Neil. Courtesy of the Daily Record.

Any image be found not to be credited appropriately, the author would be more than pleased to rectify this in future reprints.

Wikimedia Commons is a free-to-use, openly licensed media repository that serves as a central storage for images, videos and audio files from which these images were taken. The web site holds a collection of over one hundred and twenty three million freely usable media files.

Introduction

Before we kick a ba', I am well aware that this selection of Scotland's radicals may well promote debate regarding the absence…or indeed, the inclusion of many. I acknowledge the certain fact that another list of Scottish radicals equally deserving of inclusion could be assembled easily. I further concede that certain of those selected have a more tenuous relationship with Scotland than some others. But in the main, their radicalism, such as it was, was given life in Scotland or affected it even where they were born furth of that country or travelled subsequently beyond its shores.

However, in one way or another, those listed within (and I confess immediately that they are almost all men) have caused a departure from the accepted norm, have followed their own path and have caused disruption. I should say immediately that it was a priority of the author to incorporate as many women as possible in these chapters. However I was faced with considerable obstacles as history until very recently has tended to relegate the role of women to one of succour and support. This 'hidden history', in consequence, also brought about a 'silent history' but I have attempted to provide a voice for women to have their story told above the din of their male counterparts where possible. I have also had to omit many radicals where insufficient information was available; one-such being the estimable musician, poet and left-winger Freddie Anderson.

Some individuals cited herein were more successful than others. Some were better known than others. Some were celebrated for their adventurism, some incarcerated or transported. Some were put to death. I have incorporated those who were thinkers, who invented new ways of doing things, political radicals, activists, artists and I further confess that choosing and writing certain of these chapters over a glass in some of

Scotland's wonderful hostelries emboldened some of my choices, certain of my words and many of my assessments.

However, while the author has made efforts to ensure that entries are presented in neutral fashion, devoid of bias, there can be little doubt that whilst there are incomparable geniuses…courageous radicals…indubitable originals, included in this compendium, there are also a number who, upon further reflection, did not make the grade. These may form part of a second book on the subject. Paraphrasing without plagiarising is an art as much as a skill that takes some practice to master but I hope I have cleared this bar as information contained within, while largely open source, has been solicited from a vast array of articles, artificial intelligence and books and while this is certainly not an academic work and does not cite sources, my goal has been to assemble, paraphrase and summarise and I would be happy to correct or amend any troublesome or inaccurate tracts in future reprints. Equally, I have incorporated photographs under fair use but would be happy to acknowledge any which require additional recognition in any future reprint.

In ampflication of notions of radicalism, one has to go far beyond mere celebrity. I have not included, for example, Sir Malcolm Rifkind, a much respected Foreign Secretary…but radical he was not. Equally, Donald Dewar, Scotland's *first* First Minister. Important guy but no radical. Kenneth McKeller? He made the Scottish Traditional Music Hall of Fame…but gie's peace!

Nor is there significance in the order in which these individuals are arranged. I could have organised people by birth date, alphabetically, by some judgement of their importance or some other method. Instead, I registered them mostly as I remembered them from a list I made on a long train journey from Glasgow. They've been jumbled up deliberately rather than placed within nomenclatures so as to avoid any presumption that James Watt was more radical than Adam Smith or that James Connolly was more radical than Billy Connolly. The original list was subsequently supplemented by friends who took exception to an exclusion or two…and insisted upon an inclusion or two. It's more of an assemblage of facts about

Scotland's great radicals than new insights although, at least for the author, there were many.

Finally, I repeat, this book doesn't attempt to meet or seek scholarly standards. It is but a canter down the highway of Scotland's rich history of radicals who, one way or another, sought to see things done differently.

Radicals

The Merriam-Webster Dictionary tells us that the word radical was formed from the Latin adjective *radicalis*, which simply meant 'of or relating to a root.' The Latin word *radix* meant 'root.' This meaning was kept when the word *radicalis* came into English as radical, but new meanings developed too. Since a root is at the bottom of something, radical came to describe what is at the base or beginning, in other words, what is basic or fundamental. Later, radical was used to describe something that was different from the usual. That is how it has been applied in these pages.

Those individuals selected to appear here do so not just because they are famous – some are not – but they meet the above definition. In some cases, an individual has been chosen to represent a cluster of like-minded radicals (as if something of that nature was possible). So Hugh MacDiarmaid is chosen from a poets' group which might comprise Robert Garioch, Norman MacCaig, Iain Chrichton-Smith, George Mackay Brown, Jim Carruth, Liz Lochhead and Edwin Morgan. Alex Harvey is chosen over musicians and performers such as Michael Marra or David Byrne. Mungo Park has been set aside in favour of David Livingstone. Others may have made different selections.

It is a given that many radicals fail in their endeavours. Not everyone can change the world so I have been happy to include those who have exhibited radical ideas, aspirations, behaviours, new ways of doing things or have merely spent their lives swimming upstream, railing against conventional thought…those who were disruptive to the norm.

Acknowledgements

My decision to commence writing this book was accompanied by many friends offering helpful suggestions or decrying certain of those selected. I am particularly grateful to Keith Yates who poured over the list on a number of occasions and who offered some great suggestions. Equally Donnie Blair who sent me books and tracts encouraging the inclusion of some Scottish radicals – many whom I'd never even been aware of. Jim Coll sent wonderful ideas from Dunnet Head and George Cuthbert, Donald Anderson and Gerry Cairns pitched in and helped smooth out my understanding of individuals they knew much better than I.

My editor, John McManus can never go unacknowledged. Tirelessly over the years he has drawn errors and ideas to my attention whenever I place a manuscript before him and he, I'm certain, knows just how much I appreciate his efforts. A toast to him.

'So Take my hand in friendship
Be careful as you go
You're worth your weight in silver
You're worth your weight in gold
We've trusted one another
For fifty years and more
Supported one another
As years have come and gone
You're an honest man and noble
A man without a flaw
I wish you great good fortune
I wish you *Slàinte Mhath!*"

Thank you again, John.

My family, as ever, kept oot the road and allowed me space to write this book, and to the many publicans who wondered what a guy was doing with a lap top in a pub…well he was writing a book.

Contents

Scotland's Radicals

Ron Culley

Edited by John McManus

A CHAMPION FOR WOMEN'S RIGHTS AND SOCIAL JUSTICE

Mary Barbour. Activist and Politician. (1865 – 1958)

Mary Barbour was born in 1865, in Kilbarchan, a small village in Renfrewshire. She came from a working-class background. Her parents were Jean Gavin and James Rough who was a handloom weaver. As industrialisation took hold, her family, like many others, experienced economic hardship.

In the 1880s, Mary moved to Glasgow and married David Barbour, an engineer. They settled in Govan, a heavily industrialised area known for its Clydeside shipyards and factories. Like many working-class families, the Barbours lived in overcrowded and insanitary tenement housing. These poor living conditions, combined with her first-hand experience of the struggles faced by working women, fuelled Mary Barbour's passion for social reform.

The outbreak of World War One in 1914 led to a surge in demand for industrial labour, causing a massive influx of workers to cities like Glasgow. With the rising demand for housing, landlords saw an opportunity to increase rents, often without making any improvements to the already dilapidated tenement buildings. Many families, especially those with men away fighting in the war, found themselves unable to afford the rent hikes.

Mary Barbour emerged as a leader in the fight against these unjust rent increases. Alongside other activists, including Agnes Dollan and Helen Crawfurd, she helped organise the Glasgow Women's Housing Association. This group mobilised tenants, particularly women, to resist evictions and demand fair treatment.

The movement reached its peak in November 1915, when landlords attempted to evict tenants who could not pay their rent. In response, thousands of women and children took to the streets, blocking bailiffs from entering homes and organising massive demonstrations. These protests became known as the 1915 Rent Strikes, and the women involved were famously called 'Mrs. Barbour's Army.'

The movement's success forced the British government to intervene, leading to the passage of the Rent Restriction Act in December 1915. This landmark legislation froze rents at pre-war levels and protected tenants from eviction, setting a precedent for future housing policies in the UK. Mary Barbour's leadership in the rent strikes not only improved the lives of thousands of working-class families but also demonstrated the power of grassroots activism.

After the success of the rent strikes, Mary Barbour continued her activism, turning her attention to politics. In 1920, she was elected as one of Glasgow's first woman city councillors, representing the Fairfield ward in Govan as a member of the Independent Labour Party.

As a councillor, Barbour focused on issues affecting working-class families, including housing, healthcare, and child welfare. She played a key role in campaigns for better maternity care, the introduction of child welfare clinics and free school meals for impoverished children. She also advocated for improvements in public housing, pushing for the construction of modern, affordable homes to replace Glasgow's overcrowded tenements.

Barbour was deeply involved in the cooperative movement and supported initiatives that promoted collective ownership and economic fairness. She worked closely with trade unions and women's organisations, ensuring that the voices of working-class women were heard in political decision-making. Mary Barbour retired from politics in 1931 but remained active in social work. She continued to be involved in various welfare initiatives, including support for unemployed workers during the economic downturn of the 1930s.

She passed away on April 2, 1958, but her legacy as a champion of social justice lives on. In recognition of her contributions, campaigns were launched in the 21st century to honour her achievements. In 2018, the Remember Mary Barbour Association successfully campaigned for the erection of a statue in Govan, celebrating her role in the 1915 Rent Strikes. Barbour's work laid the foundation for housing rights and social welfare reforms in Scotland. Her legacy is a testament to the power of grassroots activism, demonstrating how ordinary people – especially women – can bring about significant social and political change.

THE ORATOR

James Maxton. Pacifist, Home Ruler, Red Clydesider (1885 - 1946)

James Maxton was born in Pollokshaws in Glasgow in 1885. He was brought up in Barrhead in Renfrewshire until the age of 12 where his father was a headmaster. His mother was also a schoolteacher. After being educated at Hutchesons Grammar School having won a scholarship to Glasgow University (where he described his political loyalties as lying with the Conservatives; electioneering on their behalf for the university rectorship), Maxton was encouraged to follow an academic career.

By the age of nineteen, thanks to his contact with John Maclean, he became a socialist and joined the Independent Labour Party (ILP) in Barrhead where he was immediately elected literature secretary and began acting as a propagandist on behalf of the ILP at outdoor meetings. He became a schoolteacher, first in Haghill School then in St James' School, Bridgeton, one of the poorer districts of Glasgow where his belief in socialism grew exponentially as he witnessed the dreadful poverty experienced by many of the children he taught. He became involved in the formation of teachers' unions in Scotland, including the Educational Institute of Scotland and the Scottish Socialist Teachers' Society.

Maxton went on to become one of the leading figures in the ILP, was a strong opponent of conscription during the First World War, and was imprisoned for a year in Calton Jail, Edinburgh as a result. It was while interned in this squalid and harsh prison occupying a prominent site on the rocky slope of Calton Hill in Edinburgh, that Maxton became engaged to Sarah (Sissie) McCallum, later to become Mrs Maxton and the mother of his son James. She died a year after giving birth. Young James was taken care of by his aunts who lived in Barrhead and Maxton became a regular visitor to his home town. As a conscientious objector who refused all 'war work', he spent much of the rest of the war as a 'hauder oan' to a plater on barges.

When the war ended, Maxton stood as ILP candidate for Bridgeton but was defeated by the Conservative candidate, MacCallum Scott, whom he later converted to the ILP. However, he won the seat in 1922 and became one of the ten Red Clydesiders who challenged the more complacent Labour members in Westminster. He represented Bridgeton for the next twenty-four years, although he never held office but developed a substantial reputation and was held in considerable standing in the House.

In 1927, Maxton was elected International Chairman of the League Against Imperialism at its General Council meeting in Brussels and re-elected to the same post at the 1929 Conference in Frankfurt. A prominent proponent of Home Rule for Scotland, he broke with Ramsay MacDonald and the second minority Labour government, becoming one of its most bitter critics. For many years, the ILP acted as a ginger group within the Labour Party but, as the leader of the ILP, he disaffiliated the group from the mainstream Labour Party in 1932. His skilful oratory won him wide popularity, although some biographers believed the appeal of his oratorical style somewhat detracted from the political effectiveness of his speeches.They also argued that Maxton and his parliamentarian friend and fellow ILP Member, John Wheatley were complementary: the former, the missionary and orator; the latter, the shrewd and practical politician. It was Wheatley's task to devise the strategy and tactics and to detail political programmes. It was Maxton's task to win popularity for policies and to expound their general principles to the wider public – a responsibility he took seriously and at which he was most effective.

Following the King's abdication in 1936, Maxton proposed a republican amendment to the Abdication Bill, which would have turned the UK into a republic arguing that the monarchy 'had now outlived its usefulness'.

Commentators suggest that Maxton had a preference for westerns and detective novels, and did little serious reading apart from his early study of Marxism. Some claimed indolence. However, he was widely popular as an orator who inspired human beings to work and struggle for socialism and remained the elected member for Bridgeton until his death in Largs in 1946. Winston Churchill said of him, 'He was the greatest parliamentarian of his day'.

The Maxton Papers are held in Glasgow University's digital library.

THE PHILOSOPHER OF CIVIL SOCIETY

Adam Ferguson. Philosopher (1723 – 1816)

Born in Logierait, Perthshire in 1723, Adam Ferguson was the son of a Presbyterian minister. He was educated at the University of St Andrews where he studied moral philosophy and theology. Though initially destined for the church, Ferguson's interests extended beyond theology into history, ethics, and politics. His intellectual journey led him to Edinburgh, where he became part of the vibrant Scottish Enlightenment circles that included Adam Smith, David Hume and William Robertson.

Before fully devoting himself to academia, Ferguson served as a chaplain to the Black Watch regiment during the 1745 Jacobite Rebellion. This experience exposed him to military life and provided insights into the nature of war, discipline and social organisation; themes that later appeared in his writings.

Ferguson's most influential work, '*An Essay on the History of Civil Society*', was published in 1767. In it, he examined the progression of human societies from primitive conditions to advanced civilisations. His approach was historical and sociological, marking a departure from the purely economic focus of Adam Smith's '*The Wealth of Nations*' and the individualistic rationalism of Hobbes and Locke.

Ferguson argued that human beings are naturally social creatures and that society evolves through conflict, cooperation and the struggle for survival. Unlike philosophers who saw civilisation as a steady improvement from barbarism, Ferguson believed that social and moral decay often accompanied material progress. He was particularly concerned with the weakening of civic virtue in commercial societies, warning that excessive luxury, ease, and individualism could undermine the collective good.

One of his key ideas was that conflict and competition were not inherently negative but could serve as forces for innovation and societal strength. His emphasis on civic engagement and public virtue resonated with later republican thinkers and influenced debates on democracy and governance. He was a strong advocate of civic virtue, the idea that citizens must actively participate in public life to maintain a free and stable society. Unlike Adam Smith, who emphasised the benefits of economic self-interest, Ferguson worried that unchecked capitalism could erode social cohesion. He feared that a society driven solely by commerce and private interests would lead to moral decline and political corruption.

His work was influential in shaping ideas about participatory democracy and the role of civic engagement in maintaining a just society. Some of his warnings about the dangers of commercialism foreshadowed later critiques of capitalism by thinkers like Karl Marx. However, unlike Marx, Ferguson did not advocate for class struggle but rather for a balance between economic development and communal responsibility.

The Scottish Enlightenment was characterised by an emphasis on reason, empirical observation and the study of human nature. Ferguson, alongside Adam Smith, David Hume and Dugald Stewart, contributed to this intellectual movement by exploring how societies develop and sustain themselves. His work bridged philosophy, history, and early sociology, making him one of the first thinkers to systematically analyse social structures.

Ferguson spent much of his career as a professor at the University of Edinburgh, where he taught moral philosophy. His lectures attracted students from across Europe, many of whom went on to become influential thinkers and politicians.

Ferguson's legacy lies in his contributions to the study of civil society, his emphasis on civic virtue and his insights into the dynamics of social and political life. His work remains a valuable resource for those interested in the relationship between individual liberty, economic systems and the health of democratic institutions. He was a pioneering thinker whose ideas about civil society, political engagement and the challenges of commercialism continue to resonate today. He warned against the moral and social dangers of unchecked capitalism while advocating for active citizenship and public virtue. His work provides important lessons for contemporary debates on democracy, governance and the balance between economic growth and social responsibility. He is regarded as one of the founders of modern sociology. Americans Thomas Jefferson and James Madison were familiar with Ferguson's work and drew upon his insights in their discussions of American governance.

YOU'LL NEVER WALK ALONE

William Shankly OBE. Footballer and Football Manager (1913 – 1981)

Bill Shankly was born in 1913, into a working-class family in Glenbuck, a small mining village known for producing many professional footballers despite its small size. Growing up in a close-knit community where football was a passion, Shankly quickly developed a love for the game. His early experiences in the coal mines shaped his work ethic and his belief in the value of teamwork and solidarity, qualities that would later define his managerial philosophy.

Shankly began his professional playing career with Carlisle United in 1932. He soon moved to Preston North End, where he enjoyed a successful career as a right-half and was known for his determination, tenacity and tactical awareness on the pitch. He helped Preston win the FA Cup in 1938 and earned seven caps for the Scottish national team. His playing career was interrupted by World War Two, but he continued to play in wartime matches and returned to Preston afterward, retiring as a player in 1949.

After retiring from playing, Shankly transitioned into management, beginning with Carlisle United. His managerial career took him to Grimsby Town, Workington, and Huddersfield Town. During these early years, Shankly honed his coaching philosophy, emphasising fitness, discipline, and a strong work ethic.

It was at Huddersfield that Shankly's talent for developing young players became evident. He nurtured future stars like Denis Law, demonstrating his ability to spot and cultivate talent. However, it was his move to Liverpool in 1959 that marked the turning point of his managerial career and changed the trajectory of the club forever.

When Shankly took over as manager of Liverpool, the club was languishing in the Second Division, struggling both on and off the pitch.

The facilities were outdated, the team lacked cohesion, and the club had not won a major trophy in years. Shankly saw the potential in Liverpool and set about transforming the club from top to bottom.

One of Shankly's first actions was to overhaul the club's training facilities at Melwood. He implemented new training methods, focused on fitness and ball control and introduced a strong sense of discipline and professionalism. He also made shrewd signings, bringing in players like Ian St. John and Ron Yeats who would become the backbone of his successful early teams.

Shankly's charismatic leadership and motivational skills quickly galvanised the players and the supporters. He forged a strong bond with the fans, famously referring to them as supporters of the *people's* club and fostering a sense of unity between the team and the community. His wit, passion, and understanding of the game endeared him to the Kop, Liverpool's famous supporters' section.

Under Shankly's guidance, Liverpool achieved promotion to the First Division in 1962. This was just the beginning of an era of unprecedented success. In 1964, Liverpool won the league title, their first in seventeen years. The following year, they won the FA Cup for the first time in the club's history, defeating Leeds United in the final.

Shankly's Liverpool continued to dominate English football, winning another league title in 1966 and again in 1973. The latter year also saw Liverpool claim their first European trophy, the UEFA Cup, signalling the club's arrival on the continental stage. In 1974, to the shock of fans and players alike, Shankly announced his retirement from football management. His final game in charge was a resounding victory in the FA Cup final, where Liverpool defeated Newcastle United 3-0. Shankly left behind a club transformed, both in terms of its infrastructure and its winning mentality, instilling a culture of excellence, professionalism, and a deep connection with the supporters. His famous quotes, such as "Football is not a matter of life and death… it's much more important than that," encapsulate his passion for the game and his influence on football culture.

Bill Shankly passed away on September 29, 1981, but his legacy lives on. His statue outside Anfield, Liverpool's home ground, stands as a testament to his enduring impact. Shankly is remembered not only as one of football's greatest managers but also as a man who transformed Liverpool FC into a global powerhouse.

DON ROBERTO

Robert Bontine Cunninghame Graham.
Scottish politician, writer, journalist and adventurer.
(1852 - 1936)

Robert Cunninghame Graham was the eldest son of Major William Bontine and the Hon. Anne Elizabeth Elphinstone-Fleeming, daughter of Admiral Charles Elphinstone-Fleeming of Cumbernauld and a Spanish noblewoman called Doña Catalina Paulina Alessandro de Jiménez. The first language Cunninghame Graham learned was his mother's maternal tongue, Spanish.

He spent most of his childhood on the family estate of Findlaystone in Renfrewshire and at Ardoch in Dumbartonshire. Educated at Harrow, Cunninghame Graham finished his education in Brussels before moving to Argentina for seven years to make his fortune cattle ranching. He became known as a great adventurer and gaucho, a skilled horseman, reputed to be brave and unruly and was affectionately known as *Don Roberto* on account both of his aristocratic origins and his mastery of the Spanish language. He also prospected for gold in Spain, befriended Buffalo Bill in Texas and taught fencing in Mexico City.

Returning to the UK in 1883, he became interested in politics and attended socialist meetings where he heard and met Keir Hardy. Despite his wealthy origins, Graham was converted to socialism, began to speak at public meetings and became an impressive orator. In the 1886 general election, he stood as a Liberal candidate in Lanarkshire where his election programme was extremely radical and called for the abolition of the House of Lords, universal suffrage, nationalisation of key industries and Scottish, Irish and Indian Independence. He won and was the first self-declared socialist to be elected to the House as well as being the first elected member ever suspended for swearing, having used the word, 'damn!'

Cunninghame Graham was frustrated with the House of Commons, and labelled it variously 'a factory of hot air', the 'national gasworks' and an 'asylum of incapables.'

In 1886, he helped establish the Scottish Home Rule Association, and made several attempts to persuade fellow MPs of the desirability of a Scottish Parliament. Attending a protest demonstration in London in 1887 he was beaten, arrested, and sentenced to six weeks imprisonment. For a second time he was also suspended from the House of Commons.

While in the House of Commons, Cunninghame Graham became increasingly more radical, went on to found the Scottish Labour Party with Keir Hardy in 1888. He sat in the House of Commons for only six years, but never lost his interest in politics. He was also the founder of the National Party of Scotland in 1928 and, in 1934, became the first President of the Scottish National Party shortly before his death.

He was tireless in his journalism and letter-writing, striving constantly to arouse the conscience of those in power on a whole range of social and humanitarian issues. In July 1889 he attended the Marxist Congress of the Second International in Paris and in 1890 made a speech in Calais that was considered by the authorities to be so revolutionary that he was arrested and expelled from France.

He was a man of action who embodied a host of apparently contrary positions with ease. Deeply private and loathe to reveal his inner life in his copious writings, he was sociable and gregarious. He died in Argentina in 1936, where his body lay in state for twenty-four hours, while a constant stream of people, including the President of the Republic, filed by reverently. Thousands lined the streets of Buenos Aires as his two favourite horses followed the bier with Cunninghame Graham's boots reversed in the stirrups before the coffin made its last, long journey back to Ardoch House, where it rested in the oval drawing room and where the funeral took place, prior to burial at Inchmahome Priory on the Lake of Menteith.

On his monument, there is portrait of his famous horse Pampa, which was an Argentine mustang that he rescued from pulling trams in Glasgow and thereafter rode for some 20 years. It has the inscription: 'To Pampa my black Argentine whom I rode for twenty years without a fall. May the earth lie light upon him as lightly as he trod upon its face ... Don Roberto.

PIONEER OF TELEVISION

John Logie Baird FRSE. Inventor (1888-1946)

John Logie Baird was born in 1888, in Helensburgh, into a middle-class family. His father was Reverend John Baird, the Church of Scotland minister for the local St Bride's Church, and Jessie Morrison Inglis, the daughter of a wealthy shipbuilder. Baird showed an early interest in science and technology, often experimenting with electrical devices and mechanical systems during his youth.

He attended Larchfield Academy in Helensburgh and later enrolled at the University of Glasgow, where he studied electrical engineering. However, his studies were interrupted by the outbreak of World War One. He did not serve in the military due to health issues, but continued to pursue his interests in engineering and innovation.

Baird's early career was marked by a series of inventive projects. After the war, he worked on various entrepreneurial ventures, including the development of a rust-resistant glass and a pneumatic shoe sole. While these projects did not achieve commercial success, they demonstrated his inventive spirit and determination.

Baird's interest in television began to take shape in the early 1920s. He was fascinated by the idea of transmitting moving images over long distances, a concept that had intrigued inventors for decades. Baird's approach to solving this challenge was rooted in his practical engineering skills and an unyielding passion for experimentation.

Baird's most significant breakthrough came in 1924 when he successfully transmitted the first flickering images of a human face. He used a mechanical system known as the 'Nipkow disk' which was invented by Paul Nipkow in 1884. The Nipkow disk was a rotating disk with a series of holes arranged in a spiral pattern, which scanned images line by line. Baird's adaptation of this technology enabled him to transmit rudimentary images, marking a significant step toward the development of television.

In 1925, Baird achieved another milestone by demonstrating the first live, moving television images at Selfridges department store in London. This public demonstration attracted widespread attention and established Baird as a leading figure in television innovation. The following year, he made the first transatlantic television transmission from London to New York, showcasing the potential of television as a global communication medium.

In 1927, Baird founded the Baird Television Development Company, which aimed to commercialise his television technology. He continued to refine his mechanical television system, improving image quality and developing colour and stereoscopic (3D) television. His work culminated in the first-ever television broadcast by the British Broadcasting Corporation in 1929, using Baird's technology.

Despite his early successes, Baird faced significant challenges and competition. The emergence of electronic television systems, developed by innovators like Philo Farnsworth and Vladimir Zworykin, posed a serious threat to Baird's mechanical approach. Electronic television offered superior image quality and greater scalability, which eventually led to the decline of mechanical systems. Baird continued to innovate, exploring areas such as colour television and large-screen projection systems. However, the rapid advancement of electronic television technology overshadowed his later work. By the 1930s, electronic television had become the dominant standard, and Baird's contributions were often overlooked in favour of his electronic counterparts.

John Logie Baird's contributions to television technology remain significant despite the challenges he faced. His pioneering work laid the foundation for the development of modern television, demonstrating the feasibility of transmitting moving images and inspiring future innovations. Baird's achievements were recognised later in his life, and he received several honours for his contributions to science and technology. In 2006, he was inducted into the National Inventors Hall of Fame, and his legacy is celebrated in numerous exhibitions and museums dedicated to the history of television.

John Logie Baird's pioneering work in the field of television has left an enduring legacy. His mechanical television system was the first to demonstrate the practical transmission of moving images, paving the way for the development of modern television.

HAVE YE SEEN MA RED YO-YO?

Matthew (Matt) McGinn. Singer and Songwriter (1928 - 1977)

Born the eighth child in a family of nine, Matt McGinn grew up in Glasgow's Gallowgate, in the Calton community where today the city's market called the Barras are located. He had a troubled childhood and was sent to an Approved School – a residential institution for young offenders – at the age of twelve after being convicted of theft.

He left the school and a friend introduced him to left-wing politics which McGinn credited with saving him from a life of petty crime. In 1949, he joined the Communist Party and during a Party meeting, he met his future wife, Jannette Gallagher. In 1956, McGinn went to work at the Guest, Keen & Nettlefolds, factory in Hillington in Glasgow where driveshaft and other car components were manufactured. There he encountered trade unionism and attended night classes where he educated himself so well that, at the age of thirty-one, he won a union scholarship to attend Ruskin College, part of the University of West London in Oxford from which he graduated with a diploma in Economics and Political Science. He would later qualify as a teacher in Huddersfield before returning to work in teaching in Lanarkshire and then as organiser of the Gorbals Adventure Playground, the first of its kind in Scotland.

His first foray into songwriting and musical performance came when he entered a competition in 1991 where his work, '*The Foreman O'Rourke*' was the prize-winning song in the Reynolds News Competition, judged by Bert Lloyd, Peggie Seeger and Charles Parker. A bullying foreman jumps at a worker, who steps aside and the foreman falls into the lavatory pan. The worker flushes the toilet and drowns him. The worker is waiting to hang.

His career in music began during the folk revival of the 1960s but, while others leaned towards what they perceived as traditional Scottish music, McGinn carved his own niche as a humourist as well as a singer/songwriter. His left-wing, Ruskin College background influencing him, it wasn't long before McGinn became involved with socialist politics. He became heavily involved in the anti-Polaris crusade and began to write protest songs. He was noticed by Pete Seeger who invited him to perform at New York's Carnegie Hall alongside Bob Dylan.

He became a prolific songwriter, drawing on his experiences of Glasgow life for much of his material. He was a republican, trade unionist and a member of the Communist Party of Great Britain who embraced the Folk Song Revival of the 60s and brought to this his talent as a poet, his humour and his wealth of knowledge and experience of the ordinary folk of Glasgow and West of Scotland, using his melodies as a vehicle to express and propagate his beliefs and politics.

McGinn recorded some thirty-six albums, eighteen on his own, occasionally as part of an ensemble cast along with a number of single records. His most popular recordings included, *'Red Yo-yo', 'The Rolling Hills of the Borders', 'The Butchers of Glasgow', 'The Big Effen Bee', 'Skinny Malinky Longlegs', 'Gallowgate Calypso', 'The Ibrox Disaster' and 'The Wee Kirkcudbright Centipede'.* In an attempt to deal with Glasgow's religious bigotry, he wrote a song that incorporated two of the most established songs from each side of the divide. He said, 'Since I like the words of Kevin Barry which tells of one of the finest young Irishmen who laid down their lives for their country's independence and since I find The Sash a stirring tune, I decided to combine the two into a song dedicated to Orange-Fenian unity.'

In 1975, McGinn's first novel about his time in approved school *'Fry the Little Fishes'* was published.

McGinn died on 5 January 1977, aged 48, of smoke inhalation, setting fire to his sofa after falling asleep with a lit cigarette in his hand. The post mortem revealed that there was no trace of alcohol in McGinn's blood. A Blue Plaque was installed on the exterior wall of the Auld Burnt Barns Pub in Ross Street next to where he was born.

THE FATHER OF SCOTTISH DEMOCRACY

Thomas Muir of Huntershill. Advocate and Activist (1765 - 1798)

His family originally hailing from Kirkintilloch, Thomas Muir was born in Glasgow on 24 August 1765, the son of James Muir, a merchant and Margaret Smith. He attended the University of Glasgow from the age of 12 years and graduated with an MA at the age of 17 years.

He was an Advocate in Law at the age of 22 years and practiced in Glasgow and Edinburgh. A product of the 'Scottish Enlightenment' he became a noted reformer and was a leader of Scottish 'The Friends of the People', the 'United Scotsmen' and a member of the 'United Irishmen'. Under his influence parliamentary reform societies were established all over Scotland.

Muir was arrested on 4th August 1793. The charges laid against him were that 'he attended meetings at Kirkintilloch and Milton, of a society for reform, in which he had delivered speeches in which he seditiously endeavoured to represent the government as oppressive and tyrannical; that he exhorted three people residing in Cadder, to buy and read Paine's '*Rights of Man*'; and that he circulated the work of Thomas Paine, *'A Declaration of Rights'*, to the Friends of Reform in Paisley.'

At his trial, he defended himself saying, *"What has been my crime? Not the lending to a relation of mine a copy of Mr Paine's work; not the giving away a few copies of an innocent and constitutional publication; but for having dared to be a strenuous and active advocate for an equal representation of the people, in the house of the people."*

He continued, *"From my infancy to this moment, I have devoted myself to the cause of the people. It is a good cause. It shall ultimately prevail. It shall finally triumph. As for me, I am careless and indifferent to my fate. I can look danger, and I can look death in the face, for I am shielded by the consciousness of my own rectitude. I may be condemned to languish in the recesses of a dungeon. I may be doomed to ascend the scaffold. Nothing can deprive me of the recollection of the past; nothing can destroy my inward peace of mind, arising from the remembrance of having discharged my duty."*

His trial caused a sensation and he became a renowned international figure. People around the world took an interest in his exploits because they recognised that he was one of the few people unreservedly promoting the idea of universal suffrage. Following his trial in Edinburgh, the twenty-eight years old Muir was found guilty by the draconian Lord Braxfield of having created disaffection by means of libel and seditious speeches and was banished to Botany Bay, then an open oceanic embayment (now Sydney) in Australia for fourteen years. He was held prisoner in London for eight months, some of that time in a prison ship on the Thames. Despite strenuous efforts by parliamentarians to have his sentence declared illegal, he was sent to Australia on 2 May 1794.

He escaped from Australia by securing a rowing boat and reaching an American sailing ship, *'The Otter'* which had berthed to take on supplies. He persuaded the captain to take him on board when the ship left. He'd spent sixteen months in Botany Bay before setting off on a journey across the Pacific Ocean, the Americas and the Atlantic. Caught in a sea battle between England and Spain off Cadiz, his face was badly wounded and he lost his left eye. He eventually arrived in France, where he was celebrated as a hero but never fully recovered from his injuries and died in 1799, still a young man.

Thomas Muir and Robert Burns were contemporaries. Muir's trial made headlines in the national and international newspapers and many of the ideals Burns expresses in *'A Man's A Man For A That'* are values Thomas Muir expressed and made public. As an indication of the difficult times in which these men were living Burns cautiously left his song unsigned when it was first printed in 1795.

Thomas Muir was a Scottish Martyr, an 18th Century political reformer. He is honoured by a large obelisk in Old Calton Hill Cemetery in Edinburgh that dominates the Edinburgh sky-line, a second at Nunhead Cemetery in London and a cairn in Huntershill Village in Bishopbriggs where the local library has a permanent exhibition in his honour.

The Scottish Representation of the People Act of 1832 eventually brought about the beginning of change as 5,000 electors of the 2,300,000 population increased to 65,000 voters and he was pardoned posthumously along with another four patriots in 1838.

SELECTED QUOTES

Mary Barbour

"I hope the workers will be greatly daring in their demands, not only for better homes but for a higher standard of living generally."

James Maxton (To Labour Leader Ramsay MacDonald at the dispatch box)

"Sit down, man! You're a bloody tragedy!"

"All I say is, if you cannot ride two horses you have no right to be in the bloody circus." (When opposing disaffiliation of the Scottish Independent Labour Party from the Labour Party)

"In the interests of economy they condemned hundreds of children to death and I call it murder."

Bill Shankly

"Football is not a matter of life and death... it's much more important than that!"

"A football team is like a piano. You need eight men to carry it and three who can play the damn thing."

"Take that bandage off. And what do you mean about *your* knee? It's *Liverpool's* knee!" (When Tommy Smith told him that he'd injured his knee)

"Me, havin' no education, I had to use my brains!"

John Logie Baird

"Cathode-ray tubes are the most important items in a television receiver."

"There is no hope for television by means of cathode-ray tubes."

Matt McGinn

"I couldn't play an instrument and my voice has been described as a mixture of lumpy porridge and broken glass and here I was being booked for (Carnegie Hall) the world's most celebrated concert hall!"

"It was almost my first paid engagement at a fee of two hundred dollars against Bob Dylan's sixty dollars."

"Oh the butchers of Glasgow they've a' got their pride. But they'll tell ye that Willie's the prince. For Willie the butcher, he murdered his wife…and sold her for mutton an' mince!"

"I work all day and I work all night, tae hell wi' you Jack, I'm all right. Three nights and a Sunday double time."

Thomas Muir

"Gentlemen, from my infancy to this moment I have devoted myself to the cause of the people. It is a good cause – it shall ultimately prevail – it shall finally triumph."

"I admit that I exerted every effort to procure a more equal representation of the people in the House of Commons. If that be a crime, I plead guilty to the charge. I acknowledge that I considered the issue of parliamentary reform to be essential to the salvation of my country".

"We do not, we cannot, consider ourselves as mowed and melted down into another country. Have we not distinct Courts, Judges, Juries, Laws, etc.?"

THE HOUSING CRUSADER.

John Wheatley. Socialist Politician (1869 - 1930)

John Wheatley, the eldest child of Thomas Wheatley, a labourer, and his wife, Johanna Ryan, was born in Bonmahon, County Waterford in Ireland. While aged seven, he, his parents and nine siblings moved to Braehead in Lanarkshire where he attended St Bridget's Catholic Parish School in Baillieston, about 7 miles east of Glasgow city centre where the local church and its priests were a powerful influence upon him. According to Ian.S.Wood, his biographer and a distinguished military historian, 'All his life Catholic beliefs would be a point of reference for his political thinking and activism'.

Aged fourteen, he want down to work the seams in the local pits as a miner. In 1893 he left the mine and became a publican, later joining his brother to run a grocery shop in nearby Shettleston. The business failed eight years later but Wheatley, who had been attending evening classes for many years, found work as a reporter for the Glasgow Catholic Observer, a newspaper with an substantial circulation among Roman Catholics of Irish descent in west and central Scotland. In 1906, aged thirty-seven, Wheatley was converted to socialism forming the Catholic Socialist Society and joining the Independent Labour Party.

The following year, Wheatley started a printing business called Hoxton and Walsh which dealt with Catholic church and Labour Party contracts. He also began writing and publishing political pamphlets including, *'How The Miners Are Robbed'* and '*Miners, Mines and Misery'*.

Wheatley was elected to the Lanarkshire County Council and Glasgow Corporation. His abiding interest was working class housing and he proposed a scheme for the building of municipal cottages instead of tenements in the city of Glasgow.

Wheatley was opposed to Britain's involvement in the First World War. In August 1914 he opposed Britain's declaration of war on Germany and helped to create the Glasgow branch of the Union of Democratic

Control which campaigned for a negotiated peace. The following year he played a major role in the Glasgow Rent Strike and fought against conscription. In 1920 Wheatley was now the leading political figure in Glasgow Corporation and two years later was one of the ten Labour candidates elected to represent the city in Westminster. Ramsay MacDonald, the Labour Leader disapproved of Wheatley's fiery temper - particularly when he (along with James Maxton) was suspended for referring to the Tory government's proposed cut in grants to child-welfare centres as murder. That said, MacDonald respected his administrative abilities and when he took office as PM in January 1924, he appointed Wheatley as his Minister of Health.

Wheatley viewed affordable and safe housing as fundamental to good health and was passionate about improving matters. He brought forward the Housing (Financial Provisions) Act and as historian Ian Wood pointed out: "Wheatley's Act was the only major legislative achievement of the 1924 Labour government. Until its subsidy provisions were repealed by the National Government in 1934, a substantial proportion of all rented local authority housing in Britain was built under its terms and sixty years later there were still people in Scotland who spoke of Wheatley houses. The act was a complex one, bringing together trade unions, building firms and local authorities in a scheme to tackle a housing shortage which was guaranteed central government funding provided that building standards set by the act were adhered to. The act did little for actual slum clearance but it hugely enhanced Wheatley's reputation despite the loss of a companion measure, the Building Materials Bill, which would have given central government a wide range of controls over supplies of building materials to local councils operating the Housing Act."

Labour did poorly and lost the 1924 General Election, although Wheatley retained his seat while criticising MacDonald's move to the right. As a result, despite his obvious abilities, he was not appointed to the next, successful 1929 Labour Government.

Since being appointed Minister of Health in 1924, Wheatley, began to suffer from high blood-pressure and died from a cerebral haemorrhage in1930. His burial at Glasgow's Dalbeth cemetery was the biggest political funeral the city had seen since that of John Maclean.

THE FATHER OF ECONOMICS

Adam Smith, Economist and Philosopher (1723 - 1790)

Adam Smith was born in Kirkcaldy in 1723 although the actual date and time of his birth is contested. He was to become known as *'the Father of Economics'* and '*the Founder of Moral Philosophy'*. He was the son by the second marriage of Adam Smith who was an advocate and judge in Kirkcaldy but who died two months before his birth leaving his mother, Margaret Douglas, daughter of Robert Douglas of Strathendry, a widow. Few events in Smith's early childhood are known. However Smith's biographer, John Rae records that Smith was abducted by gypsies at the age of three before being rescued after pursuit was mounted resulting in young Adam thereby being abandoned by his would-be captors. He also records that Smith was close to his mother, and attended the Burgh School of Kirkcaldy, learning Latin, mathematics, history, and writing, his school then regarded as one of the best secondary schools in Scotland at that period.

He enrolled at the University of Glasgow aged fourteen and studied moral philosophy, developing his passion for the philosophical concepts of reason, free speech and civil liberties. In 1740, while still a young man aged seventeen, he undertook postgraduate studies at Balliol College, Oxford but was very critical of their teaching writing, 'In the University of Oxford, the greater part of the public professors have, for these many years, given up altogether even the pretence of teaching' and recorded that when Oxford academics discovered him reading a copy of David Hume's *'A Treatise of Human nature'* they confiscated his book and punished him severely for reading it. Nevertheless, he took the opportunity while at Oxford to teach himself several subjects by reading widely from the shelves of the Bodleian Libraries. His time at Oxford was not a happy period and he seems to have had a nervous breakdown. His years there were spent largely in self-education from which he obtained a firm grasp of both classical and contemporary philosophy before leaving the college before graduating and returning to Scotland.

Upon his return, Smith cast about for employment. Using some connections generated by his mother's family, he was afforded an opportunity to give a series of public lectures in Edinburgh.

The lectures made a deep impression on some of Smith's contemporaries and in 1751 at the age of twenty-seven, he was appointed Professor of Logic at Glasgow University before being promoted to the better-paid Professorship of Moral Philosophy, a subject that embraced the wider fields of natural theology, political economy and ethics. During his years spent teaching at Glasgow University, Smith worked on producing some of his lectures in book form. His subsequent highly acclaimed book, '*The Theory of Moral Sentiments*' was published in 1759 and underpinned much of his later work. Four year later, in 1763, Smith moved to France to accept the position as a personal tutor to the stepson of Charles Townshend, an amateur economist who was to become a future Chancellor of the Exchequer. During his time in France, Smith met and counted as his contemporaries Benjamin Franklin and the philosophers David Hume and François-Marie Arouet, better known by his *nom de plume* M. de Voltaire who was a French enlightenment writer, philosopher, satirist, and historian. While he was in France, he worked on his book *'An Inquiry into the Nature and Causes of the Wealth of Nations'*, generally referred to by its shortened title *'The Wealth of Nations'* which was published in 1776 and is considered his *magnum opus;* his masterpiece, often referred to as 'the Bible of Capitalism'. Five editions of *The Wealth of Nations* were published during Smith's lifetime: in 1776, 1778, 1784, 1786 and 1789. Numerous editions appeared after Smith's death in 1790. Smith's ideas on free markets, assembly-line production, and gross domestic product are the basis of classical economics and influenced several authors and economists, such as Karl Marx as well as governments and organisations, settling for the first time, the earliest formulation of a comprehensive system of political economy. He argued that social harmony would emerge naturally as human beings struggled to find ways to live and work with each other and that self-interest, as if guided by an 'invisible hand' would enable bargains to be struck within a population and that a nation's resources would be drawn automatically to ends that people valued most highly. *The Wealth Of Nations* was therefore not just a study of economics but a survey of about life, welfare, political institutions, the law, and morality. The first edition sold out in six months and four more editions of the book were published during Smith's lifetime. Numerous editions appeared after his death in 1790.

He died in 1790 in Edinburgh and is buried in Canongate Kirkyard near the Scottish Parliament.

THE SCOTTISH LITERARY RENAISSANCE

Christopher Murray Grieve (Hugh MacDiarmid). Poet and Intellectual (1892 - 1978)

Christopher Murray Grieve was born in 1892, in Langholm, in the Scottish Borders. His father was a postman, and his mother was a schoolteacher, instilling in him a love of learning from an early age. Growing up in this rural environment exposed him to the natural beauty of Scotland, which would later feature prominently in his poetry.

Grieve was an academically gifted child. He attended Langholm Academy before enrolling at the University of Edinburgh, where he studied for a brief period before World War One interrupted his education. Even in his youth, he showed an intense interest in literature, politics, and the Scots language, influenced by writers like Robert Burns and European intellectuals.

The outbreak of World War I had a profound impact on Grieve. He served in the Royal Army Medical Corps in Greece where the harsh realities of war deepened his political consciousness and radicalised his worldview. After the war, Grieve returned to Scotland, married Peggy Skinner (who later left him for the local coal man) settled in the Montrose area and began writing poetry, disillusioned by British imperialism and the social inequalities he observed. His experiences abroad and at home catalysed his growing interest in Scottish nationalism and socialist politics, setting the stage for his dual career as both poet and political activist.

In the early 1920s, Grieve adopted the pseudonym Hugh MacDiarmid to distinguish his literary work from his journalistic career. This name, rich in historical and cultural resonance, symbolised his desire to reconnect with Scotland's literary past while forging a modern identity.

MacDiarmid's literary ambitions coincided with his leadership in what became known as the Scottish Literary Renaissance. This movement sought to revitalise Scottish culture particularly through the use of

Lallans (a literary form of the Scots language), blending traditional vernacular with modernist experimentation.

His seminal work, *'A Drunk Man Looks at the Thistle'* is widely regarded as one of the greatest Scottish poems of the 20th century. Using a mixture of Scots and English, MacDiarmid challenged conventional poetic forms, drawing on influences from modernist poetry, philosophy, and Scottish folklore. His poetry was revolutionary not just in its language but also in its content. He tackled themes of national identity, cultural revival, and political independence with intellectual rigour and emotional intensity.

In parallel with his literary career, MacDiarmid was deeply involved in politics, often courting controversy due to his shifting allegiances. He was a founding member of the National Party of Scotland in 1928, which later merged to become the Scottish National Party and was a passionate advocate for Scottish independence, believing that cultural revival was inseparable from political sovereignty. However, his political journey was far from straightforward. Disillusioned with the SNP's limited socialist agenda, he gravitated towards communism in the 1930s, joining the Communist Party of Great Britain. This ideological shift caused tension within nationalist circles due to his admiration for figures like Vladimir Lenin. However, his flirtation with radical leftist politics also led to his expulsion from the Communist Party during the Cold War era primarily because of his nationalist leanings. Despite these ideological contradictions, MacDiarmid's political writings remained influential. He believed that art and politics were inseparable and that poetry could be a powerful vehicle for social change. His essays and critiques, often scathing and provocative, challenged the complacency of both political and literary establishments.

In his later years, MacDiarmid continued to write prolifically, producing both poetry and essays that reflected his enduring commitment to Scotland's cultural and political future.

MacDiarmid's poetry remained challenging, often dense with allusions and complex ideas, which limited his mainstream popularity but cemented his reputation as a literary innovator.

He passed away in 1978, in Biggar, South Lanarkshire leaving behind a rich legacy that profoundly influences Scottish literature and politics that continues to shape debates around Scottish autonomy and identity in the 21st century.

SCOTLAND'S NATIONAL BARD

Robert Burns. Poet (1759 - 1796)

Born on January 25, 1759, in Alloway, Ayrshire, Robert Burns came from a farming family, and was the eldest of seven children. His father, William Burnes, was a tenant farmer, and his mother, Agnes Broun, was known for her love of traditional Scottish songs and folklore. Despite the family's financial struggles, Burns received a solid education, thanks in large part to his father's efforts to provide him with learning opportunities.

Burns' early life on the farm exposed him to the natural beauty of the Scottish countryside, which would later become a prominent theme in his poetry. The hardships and manual labor of farm life also shaped his understanding of social inequality and the struggles of the common people. These experiences deeply influenced his writing, imbuing his work with a profound empathy for the human condition.

Burns began writing poetry in his teens, drawing inspiration from the Scottish oral tradition and the works of earlier poets like Robert Fergusson and Allan Ramsay. His first collection of poems, '*Poems, Chiefly in the Scottish Dialect* was published in 1786 and was an immediate success. Known as the '*Kilmarnock Edition*', it included some of his most famous works, such as '*To a Mouse*' and '*The Cotter's Saturday Night*'. These poems reflected Burns' deep connection to rural life and his ability to capture the universal experiences of joy, sorrow, and the simple pleasures of life.

Following the success of his first publication, Burns became a literary sensation in Scotland. His work was praised for its originality, wit, and ability to convey the beauty of the Scottish dialect. Burns' poetry often celebrated the common man, criticised social injustices, and expressed a deep love for Scotland's natural landscape and cultural heritage.

Burns' poetry covers a wide range of themes, from the personal to the political. One of his most enduring themes is love. Poems like '*Ae Fond Kiss*' and '*A Red, Red Rose*' are renowned for their lyrical beauty and heartfelt expression of romantic longing. Burns' ability to convey deep emotion with simplicity and sincerity made these poems timeless classics.

Another significant theme in Burns' work is his celebration of nature. In poems such as '*To a Mouse*' and '*To a Louse*', Burns reflects on the interconnectedness of all living beings and the beauty of the natural world. His keen observation of the simple, everyday aspects of life is a hallmark of his style. Burns also had a keen interest in politics and social justice. He was a supporter of the French Revolution and an advocate for the rights of the common people. Poems like '*A Man's a Man for A' That*', express his belief in the equality of all human beings, regardless of social status. This egalitarian spirit is a recurring motif in Burns' work and resonates with his enduring popularity among working-class audiences.

In addition to his original compositions, Burns collected and preserved traditional Scottish songs and melodies. His work on '*The Scots Musical Museum*' and '*A Select Collection of Original Scottish Airs*' helped to revive and sustain Scotland's musical heritage. Songs like '*Auld Lang Syne*' and '*Scots Wha Hae*' have become integral parts of Scottish culture and are sung around the world.

Robert Burns' legacy is immense, both in Scotland and internationally. His birthday, January 25th, is celebrated annually as Burns Night, with traditional suppers that include readings of his poetry, the eating of haggis and the drinking of whisky. The event is a testament to Burns' enduring cultural significance and his role as a symbol of Scottish identity. His influence extends beyond literature into music, politics, and popular culture. His poems and songs have been adapted and performed by countless artists, and his themes of love, freedom, and equality continue to inspire new generations. Figures like Bob Dylan and Maya Angelou have cited Burns as an influence, underscoring his global impact. Burns' ability to speak to universal human experiences, coupled with his celebration of Scottish culture and language, ensures his continued relevance. His work remains a cornerstone of Scottish literature and a source of national pride. Robert Burns' contribution to literature and culture is unparalleled. His ability to capture the essence of the human spirit in verse, his celebration of Scotland's cultural heritage, and his commitment to social justice have earned him a place as one of the most beloved poets in history. Through his poetry and songs, Burns has left an indelible mark on the world, and his legacy continues to be celebrated and cherished.

In 1796 he died in Dumfries at the age of 37.

THE FATHER OF THE INDUSTRIAL REVOLUTION

James Watt FRS. FRSE. Inventor, Chemist and Engineer. (1736 - 1819)

James Watt was born in 1736 in Greenock in Renfrewshire, the eldest of five children. His mother was well-educated and his father, a shipwright, was Greenock's most senior Bailie, an important municipal officer and magistrate. His parents were Presbyterians but despite Watt''s religious upbringing he later became a *deist* - a philosophy that asserts that empirical reason and observation of the natural world requires exclusively logical and reliable evidence to determine the existence of a supreme being as the creator of the universe.

Watt was home-educated by his mother, before going on to attend Greenock Grammar School where he exhibited an aptitude for mathematics but suffered prolonged bouts of ill-health as a child and in adulthood from frequent headaches.

After leaving school, Watt worked in the workshops of his father's businesses, creating engineering models. However, after his father's business experienced difficulties, Watt left Greenock to seek employment as a mathematical instrument maker in Glasgow. Money was tight but when some complex astronomical instruments arrived in Glasgow, Watt was asked to restore them. This he did so expertly that he received a handsome wage and was asked in 1757 by three professors to set up a small workshop in the Macfarlane Observatory. Two of these professors, the 'Father of Economics', Adam Smith and the equally famous Scottish chemist, Joseph Black, befriended the young man.

In 1712 the atmospheric engine was invented by Thomas Newcomen which allowed atmospheric pressure to push a piston into a cylinder. It was historically significant as the first practical device to harness steam to produce mechanical work. However it was completely inefficient. Watt's invention understood that contemporary engine designs wasted a great deal of energy and he adapted his engine to produce rotary motion, hugely broadening its use beyond pumping water. Watt's engine rotated a shaft instead of providing the simple up-and-down motion of the pump. He improved the design further by ensuring that steam pushed the piston down as the vacuum simultaneously pulled it in. Thus, Watt combined theoretical knowledge of science with the ability to apply it practically and transformed the steam engine – the most significant invention of the Industrial Revolution. On 5 January 1769, he took out the famous patent for *'A New Invented Method of Lessening the consumption of Steam and Fuel in Fire Engines.'* Demands for his engine came quickly from paper mills, flour mills, cotton mills, iron mills, distilleries, canals, and waterworks. By 1790 Watt was a wealthy man, having received £76,000 in royalties on his patents in eleven years. However, the steam engine did not absorb all his attention. He was a member of the Lunar Society in Birmingham, a group of writers and scientists who wished to advance the sciences and the arts. Watt was often involved in legal proceedings to protect his patents. In 1785 he was elected a fellow of the Royal Society of London at which point he began to take holidays and bought an estate at Doldowlod in Mid-Wales near Rhayader. In 1800 he retired to his house in Handsworth where he devoted himself entirely to research work. He patented several other important inventions including the rotary engine, the double-action engine and the steam indicator, which records the steam pressure inside the engine.

Watt's first wife, Margaret, died in childbirth in 1773, leaving him with two young children. He married Ann in 1776 and had a son and a daughter, each of whom died of consumption before their father's death.

Without Watt there would have been no locomotives, steam ships or factories where machines were energised by coal. Watt was, however, much more – a scientist who also conceived the concept of horse-power, who made the first commercial copying machine and gave his name to a unit of power – the Watt. His inventions were influenced and shaped by friends in the Scottish Enlightenment period, but his business interests were interconnected with transatlantic slavery and, in a revolutionary age, he was politically conservative. He died in 1819 in Heathfield, near Birmingham, aged 83 and was buried at nearby St. Mary's Church.

The Scottish Science Hall of Fame voted James Watt the eighth most popular Scottish scientist from the past.

GUARDIAN OF SCOTLAND

William Wallace. Soldier and Freedom-fighter (1270 - 1305)

Much of William Wallace's early life remains obscure, with historical accounts providing limited details about his upbringing. Born around 1270 in Elderslie, Renfrewshire, Wallace was probably the son of a minor nobleman or knight, which afforded him some education and training in arms. The historical context of Wallace's early years was marked by the death of Alexander III of Scotland in 1286, which plunged the nation into a succession crisis and eventually led to English intervention.

The struggle for the Scottish crown, exacerbated by the competing claims and lack of a clear successor, set the stage for King Edward I of England's attempts to assert control over Scotland. In 1296, Edward invaded Scotland, deposing King John Balliol and imposing English rule. It was against this backdrop of foreign occupation and national unrest that Wallace emerged as a key figure in the fight for Scotland's independence.

William Wallace's rise to prominence began in 1297 when he led a series of uprisings against English garrisons and officials. The precise motivations for Wallace's rebellion are unclear, but it is widely believed that personal grievances, possibly including the killing of a family member by the English, played a role in galvanising his resistance.

Wallace's most significant military achievement came at the Battle of Stirling Bridge on September 11, 1297. Alongside Andrew Moray, another Scottish leader, Wallace orchestrated a tactical masterstroke against a larger and better-equipped English army. The Scots used the natural terrain of the narrow Stirling Bridge to their advantage, effectively trapping and decimating the English forces as they attempted to cross. The victory at Stirling Bridge was not only a major military success but also a symbolic triumph that demonstrated Scotland's resilience and capability to defy English supremacy.

Following the victory, Wallace was appointed Guardian of Scotland, a position that underscored his leadership and commitment to the cause of Scottish independence. As Guardian, Wallace sought to consolidate Scottish resistance and strengthen the nation's defences, though his tenure was marked by ongoing challenges and internal divisions.

Wallace's fortunes took a drastic turn in 1298 at the Battle of Falkirk. King Edward I, determined to crush the Scottish rebellion, personally led a formidable English army against Wallace's forces. Despite Wallace's strategic use of schiltrons, tightly packed formations of spearmen, the Scots were overwhelmed by the superior numbers and tactics of the English. The defeat at Falkirk was a severe blow to the Scottish resistance and marked the beginning of Wallace's decline in power.

Following the loss at Falkirk, Wallace resigned as Guardian and continued to fight as a guerrilla leader, employing hit-and-run tactics against English forces. However, his influence waned as Scotland's nobility, including figures like Robert the Bruce, assumed greater roles in the struggle for independence.

In 1305, after several years of evading capture, Wallace was betrayed and handed over to the English authorities. He was taken to London, where he faced a show trial for treason against King Edward I. Despite his steadfast defence, arguing that he could not be a traitor since he had never sworn allegiance to Edward, Wallace was condemned to death.

On August 23, 1305, Wallace was executed in a brutal and symbolic manner. He was hanged, drawn, and quartered, a punishment reserved for traitors. His execution was intended to serve as a warning to other would-be rebels but instead, it immortalised him as a martyr for the Scottish cause. William Wallace's legacy endures as a symbol of Scottish nationalism and resistance. His life and actions have been romanticised in literature, art, and film, most notably in the 1995 movie "*Braveheart*," which brought his story to an international audience. While the film takes considerable liberties with historical accuracy, it captures the spirit of Wallace's defiance and the enduring quest for freedom that he represents. Wallace's memory is honoured in various ways across Scotland; the National Wallace Monument in Stirling stands as a testament to his contributions and sacrifices. His story continues to inspire those who value independence, courage, and the struggle for self-determination, cementing his legacy as one of Scotland's most celebrated patriots.

JOHN OF THE MOUNTAINS

John Muir. Traveler and Ecologist (1838 - 1914).

John Muir was born in a three-story stone building at 126 High Street, now preserved as a museum in Dunbar, a small town on the North Sea coast in East Lothian, approximately thirty miles east of Edinburgh. He was the third of eight children of Daniel Muir and Ann Gilrye. From the age of three until the age of eleven he attended the local schools in town. In 1849, the Muir family emigrated to the United States, settling at Hickory Hill Farm near Portage, Wisconsin. In 1860, he traveled the short distance south to the University of Wisconsin-Madison, where he studied chemistry and developed a lasting interest in the subject. That said, he was never a traditional student, as records showed his class status as 'an irregular gent' who never graduated but learned enough geology and botany to inform his later travels throughout America and beyond.

The American Civil War commenced in 1861 and in 1863, his brother, Daniel headed to Canada to avoid the draft. Muir also left Madison, travelled to the same region in 1864 and spent that year exploring the woods and swamps and collecting plants. Muir, with his brother in tow, took employment with the Trout family in an area called Trout Hollow in Ontario, on the Bighead River and while there he continued exploring the local environment.

One year after the Civil War ended, Muir returned to Indianapolis in the United States and commenced work in a wagon-wheel factory where he proved invaluable to his employers because of his ability to improve machines and processes. He was promoted to supervisor, but an industrial injury cut the cornea in his right eye and his left eye also failed. It took six weeks to regain his sight but once recovered he determined to change his life and follow his dream of the exploration and study of plants. Thus, he began his years of wanderlust and walked a thousand miles from Indianapolis to the Gulf of Mexico before sailing to Cuba and later to

Panama. He trekked across the Isthmus and sailed up the West Coast to San Francisco in 1868. Arriving there, although he would travel around the world, California would become his home base.

His journeys through the Sierra Nevada and Yosemite, living off the land, inspired him and, in 1871 he found living glaciers in the Sierra and conceived his then-contentious theory of the glaciation of Yosemite Valley. In 1874, a series of articles entitled 'Studies in the Sierra' launched a successful career as a writer on the environment, bringing a procession of famous people to the log cabin he called home. As his fame grew he travelled to Alaska before, in 1880, marrying Louie Strentzel and moving to Martinez, California where the couple raised their two daughters, Wanda and Helen. His wanderlust, however, was unrequited and took him to Alaska, Australia, South America, Africa, Europe, China, Japan, returning always to the Sierra Nevada mountain range. He envisioned the Yosemite area and the Sierra as pristine lands and considered the greatest threat to the Yosemite area and the Sierra was domesticated livestock - especially domestic sheep, which he referred to as 'hoofed locusts'.

Robert Johnson, the editor of *The Century* magazine, agreed to publish any article Muir wrote and also agreed to twist arms to introduce a bill to Congress to make the Yosemite area into a National Park.

In 1903, President Theodore Roosevelt accompanied Muir on a visit to Yosemite where the President experienced the magnificent splendour of the mountain range. They camped together and Roosevelt later said, 'Lying out at night under those giant Sequoias was like lying in a temple built by no hand of man, a temple grander than any human architect could by any possibility build'. During his lifetime John Muir published over 300 articles and 12 books. He co-founded the Sierra Club which has over two million members and which helped establish a number of national parks after he died. Muir was a towering figure in the American ecology movement and has been called the 'Patron saint of the American wilderness'.

Muir never forgot his Scottish roots. He greatly admired the works of Scottish essayist, historian and philosopher Thomas Carlisle and the poetry of Robert Burns. Indeed, he was known to carry a collection of poems by Burns during his travels through the American wilderness.

He returned to Scotland on a trip in 1893 and never lost his Scottish accent.

TWEEDS IN THE MOTHER OF PARLIAMENTS

Keir Hardy. Politician (1856 - 1915)

In 1856, James Keir Hardie was born in Legbrannoch, near Motherwell in Lanarkshire, the illegitimate son of William Aitken who was a miner and Mary Kerr, a farm servant, daughter of James Keir and Agnes Paterson. Mary Keir later married David Hardie, a ship's carpenter who was an early trade unionist.

Young Keir Hardie's early life was difficult and the family were forced to move frequently in search of regular employment in shipbuilding. Hardie was sent to work first as a messenger boy, then as a baker's delivery boy aged eight without any schooling. He subsequently found somewhat dangerous employment heating rivets in the shipyards The work was tough and unforgiving for children. His family's precarious financial situation worsened when a lockout occurred at Clydeside shipyard forcing the workers to be sent home for a period lasting six months. With his father out of work, young Keir became the sole breadwinner. By the age of eleven, he was a coal miner.

Aged seventeen he had taught himself to read and write. In the late 1870s he was fired and blacklisted by the Lanarkshire mine-owners for his strike activity, forcing a move to Ayrshire

He then began employment as a journalist with the Cumnock News in 1882. During this time he became actively involved with the Cumnock community, founding a Good Templar Lodge promoting the temperance movement and was also involved with local societies and churches. From 1881 he helped to form miners' unions on a county basis and, in 1886 was offered the post of Secretary to the newly formed Ayrshire Miners' Union.

In 1881 he led the first ever strike of Lanarkshire miners. Meanwhile, Hardie earned his living as a journalist. In his own newspapers, The Miner (1887–89) and the Labour Leader (from 1889). He expressed Christian socialist views on labour and on wider political issues and in 1892, Hardie, disillusioned with the Liberals, questioning Gladstone's economic policies and the impact on the working classes, won an election as an Independent

Labour Party candidate in West Ham in East London. Taking his seat in parliament, he marked himself out as a radical both by his dress - he wore a tweed suit when most members of parliament wore more formal dress - and the subjects he advocated, including women's rights, free schooling, old age pensions, Indian self-rule, the abolition of the House of Lords and Home Rule for Scotland.

In the 1890's, working-class representation in political office became a great concern for many Britons. At that time, those who sought the election of working men and their advocates to the UK Parliament saw the Liberal Party as the main vehicle for achieving this. However, at a TUC meeting in September 1892, a call was issued for a meeting of advocates of an independent labour organisation. A conference was held in Bradford the following year which proved to be the foundation conference of the Independent Labour Party. Member of Parliament, Keir Hardie was elected as its first chairman. In 1895, with finance tight, just twenty-eight candidates ran under the ILP banner. None was elected however, with even popular party leader Hardie also going down to defeat in a straight fight with the Conservatives.

Reelected as an MP, this time for Merthyr Tydfil in Wales in 1900, he was elected first chairman of the Parliamentary Labour Party but resigned from the post in 1907. Both within and outwith Parliament, he campaigned tirelessly for the unemployed, free schooling, pensions, Indian self-rule and, perhaps most of all, women's rights. Hardie was also a pacifist and outspoken in his criticism of the First World War.

Hardie was an internationalist and vociferous critic of the British Government in India, frequently calling for Indian self-rule in Parliament. In 1907, he toured India and gave numerous speeches there, exposing the corruption of the Raj, speaking out in favour of Indian self-determination and against racism and advocating non-violent agitation.

Hardie's tour of India alarmed the British authorities and was stirred up by the press. There were calls for him to be deported amid accusations of sedition.

He died in September 1915 aged 59 of pneumonia at 8 South Park Terrace in the west end of Glasgow. No political representatives attended his funeral and the press condemned his politics and legacy. No blue plaque adorns the doorway of the somewhat anonymous Georgian building in which he passed away.

A bronze bust of James Keir Hardie, stands on a pink granite plinth outside Cumnock Town Hall since he lived for the majority of his life there. The National Keir Hardie Memorial Committee commissioned the sculptor Benno Schotz RSA, to create the bronze bust.

The memorial bust was accepted by provost Nan Hardie Hughes, Keir Hardie's daughter, in August 1939, on the eve of World War Two.

THE BOSS

Sir Alexander (Alex) Chapman Ferguson. Footballer and Football Manager (1941-)

Sir Alexander Chapman Ferguson, commonly known as Sir Alex Ferguson, was born on December 31, 1941, in the Govan district of Glasgow. Ferguson grew up in a working-class family. He developed a passion for football early on, playing as a forward for various youth teams such as Harmony Row, in Govan. His professional playing career began with Queen's Park in 1957. Although his time at Queen's Park was modest, it provided the foundation for his future in football.

Ferguson later played for St. Johnstone, Dunfermline Athletic, Rangers, Falkirk, and Ayr United, earning a reputation as a hardworking and determined forward. He achieved an International cap for Scotland but it was during this period that he began to cultivate his understanding of the game, laying the groundwork for his future success as a manager.

His managerial journey began with East Stirlingshire in 1974, where he quickly made a name for himself despite limited resources. His time at St. Mirren, starting in 1974, was more notable as he led the club to the Scottish First Division title in 1977. His success at St. Mirren caught the attention of Aberdeen, where he was appointed manager in 1978.

At Aberdeen, Ferguson truly began to showcase his managerial prowess. Under his leadership, Aberdeen broke the dominance of the Old Firm (Celtic and Rangers) in Scottish football. Ferguson guided the club to three Scottish league titles, four Scottish Cups, and a League Cup. The pinnacle of his success at Aberdeen came in 1983 when the club won the European Cup Winners' Cup, defeating Real Madrid in the final. This victory established Ferguson as a top-tier manager and brought him to the attention of clubs across Europe.

Ferguson took over as manager of Manchester United in November 1986. The club was struggling at the time, having not won the league since 1967. His early years at United were challenging, with inconsistent performances and mounting pressure. However, Ferguson's determination and long-term vision paid off, and he gradually built a team capable of competing at the highest level.

The turning point came in 1990 when United won the FA Cup, providing Ferguson with the time and confidence to implement his ideas fully. Over the next two decades, he led Manchester United to unprecedented success. Under his management, the club won 13 Premier League titles, 5 FA Cups, 4 League Cups, and 2 UEFA Champions League titles. His ability to rebuild and reinvent his team over the years ensured continued success.

Ferguson's tenure was marked by several notable achievements, including the famous treble-winning season of 1998-1999, when Manchester United won the Premier League, FA Cup, and UEFA Champions League. Ferguson's management style was characterised by his strong leadership, discipline, and a keen eye for talent. He was known for his 'hairdryer treatment,' a term used to describe his fiery temper and intense motivational talks. Despite his demanding nature, Ferguson was also deeply committed to the welfare of his players, often acting as a mentor and father figure.

One of Ferguson's greatest strengths was his adaptability. He was able to evolve with the changing dynamics of football, embracing new tactics, training methods, and sports science. His ability to stay ahead of the curve allowed him to maintain Manchester United's dominance both domestically and in Europe.

Sir Alex Ferguson retired from management in 2013, ending a remarkable twenty-six year tenure at Manchester United, allowing his burgeoning interest in horse-racing to take hold. His legacy is enshrined not only in the numerous trophies and accolades but also in the cultural and institutional transformation of the club. Under his guidance, Manchester United became one of the most commercially successful and widely supported football clubs in the world. Even after retiring, Ferguson remained an influential figure in football. His expertise and insights are still sought after by managers, players, and football enthusiasts worldwide.

Sir Alex Ferguson's contribution to football is unparalleled. His extraordinary career is a testament to his resilience, strategic genius and unwavering commitment to excellence. As one of the most decorated and respected managers in the history of the sport, Ferguson's legacy continues to inspire future generations of players, managers and fans.

SELECTED QUOTES

Adam Smith

"It is not from the benevolence of the butcher, the brewer, or the baker, that we expect our dinner, but from their regard to their own interest. We address ourselves, not to their humanity but to their self-love and never talk to them of our necessities but of their advantages."

Hugh MacDairmid

"The rose of all the world is not for me.
I want for my part
Only the little white rose of Scotland
That smells sharp and sweet - and breaks the heart."

"It is time we in Scotland put England in its proper place and instead of our leaning on England and taking inspiration from her, we should lean and turn to Europe, for it is there our future prosperity lies."

Robert Burns

"Oh wad some power the giftie gie us, to see ourselves as ithers see us."

"Man's inhumanity to man makes countless thousands mourn!"

"The best laid schemes o' mice an' men gang aft agley."

"Then gently scan your brother man, still gentler sister woman, though they may gang a kennin' wrang, to step aside is human."

"I have often said to myself, what are the boasted advantages which my country reaps from a certain Union that counterbalance the annihilation of her Independence and even her very name!"

William Wallace (Attrib.)

"When I was a boy, the priest, my uncle, carefully inculcated upon me this proverb, which I then learned and have ever since kept in my mind: *'Dico tibi verum, Libertas optima rerum; Nunquam servili, sub nexu vivito, fili.'* "I tell you a truth: Liberty is the best of things, my son; never live under any slavish bond.

John Muir

"The world is big and I want to have a good look at it before it gets dark."

"The clearest way into the Universe is through a forest wilderness."

"On my first long walk from Indiana to the Gulf of Mexico I carried a copy of Burns poems and songs and sang them all the way. The whole country and the people, beasts and birds seemed to like them."

"Any fool can destroy trees. It took more than three thousand years to make some of those trees in the Western Woods".

Sir Alex Ferguson

"I feel sympathy for the working class lad. I've always championed about ticket prices and try to equate that to people's salaries."

"Myths grow all the time. If I was to listen to the number of times I've thrown teacups then we've gone through some crockery in this place. It's completely exaggerated, but I don't like people arguing back with me."

"It's squeaky bum time!"

"He was certainly full of it, calling me 'Boss' and Big Man' when we had our post-match drink after the first leg. But it would help if his greetings were accompanied by a decent glass of wine. What he gave me was paint-stripper." (Ferguson's first impressions of Jose Mourinho)

THE BIG YIN

Sir William (Billy) Connolly. Actor, Comedian and Artist. (1942 -)

Billy Connolly was born in 1942 in Glasgow, to a working-class family. His father, William Connolly, was in the Royal Air Force during World War Two, and his mother, Mary, left the family when he was young, leaving him and his sister Florence to be raised by their aunts in a strict Catholic household. Growing up in a tough environment, Connolly experienced hardship and abuse, which he later spoke about in his autobiographies and stand-up routines. However, he found solace in humour and music, which would become his escape from a difficult childhood.

At the age of 15, Connolly left school and became an apprentice welder in the Glasgow shipyards, a job that exposed him to the camaraderie and humour of working-class life; an experience that would later inform much of his comedy. During this time, he also developed a love for folk music and learned to play the banjo and guitar, often playing in sessions in the Scotia Bar in Glasgow with friends and other patter merchants.

Connolly initially pursued a career in music, becoming a folk singer in the 1960s. He formed a duo with Tam Harvey calling themselves, *The Humblebums*, which later included the renowned singer-songwriter Gerry Rafferty. The group enjoyed some success, but Connolly's comedic interludes during performances started gaining more attention than the music itself.

By the early 1970s, Connolly had fully transitioned into stand-up comedy. His breakthrough moment came in 1975 when he appeared on *The Michael Parkinson Show*, a popular British talk show. His natural storytelling ability and irreverent humour won over audiences instantly. His joke about a man who murdered his wife became legendary and propelled him to national fame.

Following his television breakthrough, Connolly became a household name. He developed a unique comedic style that blended storytelling, observational humour, and personal anecdotes delivered in his thick

Glaswegian accent. His performances felt spontaneous, as he would frequently go off on hilarious tangents, making each show feel fresh and unscripted. In the 1980s and 1990s, Connolly's popularity soared internationally. He toured extensively across the UK, Australia, Canada and the United States, earning him a global fan base. His ability to find humour in everyday situations, combined with his fearless approach to taboo subjects made him one of the most influential comedians of his generation.

Beyond stand-up comedy, Connolly proved to be a talented actor. His acting career took off in the late 1980s and he starred in numerous films and TV shows. Some of his most notable roles included *Mrs. Brown* in which he played John Brown, the loyal servant to Queen Victoria (played by Judi Dench). His performance earned critical acclaim, showing his ability to handle serious dramatic roles. In '*The Boondock Saints',* he portrayed *Il Duce*, a ruthless assassin in this cult action film. In '*The Man Who Sued God'*, Connolly played the lead role in this Australian film, tackling themes of religion and justice with his trademark wit and in '*The Last Samurai',* he appeared alongside Tom Cruise in this historical epic, playing a tough Scottish sergeant. Additionally, he lent his voice to animated films, including '*Brave*', where he voiced King Fergus, delighting audiences with his humour and distinctive voice.

Connolly has been married to Pamela Stephenson, an actress, psychologist, and writer, since 1989. She has played a crucial role in supporting him throughout his career and health struggles. In 2013, Connolly was diagnosed with Parkinson's disease, a progressive neurological condition that affects movement and speech. Although the diagnosis led him to retire from stand-up comedy, he continued to make television appearances and create art. Despite the challenges of his illness, Connolly remains positive and humorous about life. He has spoken openly about aging and his condition, inspiring many with his resilience and humour.Over the years, Connolly has received numerous accolades for his contributions to entertainment, including a knighthood in 2017 for services to entertainment and charity, multiple BAFTA and British Comedy Awards for his influence on stand-up comedy, induction into the Scottish Hall of Fame and various lifetime achievement awards. His legacy in comedy is profound. He revolutionised stand-up with his free-flowing, storytelling approach, paving the way for modern comedians who embrace improvisation. His humour is often laced with profanity but even in retirement, his influence on comedy, film, and popular culture remains as strong as ever.

FRANCO'S WOULD-BE ASSASSIN

Stuart Christie. Anarchist, Writer and Publisher (1946 - 2020).

Stuart Christie was born on the banks of the River Clyde in the Partick area of Glasgow to a hairdresser and a Glaswegian trawlerman and was raised in nearby Blantyre by his mother and grandparents, becoming an anarchist at a young age. He ascribed this to his grandmother's influence: 'Basically, what she did was provide a moral barometer which married almost exactly with that of Libertarian Socialism and Anarchism, and she provided the star which I followed.' He joined the Anarchist Federation in Glasgow in 1962, at the age of sixteen and became active in the Campaign for Nuclear Disarmament before becoming attracted to the more militant approach of the Committee of One Hundred and the Direct Action Committee which took part in a series of confrontations at the Faslane Naval Base on the Clyde.

As a teenager, Christie gravitated toward anarchism, a political philosophy that advocates for a stateless society based on voluntary cooperation and mutual aid. His political awakening coincided with the tumultuous 1960s, a decade marked by widespread social and political upheaval. Inspired by the Spanish anarchists of the 1930s and the broader global resistance to fascism, Christie quickly became an ardent activist.

Christie's life took a dramatic turn in 1964 when, at the age of 18, he traveled to Spain to join the resistance against the fascist regime of General Francisco Franco. Franco's dictatorship had ruled Spain with an iron fist since the end of the Spanish Civil War in 1939, crushing dissent and outlawing political opposition, including anarchist groups. Christie, inspired by the Spanish anarchists' legacy, volunteered for an audacious mission to assassinate Franco. He joined the '*Defensa Interior*', a clandestine anarchist organisation dedicated to combating Franco's regime.

Christie smuggled explosives into Spain with the intention of using them in an attack against Franco. However, he was arrested in Madrid in 1964, before the mission could be carried out. The arrest marked the beginning of a high-profile trial that thrust Christie into the international spotlight. He was sentenced to twenty years in prison but served only three after international campaigns for his release, led by figures such as philosopher Bertrand Russell, drew widespread attention. His imprisonment underscored the brutal repression faced by political dissidents in Francoist Spain but also solidified his reputation as a committed anarchist willing to risk his life for his beliefs.

After his release in 1967, Christie returned to Britain where he continued his activism. He became involved in a variety of anarchist movements, campaigning for workers' rights, anti-militarism and the abolition of authoritarian institutions. He was particularly critical of state power, capitalism and imperialism, viewing them as interconnected systems of oppression. He was also involved with the Angry Brigade and was arrested and remanded but was acquitted of all charges of small bomb attacks targeting banks, embassies, the homes of Conservative MPs and a BBC outside broadcast vehicle between 1970 and 1972.

In 1969, Christie co-founded the *Anarchist Black Cross*, a group dedicated to supporting political prisoners and opposing state repression. This initiative became a vital part of the international anarchist movement, providing solidarity to activists who had been jailed for their political activities. Through the organisation, Christie helped raise awareness of the plight of prisoners, connecting their struggles to broader issues of systemic injustice.

Christie was not only an activist but also a prolific writer and publisher. In the 1970s, he co-founded '*Cienfuegos Press*', an anarchist publishing house that produced books, pamphlets, and periodicals on a wide range of topics. The press was instrumental in revitalising anarchist literature, making important historical and contemporary works accessible to a new generation of readers. Christie also authored several books, including '*The Christie File*' and '*Granny Made Me an Anarchist*' ; a memoir that combines personal anecdotes with political analysis, offering insight into the motivations and struggles of an anarchist activist. Stuart Christie remained active in anarchist circles until his death on August 15, 2020. His life and work had a profound impact on anarchist movements in Britain and beyond. He was not only a participant in the struggles of his time but also a chronicler and theorist who sought to understand and articulate the principles of anarchism in a changing world. Christie's legacy lies in his unwavering commitment to the ideals of freedom and justice. He lived by the belief that ordinary people have the power to resist oppression and create a more equitable society. His efforts to challenge authoritarianism, support political prisoners and promote anarchist ideas continue to inspire activists today.

"JOHN, YOU'RE IMMORTAL!"

John (Jock) Stein CBE. Footballer and Football Manager. (1922 - 1985).

Jock Stein was born in 1922 in Burnbank, Hamilton amid the surrounding coalfields of Lanarkshire and was almost certainly destined to become fodder for the dark mine-workings that criss-crossed the depths of that county's bleak landscape. In 1937, he left Greenfield school in Hamilton and after a short time working in a carpet factory, he went down the pits to become a miner as did as many in his community.

The next year he joined Blantyre Victoria Junior Football Club but started as a part-time professional player with Albion Rovers the following year. He continued to work as a miner during the week while playing as centre-half on Saturday and made a name for himself as a tough defender going on to make over 200 appearances for the club.

In 1950, he signed for non-league Welsh club Llanelli Town and, for the first time in his career, he became a full-time professional footballer on a wage of £12 per week. However, he had left his wife Jean and young daughter Ray behind in Lanarkshire and he was soon keen to return to Scotland. In 1951, Celtic bought him for £1,200.

In 1953, he captained Celtic to success in the Coronation Cup by beating Arsenal, Manchester United and Hibernian to become unofficial champions of Britain. The following year, he captained Celtic to their first League championship since 1938 and their first League and Scottish Cup double since 1914. He retired formally in January 1957 as an ankle injury suffered in a league cup against Rangers led to the end of his playing career having played a hundred and forty-eight league and cup games for Celtic, mostly as captain.

After he retired from playing, he was given the role of coaching the reserve and youth players and was responsible for persuading the board to purchase nearby Barrowfield as a training ground. In 1958, he managed the reserve team to win the Second Eleven Cup with an 8-2 aggregate triumph over rivals Glasgow Rangers, his first success as a manager. Despite the very poor performances of the Celtic first team, his unquestioned abilities were overlooked by the Board and he decided to move on.

In 1960, Stein was appointed manager of Dunfermline who were mired in a battle against relegation having not won in four months. They won their first six matches under Stein who then guided them to their first Scottish Cup triumph winning 2–0 in a replayed final against his old team, Celtic. This success resulted in job offers from Newcastle United and Hibs but each was rejected by Stein although, two years later, he accepted a Hibs offer and took over managership of the club whom he then led to victory in the Summer Cup, their first trophy in ten years. Having been offered a job at Wolverhampton Wanderers, he contacted the Celtic chairman, Bob Kelly 'for advice', hoping to be invited back to Celtic but this was not forthcoming - according to his later captain, Billy McNeill, on grounds of sectarianism as Stein was a Protestant. However after some manoeuvring, Kelly eventually agreed to offer Stein full powers over team selection and he became manager in 1965. In his first season, Celtic reached the semi-finals of the UEFA Cup Winners' Cup, but were beaten controversially 2–1 on aggregate by Liverpool. Stein also went on to win the league championship for the first time in 12 years. Celtic won the championship again the following year and reached the final of the European Cup against serial winners Inter Milan in Lisbon. Celtic won 2-1 playing attractive attacking football prompting Liverpool manager Bill Shankly to embrace Stein after the final whistle saying, "John, you're immortal!" In winning club football's most prestigious trophy, Stein became the first man not only to guide a Scottish club to become champions of Europe, but also the first to achieve this honour with a British club. Furthermore, he became the first manager to win the European Treble and remains the only manager to win the fabled Quadruple, thanks to his side's earlier League Cup success over Rangers. All of this was achieved with Scottish-born players each of whom were born within 30 miles of Parkhead, many of them within the long shadow of the stadium. Only Bobby Lennox from nearby Saltcoats could be considered a commuter.

The 70s brought continued success in Scotland. During this time Stein's Celtic completed a world equaling record of nine consecutive league championships. In 1975 he was badly injured in a car crash and almost died but eventually recovered and returned to management. However his track-suit days were over and Celtic floundered. Stein resigned the following season and rejected a Board offer of managing Celtic Pools. He accepted the position of Manager of Leeds United but early results were mixed and Stein apparently missed the pressure of big games against foreign opposition. In consequence, when Ally Macleod resigned after a disappointing World Cup, Stein accepted the role of National Manager. After an indifferent start, Scotlands' form improved in their successful qualifying campaign for the 1982 World Cup. They finished top of their group only losing once. Scotland travelled to Spain in the summer of 1982 in what would be the only occasion Stein would manage a side at the finals of major international tournament. Scotland went out on goal difference but Stein commented after the final match: "I am very disappointed we have not qualified…but I think we have done Scotland proud, both on and off the field."

Scotland began their qualifying campaign for the 1986 World Cup successfully but went into their last qualifying tie, away to Wales in Cardiff, needing at least a draw to secure a play-off spot. With nine minutes left, Davie Cooper scored to make the score 1–1, securing a qualification play-off against Australia. Stein, who had been in poor health and who had stopped taking medication, suffered a fatal fluid build-up in his lungs and died at the end of the game. He was 62 years old.

THE MARXIST-LENINIST BANK ROBBER

Matthew (Matt) Lygate. Marxist Revolutionary. (1938 - 2012)

Matt Lygate was born in the dockland area of Glasgow's Govan and was educated at St Gerards' Roman Catholic Secondary School, leaving aged fifteen. As a teenager, he moved to Sunderland with his family and became a well-regarded tailor's cutter. Whilst still in his teens, he joined the Communist Party of Great Britain and when required to undertake National Service, he refused to join the British Army because he considered it imperialist. He absconded to New Zealand where he spent six years travelling extensively before returning to Scotland. He was also a devout Christian, believing that Christ was himself a revolutionary socialist.

Settling in Glasgow, he became heavily involved and was a leading figure in the Scottish and Irish republican and socialist movements and was increasingly drawn into the political orbit of dissident Communist Party members and Scottish Nationalists. He was a founder of the Workers Party of Scotland which was a Marxist-Leninist Republican party advocating the establishment of a Scottish Socialist Republic in the same tradition of John Maclean. He was also inspired by and was instrumental in the establishment of the John Maclean Society which did much work to resurrect the memory and life's work of Maclean.

The Workers' Party of Scotland declared itself to be based fundamentally upon the Communist Manifesto of Marx and Engels, the subsequent development of Marxism by Lenin, Stalin and John Maclean and were also great admirers of William Wallace: "We have persistently upheld the memory and example of our heroic and martyred William Wallace, a highly successful pioneer in guerrilla warfare because he was a man of and for the people." He supported the revival of Gaelic and published works of Mao Tse-tung in Gaelic. In 1969 Lygate stood as the Workers' Party of Scotland candidate in a by-election in the Gorbals, a constituency rich in historical symbolism for the party. Nevertheless, Lygate secured only seven votes, losing badly.

Lygate and other party members, aware that funds were low, decided to make two bank robberies to finance political activities and in 1971 Lygate, together with William McPherson, Colin Lawson and Ian Doran committed two robberies, bringing the movement fourteen thousand pounds. Police initially found no evidence but McPherson and Doran, who were professional criminals, made two more robberies without consulting the others and during one of them, a shot was fired with a sawn-off shotgun which gave the police clues that led to the arrest of all four. Compounding the felony was a police raid on Lygate's Paisley Road bookshop where the police uncovered the proceeds of the robberies in a shoebox.

It transpired that the judge, Lord Dunpark, thought that the defendants should have been charged with treason which was reflected in his sentencing of Lygate - to twenty-four years in prison. Lygate pleaded not guilty, arguing that he robbed capitalist institutions who had robbed the working-class and saw the trial as his opportunity to emulate his hero John Maclean, whose speech on being jailed for sedition during World War One was, and remains, one of the great classics of socialist oratory. Upon being sentenced in the public gallery Lygate clenched his fist and shouted, "Long live the workers of Scotland!". However, Lygate failed to move the judge, was taken down and not released for eleven years. The sentence given to him was on par with the Great Train Robbers. A lawyer commented that he had been given eight years for robbery and sixteen for his politics. In prison, Lygate still opposed the Crown, refused to wear his prison uniform and spent time on hunger strike. He devoted much of his time to teaching his fellow inmates how to read and write. Upon discharge, Lygate established a small printing business named the Phoenix Press and embarked upon a family life that would raise three children. Lygate was nominated to become Rector of Glasgow University but was the first of the six candidates to be knocked out. He was nominated for honorary degrees at Glasgow and Edinburgh Universities but rejected both believing that they might adulterate his working class background.

Lygate sustained a lifelong love of art, poetry and nature. He contracted Alzheimer's disease in his final years, an ailment that he fought, still retaining the capacity to recite the poems of Robert Burns but in January, 2012, he stepped in front of a train and brought his life to an end, aged seventy-four.

'ALL HAIL, THE SCOTTISH WORKERS' REPUBLIC!'

John Maclean. Socialist. Chair of the Third All-Russian Congress of Soviets, Bolshevik Consul in Scotland. (1879 - 1923)

John Maclean was born in Pollokshaws, Glasgow. His father, Daniel was a potter who hailed from Borrowstounness (usually referred to as Bo'ness) near Falkirk and his mother hailed from Corpach near Fort William.

Maclean's burgeoning interest in politics first derived via the Pollokshields Progressive Union where he became convinced that the standard of living of the working people could only be improved by a social revolution and in consequence, it was as a Marxist that he joined the Social Democratic Federation and gave a series of local speeches that led to the establishment of a branch in his community of Pollokshields. In 1904, he graduated from Glasgow University with a Master of Arts degree, thereafter often using the letters M.A. after his name when his work was published. He married Agnes Wood in 1909 but they became estranged in 1919 as she was 'unable to stand the pressures and insecurity of living with a man who lived only for the revolution'.

As World War One loomed, he worked with others on the Clyde Workers' Committee to oppose hostilities as he felt it was a war of imperialism that divided workers from one another. His politics made him well known to the authorities of the day, and in 1915, he was arrested under the *Defence of the Realm Act*, convicted and sentenced to three years; initially in Calton Jail in Edinburgh then north to Peterhead although he served only eight months and was summarily dismissed from his teaching position in Lorne Street Primary School. Unemployed, he began to lecture on Marxism whilst organising anti-war activities which saw him again imprisoned in 1918 having been convicted of six separate offences of sedition. Maclean famously conducted his own defence and in a defiant manner, refusing to plead, made his famous speech from the dock, saying, "I am not here, then, as the accused; I am here as the *accuser* of capitalism dripping with blood from head to foot." He was imprisoned for five years in Peterhead Prison, but was released having served only fourteen months of his sentence following a public campaign against his custodial sentence. Following the armistice on 11 November, he returned to Glasgow to a tumultuous welcome.

During his imprisonment in Peterhead he was on hunger strike believing the food was drugged so he could be diagnosed as mentally incapable and was force-fed. His health suffered. Shortly after his release, still unwell, he stood as the official Labour Party candidate at the general election for the constituency of Glasgow Gorbals but failed to unseat the sitting MP. During the Irish Easter Rising in 1916, Maclean was a supporter of Home Rule for Ireland and later became committed to Irish independence as part of a worldwide anti-imperialist struggle. Initially, he distanced himself from the Irish armed struggle because he viewed it was in contradiction with his Pacifist principles but as a consequence of visits to Ireland, his attitude was radicalised and he gave up his opposition to blood being spilled. Despite his long membership of the British Socialist Party, when it merged into the newly formed Communist Party of Great Britain, Maclean was secretly expelled, after declaring that Moscow should not dictate to Glasgow and declared himself in favour of a Scottish Workers' Republic, issuing a famous pamphlet entitled, *'All Hail, the Scottish Workers' Republic!'*. In it he argued that the British Empire was the greatest menace to the human race. "The best interest of humanity can therefore be served by the break-up of the British empire. The Irish, the Indians and others are playing their part. Why ought not the Scottish?" In 1923 he founded the Scottish Workers' Republican Party which combined communist ideologies with Home Rule for Scotland.

Maclean died at home in Pollokshaws, Glasgow on 30 November 1923, although other sources suggest that he collapsed while giving an outdoor speech and died of pneumonia. He was only forty-four years old. His reputation was such that his funeral became known as the largest Glasgow had ever seen. Vladimir Lenin described him as one of the "best-known names of the isolated heroes who have taken upon themselves the arduous role of forerunners of the world revolution". The Soviet Union honoured Maclean with an avenue in central Leningrad - *Maklin Prospekt* and in 1979, on the centenary of his birth, issued a four kopek commemorative postage stamp depicting his image. In *'Stony Limits and Other Poems'*, Hugh MacDiarmid declared that, "Of all Maclean's foes not one was his peer" and proclaimed that, "Next to Burns, Maclean was the greatest-ever Scot".

He is buried in Eastwood New Cemetery where the author maintains his grave.

SELECTED QUOTES

Billy Connolly

"My definition of an intellectual is someone who can listen to the William Tell Overture without thinking of the Lone Ranger."

"I've always wanted to go to Switzerland to see what the army does with those wee red knives."

"I don't know why I should have to learn Algebra... I'm never likely to go there."

"Still, we gave the Americans Andrew Carnegie about whom it was said that he gave away money about as silently as a waiter falling down a flight of stairs with a tray of glasses.

Stuart Christie

"My Granny made me an anarchist!"

"I had to do more than just demonstrate and leaflet."

Jock Stein

"The secret of being a good manager is to keep the six players who hate you away from the five who are undecided."

"Football is not like that. If form was the only factor we would all win the pools every week."

"There is not a prouder man on God's Earth than me at this moment. Winning was important, aye, but it was the way that we have won that has filled me with satisfaction. We did it by playing football. Pure, beautiful, inventive football. There was not a negative thought in our heads. Inter played right into our hands; it's so sad to see such gifted players shackled by a system that restricts their freedom to think and to act. Our fans would never accept that sort of sterile approach. Our objective is always to try to win with style."

Matt Lygate

"I will be released very soon, when the revolution comes."

"I am not a Trotskyist. I was a Maoist in the sixties. But now I am a Marxist-Leninist and an anarchist in the true sense."

John Maclean

"I wish no harm to any human being, but I, as one man, am going to exercise my freedom of speech. No human being on the face of the earth, no government is going to take from me my right to speak, my right to protest against wrong, my right to do everything that is for the benefit of mankind."

"I am not here, then, as the accused; I am here as the accuser of capitalism dripping with blood from head to foot."

"I have taken up unconstitutional action at this time because of the abnormal circumstances and because precedent has been given by the British government. I am a socialist and have been fighting and will fight for an absolute reconstruction of society for the benefit of all. I am proud of my conduct. I have squared my conduct with my intellect, and if everyone had done so this war would not have taken place."

"The only war that is worth waging is the class war"!

"I for one am out for a Scottish Socialist Workers' Republic".

THE OPEN UNIVERSITY

Janet "Jennie" Lee. Baroness Lee of Asheridge. Politician (1904 - 1988)

Jennie Lee was born in 1904, in Lochgelly, Fife to Euphemia Greig and James Lee. James was a miner who held the post of fire and safety officer. Later he was a hotelier. She had a younger brother, Tommy and was deeply influenced by her family's strong ties to the Independent Labour Party (ILP). Her grandfather, Michael Lee, was a notable trade unionist and a founding member of the Fife-shire ILP federation, while her father, James Lee, was an active ILP member.

Demonstrating academic prowess from a young age, Jennie attended Beath High School, where she excelled and became dux of the school in her final year. Her academic achievements earned her support from the Carnegie Trust, Fife County Council, and the Fife Education Authority, enabling her to attend the University of Edinburgh. There, she initially studied education, earning a teacher's diploma and later pursued law, obtaining an LL.B in 1927.

Jennie's political career commenced with her deep involvement in the ILP, reflecting her family's socialist inclinations. In 1929, at the age of twenty-four, she was elected as the Member of Parliament for North Lanarkshire in a by-election, becoming the youngest woman then ever elected to the House of Commons. Notably, at that time, women under thirty were not yet eligible to vote, highlighting the significance of her achievement. Her maiden speech was an attack on the budget proposals of Winston Churchill. She accused him of 'cant, corruption and incompetence'. Churchill was so impressed he offered his congratulations after their exchange in the Commons. Her tenure in Parliament was marked by her passionate advocacy for socialist policies and her commitment to representing working-class interests. However, in 1931, during a period of political upheaval and economic depression, she lost her seat amid a Conservative landslide. Undeterred, Jennie continued her activism through journalism and lecturing, both domestically and internationally, maintaining her dedication to socialist ideals.

In 1934, Jennie married Aneurin "Nye" Bevan, a fellow Labour politician and a leading figure in the party. Their partnership was both personal and political, with both sharing a deep commitment to socialist principles and public service. During World War Two, Jennie contributed to the war effort by working in the Ministry of Aircraft Production and serving as a political correspondent while also lecturing in America, Canada and Europe.

Jennie's political career saw a resurgence in 1945 when she was elected as the MP for Cannock, Staffordshire, a position she held until 1970. Her return to Parliament coincided with a period of significant social reform in post-war Britain. In 1964, under Prime Minister Harold Wilson's Labour government, she was appointed Minister for the Arts. In this role, she was a formidable advocate for the arts, successfully campaigning for increased government funding, supporting the film industry and abolishing theatre censorship by the Lord Chamberlain.

One of Jennie's most enduring legacies is her pivotal role in the establishment of the Open University. She championed the concept of a 'University of the Air,' advocating for a correspondence university that utilised television and radio to provide higher education opportunities to adults who had previously been denied access. Her vision was rooted in the principle of open access, ensuring that enrolment was open to everyone, irrespective of educational qualifications. This groundbreaking initiative democratised higher education in the UK, providing flexible learning opportunities to countless individuals.

In recognition of her contributions, Jennie was appointed a Privy Councillor in 1966 and, upon her retirement from the House of Commons in 1970, was granted a life peerage as Baroness Lee of Asheridge. She continued to be an active member of the House of Lords until the mid-1980s, advocating for the causes she held dear. Her autobiography, '*My Life with Nye*', published in 1980, offers personal insights into her life and her partnership with Aneurin Bevan.

Baroness Lee's legacy is commemorated through various memorials, including a plaque on Buccleuch Place in Edinburgh and the Jennie Lee Building of the Open University in Drumsheugh Gardens. Her life's work exemplifies a steadfast commitment to social justice, education, and the arts, leaving an indelible mark on British society.

She passed away on November 16, 1988, in London, at the age of 84. Her contributions to politics, education, and the arts continue to resonate, reflecting her enduring impact on the fabric of British public life.

A RADICAL STORY-TELLER

Robert Louis Stevenson. Author (1850 - 1894)

Robert Louis Stevenson was born at 8 Howard Place, Edinburgh, in 1850 to Thomas Stevenson, a leading lighthouse engineer and his wife, Margaret Isabella *nee* Balfour. Stevenson was marked from childhood by chronic ill health - tuberculosis, asthma and fragile lungs would dog him all his life. This physical health insecurity coupled with an upbringing steeped in the Presbyterian moralism of mid-Victorian Scotland, sharpened his sensitivity to questions of suffering, authority and human need. After enrolling at Edinburgh University to study engineering (and later law), he drifted instead toward the bohemian set of literary Edinburgh, where he absorbed radical currents ranging from Scottish romantic nationalism to the early stirrings of socialism. A decisive moment came in 1873 when Stevenson published his first poems, *'An Old Song Re-Sung'* among them, in the family journal, quietly asserting his artistic ambitions against paternal disapproval. Soon afterwards, following bouts of illness, he undertook a voyage to the Continent, gathering material for what would become his first travel narratives and laying the groundwork for a life lived in perpetual motion.

Stevenson's travel books - *'An Inland Voyage'* in1878, *'Travels with a Donkey in the Cévennes'* written in 1879 and later, *'Mediterranean Sketches'* - are more than guidebooks or picturesque reminiscences. They embody a subtle critique of urban industrialism and social conformity. In the Cévennes, for instance, his decision to carry his own provisions and choose his own path - rather than rely on coach or guide - becomes a metaphor for self-reliance and resistance to the commodification of nature. His habit of seeking out the poor, isolated and politically marginalised transforms his narrative into a compassionate survey of those left behind by progress.

By positing the dignity of simple living - and by wagging a literary finger at Victorian propriety - Stevenson's travelogues recast tourism as an act of solidarity with the rural poor rather than as a spectacle. His radicalism here is personal and ethical; he urges readers to question the costs of empire and industrial wealth, to consider alternate ways of being in the world.

In fiction, Stevenson's radical edge takes on a darker hue. *'Dr Jekyll and Mr Hyde'* written in 1886 dramatises the duality of human nature, exposing the thin veneer of civilised respectability that masks humanity's capacity for violence. Published anonymously, it arrived at a moment when debates over heredity, criminal anthropology and the social determinants of behaviour were stirring the public imagination. Stevenson invited readers to confront the uncomfortable idea that good and evil coexist within each individual, destabilising the era's easier moral certainties.

Similarly, adventure tales like *'Treasure Island'* in 1883 and *'Kidnapped'* three years later revel in the allure of the frontier - uncharted seas, unclaimed islands, the possibilities of reinvention beyond the bounds of polite society. Yet these stories never shy away from brutality; pirates kill without hesitation and captains abuse their authority. In so doing, Stevenson critiques imperial hierarchies and exposes the fragility of any social order built on coercion.

Less well known is Stevenson's involvement with contemporary political causes. In Samoa, where he settled in 1889 in pursuit of better health, he took up the cause of indigenous Samoans against the colonial ambitions of Germany, Britain and the United States. Earning the affectionate title *'Tusitala'* (teller of tales) from the local population, he lent his pen to petitions and public letters, advocating respect for Samoan governance and warning of the abuses of naval gunboat diplomacy. Even as a celebrated author, Stevenson refused to remain neutral; his writings from Samoa blend travelogue, political analysis and passionate plea for justice.

Back in Britain, he maintained friendships with literary radicals such as H. G. Wells and George Bernard Shaw, engaged in lively correspondence on socialism and the 'forward movement' in British politics, and counselled working-class writers on the craft of storytelling. Although never a party-politician, his circle placed him squarely among the intellectual avant-garde of late Victorian liberalism. Robert Louis Stevenson died on December 3, 1894, aged only forty-four on the Samoan island of Upolu. Perhaps Stevenson's greatest radical achievement was to demonstrate that a storyteller could be both entertainer and moral provocateur: that thrilling sea chases and buried treasure need not distract from deeper questions about power, identity and human solidarity.

SCOTLAND'S ONLY WORLD CUP WINNER.

Rose Peralta (nee Reilly) MBE. Footballer (1955 -)

Rose Reilly was born in Kilmarnock and brought up in Stewarton in Ayrshire. In a community where football was predominantly considered a male sport, Rose defied societal norms and expectations by playing with boys on the streets and in local teams. She was allowed to play for Stewarton United on the provision that she cut her hair short and called herself Ross. Her talent was such that she attracted the interest of scouts from Glasgow Celtic.

However, opportunities for girls to play football in Scotland in the 1960s and 70s were extremely limited. Women's football was not taken seriously and the infrastructure to support aspiring female athletes was practically non-existent.

Despite her undeniable talent, Reilly faced significant obstacles in Scotland. The Scottish Football Association not only refused to support women's football but also actively discouraged it. Women's teams were marginalised and matches were often played in poor conditions with minimal resources. Reilly was forced to contend with societal attitudes that deemed football an unsuitable sport for women.

In consequence, at the age of seventeen, Reilly made the bold decision to leave Scotland in search of better opportunities abroad. This decision marked the beginning of her journey to greatness but also highlighted the challenges faced by female footballers who lacked the support and recognition they deserved in their own countries.

Her move to Italy proved to be a turning point in her career. In Italy, women's football was beginning to gain traction, and Reilly quickly established herself as one of the top players in the league. She joined AC Milan's women's team before moving to Catania and later Reggiana. Her success in Italy was extraordinary as she became a prolific goal scorer and an integral part of her teams. She won *Serie A* titles and numerous domestic cups, earning widespread acclaim for her skill, vision, and determination.

While playing in Italy, Reilly achieved an incredible milestone that underscored her exceptional talent. In 1983, she was named the Best Female Footballer in the World, a recognition of her outstanding contributions to the sport. Her achievements on the field were a testament not only to her abilities but also to her perseverance in the face of adversity.

One of the most remarkable aspects of Rose Reilly's career was her unique international experience. Initially, she played for the Scottish women's national team, debuting in 1972 and scoring a goal in her first match. However, due to the lack of support from the SFA and her frustration with the state of women's football in Scotland, Reilly made the controversial decision to switch allegiances and began representing the Italian women's national team after becoming a naturalised Italian citizen. This move was significant, as it allowed her to compete at a higher level on the international stage. With Italy, Reilly enjoyed considerable success, including winning the 1984 *Mundialito*, al precursor to the Women's World Cup. Her versatility, leadership, and skill made her an invaluable player for both Scotland and Italy during her career. Rose Reilly's career paved the way for future generations of female footballers. Her success challenged stereotypes and demonstrated that women's football could produce players of extraordinary skill and professionalism. Despite the challenges she faced, Reilly never lost her love for the game or her determination to succeed. In recognition of her contributions to football, Reilly has received numerous accolades in her later years. In 2007, she was inducted into the Scottish Football Hall of Fame, a long-overdue acknowledgment of her impact on the sport. She has also been celebrated as a role model for young athletes, particularly in Scotland, where her story continues to inspire.

Rose Reilly's journey from a small town in Scotland to becoming one of the world's greatest women footballers is a testament to her talent, determination, and passion for the game. In an era when women's football was marginalised and undervalued, she overcame significant obstacles to achieve international success and pave the way for future generations.

Today, Rose Reilly's name is synonymous with excellence in women's football and her story remains a powerful inspiration for anyone striving to break barriers and achieve greatness. Married to Argentinian, Norberto Peralta, she lives with him and her daughter in Stewarton.

THE SCIENTIFIC ENGINEER

William Thomson, 1st Baron Kelvin: Physicist and Engineer (1824 - 1907)

William Thomson was born in 1824 in Belfast, Ireland. His father, James Thomson, was a mathematics professor at the Royal Belfast Academical Institution and later at the University of Glasgow. Under his father's guidance, young William displayed extraordinary mathematical talent from an early age. His upbringing in an intellectually stimulating environment nurtured his fascination with science and mathematics, setting the stage for his future achievements. At just ten years old, Thomson enrolled at the University of Glasgow, an astonishing feat even by 19th-century standards. There, he excelled in mathematics and physics, quickly outpacing his peers. In 1841, at the age of 17, he continued his studies at Cambridge University, where he distinguished himself as one of the university's top students, earning numerous academic honours. After Cambridge, he spent time in Paris, studying under the renowned physicist Jean-Baptiste Joseph Fourier, whose work on heat conduction greatly influenced Thomson's later research.

One of Thomson's most significant contributions to science was in the field of thermodynamics, the study of heat, energy and work. His work helped establish the laws of thermodynamics which are fundamental principles governing the behaviour of energy in physical systems.Thomson introduced the concept of an absolute temperature scale in 1848. Unlike the Celsius or Fahrenheit scales, which are based on arbitrary reference points like the freezing and boiling points of water, Thomson's scale was grounded in the fundamental properties of nature. This scale, which later became known as the Kelvin scale, starts at absolute zero, the theoretical temperature at which all molecular motion ceases. The Kelvin scale is still used today in scientific disciplines worldwide, particularly in physics and engineering.

Thomson also played a pivotal role in formulating the Second Law of Thermodynamics, which states that the total entropy of an isolated system can never decrease over time. This principle has far-reaching implications, from understanding why heat flows from hot to cold objects to the fundamental nature of time and the eventual fate of the universe. His insights into thermodynamics not only advanced theoretical physics but also had practical applications in engineering, particularly in the design of more efficient heat engines. While Thomson's theoretical work was groundbreaking, he was equally influential as an engineer and inventor. Perhaps his most famous engineering achievement was his role in the successful laying of the transatlantic telegraph cable, which revolutionised global communication.

Thomson developed new methods to improve signal transmission including the invention of the mirror galvanometer, a highly sensitive instrument capable of detecting weak electrical signals with great precision. In 1866, after several failed attempts, the transatlantic telegraph cable was successfully laid, connecting Europe and North America for the first time. This achievement drastically reduced the time it took to send messages across the ocean from weeks to mere minutes, ushering in a new era of global communication. For his contributions, Thomson was knighted by Queen Victoria and later elevated to the peerage as Baron Kelvin of Largs, becoming the first scientist to receive a British hereditary title based on scientific achievement.

In addition to his work in thermodynamics and engineering, Lord Kelvin made significant contributions to the study of electromagnetism and mathematical physics. He collaborated with James Clerk Maxwell whose equations unified the theories of electricity and magnetism into a single framework. Kelvin's mathematical rigour and analytical skills were instrumental in refining and expanding Maxwell's theories, helping to establish the foundations of modern electromagnetic theory. Kelvin also explored the behaviour of fluid dynamics, wave motion, and the mathematical analysis of energy. His interest in the ether theory - an obsolete concept that proposed a medium for light waves to travel contributed to the scientific discourse that eventually led to Einstein's theory of relativity.

Lord Kelvin continued his scientific pursuits well into his later years. He served as a professor of Natural Philosophy at the University of

Glasgow for over fifty years, mentoring generations of students and influencing countless future scientists and engineers. His passion for teaching was matched by his enthusiasm for invention, holding over seventy patents for devices ranging from electrical instruments to maritime navigational tools. Lord Kelvin passed away on December 17, 1907, at the age of 83. He was buried in Westminster Abbey, near the graves of other scientific luminaries like Isaac Newton and Charles Darwin, a testament to his status as one of the greatest scientists in history.

THE CENTENARIAN FIREBRAND

Emanuel Shinwell. Politician and Activist (1884 - 1986)

Emanuel Shinwell was born in London in 1884, to Jewish immigrants from Poland. His family soon moved to Glasgow, where he grew up in relative poverty. His father was a tailor, and the family struggled financially, giving young Shinwell firsthand experience of working-class hardship. This background played a crucial role in shaping his political outlook.

At a young age, Shinwell left school to work and help support his family. He started as an apprentice in the clothing industry before moving into trade union activism. His involvement in workers' rights began when he joined the Amalgamated Union of Operatives. He later transitioned into work related to the dockers and seamen, becoming a prominent figure in Glasgow's Labour movement.

He gained prominence during the early 20th century as an organiser for the Seamen's Union and became known for his militant stance on workers' rights, often engaging in strikes and labor disputes. One of his most famous early conflicts was the 1919 Glasgow dockers' strike, during which he was imprisoned for inciting riotous behaviour. His arrest and imprisonment only bolstered his reputation among workers, who saw him as a fearless champion of their cause.

He was first elected as a Labour Member of Parliament for Linlithgow in 1922. Although he lost his seat in 1924, he returned to Parliament in 1928 and remained a fixture in British politics for decades. He was a staunch advocate for the working class, often clashing with political opponents and even members of his own party over labor issues.

During the 1929 - 1931 Labour government, Shinwell served as Secretary for Mines, where he began pushing for reforms in the coal industry. However, his tenure was short-lived due to the economic crisis and the fall of the Labour government in 1931. Like many left-wing Labour MPs, he opposed Ramsay MacDonald's decision to form a National

Government and subsequently lost his seat. After returning to Parliament in 1935, Shinwell became a vocal critic of appeasement policies toward Nazi Germany. During World War II, he worked within the government to support the war effort while continuing to advocate for post-war socialist policies.

Shinwell's most significant political achievements came during the post-war Attlee government (1945 - 1951). As Minister of Fuel and Power, he played a leading role in the nationalisation of the coal industry in 1947. This was a landmark policy of the Labour government, aimed at improving the working conditions and economic security of coal miners. Shinwell worked closely with trade unions to oversee the transition of coal production from private ownership to state control under the National Coal Board.

Despite the ambitious goals of nationalisation, the transition was challenging. Britain faced severe fuel shortages, and Shinwell came under heavy criticism for his handling of the situation, particularly during the harsh winter of 1947. Nevertheless, he remained a strong defender of Labour's policies and continued to push for expanded nationalisation in other sectors.

After his tenure in the Ministry of Fuel and Power, Shinwell held several key positions, including Minister of Defence. His time in this role was marked by Cold War tensions, the early years of NATO, and Britain's involvement in the Korean War. Although he was not a military expert, he worked to modernise Britain's armed forces and strengthen its defence alliances.

Following Labour's defeat in 1951, Shinwell remained an influential figure within the party. He served as Chairman of the Labour Party and continued to advocate for socialist policies, though he gradually moved toward the political centre as the party evolved.

In 1970, after serving as an MP for various constituencies, Shinwell was made a life peer, becoming Baron Shinwell of Easington. He remained active in the House of Lords well into his 90s, making him one of Britain's longest-serving politicians.

Emanuel Shinwell's was a fiery orator, often engaging in heated debates with political opponents. His role in nationalising coal and his contributions to defence policy during the early Cold War years remain key aspects of his legacy.

Shinwell passed away on May 8, 1986, at the age of 101, making him one of the longest-lived British politicians. His life and work remain an important chapter in the history of British Labour politics.

THE DREAM SHALL NEVER DIE.

Alexander (Alex) Elliot Anderson Salmond. Politician (1954 - 2024)

Alexander Salmond was born at his parents' home at 101 Preston Road, Linlithgow on 31 December 1954, the second of four children born to Robert Fyfe Findlay Salmond and Mary Stewart Salmond both of whom were civil servants. Salmond grew up in a working-class family in Linlithgow, attending Linlithgow Academy before studying economics and history at the University of St Andrews. His interest in politics began during his university years, where he became involved in student activism. After graduating, he worked as an economist for the Royal Bank of Scotland. Salmond married Moira McGlashan in 1981. She was a senior civil servant seventeen years his senior and became his boss when he joined the Scottish Office. They had no children.

Salmond joined the SNP in the 1970s when the party was still relatively marginal in Scottish politics and was elected as Member of Parliament for Banff and Buchan in 1987, marking the start of his rise to prominence. Known for his sharp debating skills and strategic thinking, Salmond quickly became a leading voice within the SNP, advocating for Scottish independence and greater autonomy within the United Kingdom.

In 1990, Salmond was elected leader of the SNP, a position he would hold until 2000 and again from 2004 to 2014. His leadership transformed the party from a fringe political movement into a dominant force in Scottish politics. He was instrumental in modernising the SNP, broadening its appeal beyond its traditional base to attract a wider range of voters.

The establishment of the Scottish Parliament in 1999 provided Salmond with a new political arena. Although the SNP did not initially gain control, Salmond continued to push for independence, arguing that Scotland needed full control over its own affairs. In 2007, the SNP won a narrow victory in the Scottish Parliament elections, and Salmond became First Minister. This was a historic moment, marking the first time the SNP had led the government. Despite leading a minority government, Salmond's administration focused on improving public services, promoting renewable energy and advocating for independence.

His government introduced policies, such as free university tuition and free prescriptions, which helped boost the SNP's popularity. In 2011, the party won a landslide victory, securing a majority in the Scottish Parliament. This was a remarkable achievement given the proportional representation system designed to prevent single-party majorities. The 2014 independence referendum was the defining moment of Salmond's career. Salmond led the 'Yes Scotland' campaign, arguing that independence would allow Scotland to control its own economy, welfare system, and foreign policy.

The campaign was marked by passionate debate and high voter engagement, with an unprecedented turnout of 84.6%. Ultimately, the 'No' side won, with 55% of voters choosing to remain in the UK. Although the result was a setback for Salmond, the referendum significantly increased political awareness and engagement in Scotland.

Following the defeat, Salmond resigned as First Minister and leader of the SNP, passing the baton to his deputy, Nicola Sturgeon. His departure marked the end of an era, but his influence on Scottish politics remained profound. After stepping down as First Minister, Salmond returned to Westminster as MP for Gordon from 2015 to 2017. During this period, he continued to advocate for Scottish independence and played a key role in debates about Brexit and its implications for Scotland.

However, Salmond's legacy became more complex in 2018 when allegations of sexual misconduct were made against him. He denied the charges and was acquitted of all criminal charges in a high-profile trial in 2020. The case led to a public rift between Salmond and his successor, First Minister Nicola Sturgeon, over how the allegations were handled, creating divisions within the SNP and the broader independence movement.

In 2021, Salmond launched a new political party, *Alba*, aimed at advancing the cause of Scottish independence.

Salmond's political career transformed the SNP into a mainstream party and brought the issue of independence to the forefront of Scottish politics.. His career has not been without controversy but his contribution to Scotland's history is undeniable.

Salmond died on 12 October 2024, at the age of sixty-nine when in Ohrid, North Macedonia and is buried in Strichen Cemetery, Aberdeenshire.

HECTOR THE HERO.

Major General Sir Hector Archibald MacDonald. Soldier (1853 - 1903)

Hector MacDonald was born on a farm at Rootfield, on the Black Isle near Dingwall just north of Inverness. His father William was both a stonemason and crofter and his mother, Ann, a housewife. The family all spoke Scots Gaelic.

At the age of 15, MacDonald was an apprentice draper in Dingwall before, aged seventeen, joining the 92nd Gordon Highlanders by adding a year to his age. He rose rapidly through the non-commissioned ranks, and was promoted to Colour-sergeant when his bravery in the presence of the enemy during the Afghan War led to him being offered the choice of being recommended for the Victoria Cross or commissioned in his regiment. He chose the latter and was further promoted to the commissioned ranks as a Captain Lieutenant. During the First Boer War he was made prisoner but his bravery so impressed General Joubert, the commandant-general of the Boer forces that he gave him back his sword. During the Mahdist War in Sudan, MacDonald commanded a brigade of the Egyptian army in a series of battles including those at Altbara, Dongola and Omdurman following which he became a household name in Britain. He received a brevet promotion (a promotion which carries temporary status but not the appropriate salary) to Colonel and was also appointed as an aide-de-camp to Queen Victoria. He was nicknamed, 'Hector of the Battles'.

A year later, in1899, MacDonald received the temporary rank of Brigadier General and was sent to command matters in the India's Punjab but shortly thereafter, following the outbreak of war in South Africa, he was ordered there to command the Highland Brigade and received the substantive rank of colonel before, only some days after assuming that rank and full command of the Highland brigade, he was promoted to the rank of Major General. A year later following operations in Pretoria and Bloemfontein, he was knighted for his services.

When early in 1902 he was appointed Commander-in-Chief of British troops in Ceylon he caused some consternation by yelling at the Governor to get off the parade ground, compounding the process of alienation by declining the social invitations of the British community and consorting instead with the locals. Insisting on better standards of dress and behaviour in respect of the children of important British planters, he further distanced himself from the local establishment. Shortly thereafter the Governor and a local tea-planter advised that MacDonald was consorting with locals in a club and that they suspected homosexuality. According to Robert Hyam in his book, *'Empire and Sexuality'*, MacDonald 'was probably told by the King when in London that the best thing he could do was to shoot himself'. However, the, Commander-in-Chief of the Army, advised MacDonald to go back to Ceylon and face a court martial to clear his name. MacDonald, reading of his charges in a morning newspaper over breakfast in his hotel in Paris, returned to his room and shot himself.

MacDonald had alone risen through the ranks to Major General and was knighted by his own efforts as opposed to the Eton, Oxbridge and family connections utilised by other senior officers. The suicide of the war hero caused great public shock particularly when it was made public that MacDonald had had a wife and a son.

MacDonald's funeral was held at Dean Cemetery in Edinburgh and 30,000 people turned up to pay their final respects. In the weeks following, thousands more from all over the world came to say farewell. A one hundred foot high memorial was erected above Dingwall. In 1907, James Scott Skinner, one of the most influential fiddlers in Scottish traditional music wrote a tune in his honour called *'Hector the Hero'* and Scottish poet Robert Service wrote his poem '*Fighting Mac'*.

A Government Commission released a report on the tragedy on 29 June 1903: *'In reference to the grave charges made against the late Sir Hector MacDonald, we, the appointed and undersigned Commissioners, individually and collectively declare on oath that, after the most careful, minute, and exhaustive inquiry and investigation of the whole circumstances and facts connected with the sudden and unexpected death of the late Sir Hector MacDonald, unanimously and unmistakably find absolutely no reason or crime whatsoever which would create feelings such as would determine suicide, in preference to conviction of any crime affecting the moral and irreproachable character of so brave, so fearless, so glorious and unparalleled a hero: and we firmly believe the cause which gave rise to the inhuman and cruel suggestions of crime were prompted through vulgar feelings of spite and jealousy in his rising to such a high rank of distinction in the British Army. We find the late Sir Hector MacDonald has been cruelly assassinated by vile and slandering tongues.'*

THE SCOTTISH RADICAL WAR OF 1820

John Baird, Andrew Hardie, and James (Purly) Wilson. Political Activists Circa (1820)

The Scottish Radical War of 1820 was a pivotal event in Scotland's history, marked by a brief but intense insurrection driven by demands for political reform and workers' rights. Amidst growing economic hardship, political repression, and the influence of revolutionary movements across Europe, Scottish radicals sought to challenge the existing power structures. Central to this movement were John Baird, Andrew Hardie, and James (Purly) Wilson, who played crucial roles in organising, leading, and inspiring the radicals during the uprising. Their actions not only shaped the events of 1820 but also left a lasting legacy in the history of political reform in Scotland.

John Baird was a former soldier in the British Army and his military experience made him an invaluable figure during the Radical War. Born around 1790, Baird had served in the Napoleonic Wars, gaining combat knowledge and leadership skills. His background distinguished him from many other radicals, most of whom were weavers, artisans, and labourers with little to no military training.

Baird' s role in the Radical War was primarily as a military commander. He was tasked with leading one of the key radical forces during the attempted uprising. On April 5, 1820, Baird, alongside Andrew Hardie, led a group of radicals from Glasgow and surrounding areas with the objective of seizing the Carron Ironworks near Falkirk. The Carron Company was a symbol of industrial power and was known for producing armaments, making it a strategic target. The radicals believed that capturing the ironworks would not only arm them but also inspire a broader uprising across Scotland.

However, Baird's leadership faced significant challenges. The radical movement had been infiltrated by government agents and informers who deliberately spread misinformation and exaggerated the extent of support for the uprising. This led Baird and his men to believe they were part of a larger, coordinated revolt when in reality the government was well-prepared to suppress them. The march to Carron Ironworks ended in disaster when the radicals encountered government forces at Bonnymuir on April 5. Despite Baird's efforts to organise and inspire his poorly armed and inexperienced men, the radicals were quickly overwhelmed by the disciplined troops. Baird fought bravely but was captured alongside Hardie and other key leaders. After his capture, he was executed on September 8, 1820 and became a martyr for the movement.

Andrew Hardie was another central figure in the Radical War, serving alongside John Baird as a co-leader of the radical forces at Bonnymuir. His passion for reform and justice made him a charismatic leader, capable of inspiring others to join the cause.

Hardie co-led the group that marched towards Carron Ironworks, sharing the responsibility for organising the radicals and maintaining morale. Hardie's leadership was marked by his fervent belief in the principles of democracy and social justice. Following their defeat at Bonnymuir, Hardie was captured alongside Baird. During their trial for treason in Stirling, Hardie's speeches reflected his unyielding commitment to the radical cause. Hardie's execution by hanging and beheading on the same day as Baird cemented his status as a martyr. His courage in the face of death demonstrated the depth of conviction within the radical movement. Like Baird, Hardie's legacy lived on, symbolising the enduring struggle for political representation and workers' rights in Scotland.While John Baird and Andrew Hardie are often remembered for their leadership during the actual insurrection, James (Purly) Wilson played a vital role as a grassroots organiser within the radical movement. Wilson's nickname 'Purly' referred to his occupation as a weaver, a common trade among radicals at the time. Weavers were particularly active in the movement due to the economic hardships they faced during the post-Napoleonic War depression, which saw wages fall and unemployment rise. Wilson's role focused on mobilising support, organising meetings, and spreading radical ideas among the working class. He was part of a network of radicals who communicated through secret societies, pamphlets and word of mouth. Unlike Baird and Hardie, Wilson did not lead armed forces during the uprising and was imprisoned, not executed like Baird and Hardie. The Scottish Radical War of 1820 was a defining moment in the history of political reform in Scotland. Figures like John Baird, Andrew Hardie, and

James (Purly) Wilson played distinct but complementary roles in the movement. Baird provided military leadership, Hardie embodied ideological defiance, and Wilson ensured grassroots organisation. Their sacrifices and contributions highlighted the widespread desire for political change among Scotland's working class. A sizeable monumental gravestone in Glasgow's Sighthill Cemetery marks their interment.

THE TARTAN WHIRLWIND

Gwendoline Emily Meachum (Wendy Wood). Artist and Political Activist (1892 - 1981)

Gwendoline Emily Meachum was born to Scottish parents in Kent in 1892. Her maternal grandmother was a highland crofter's daughter called Eilidh Ross, who spoke Gaelic rather than English. Eilidh Ross died in childbirth delivering Wendy's mother who subsequently imbued her with stories of William Wallace and Scotland before the family moved to South Africa where she grew up. As a child, her family holidayed in Scotland and she was encouraged to think of it as her home. When challenged as to her legitimacy as a Scot, she would reply "One does not have to have to be a horse to have been born in a stable".

Wood went to school in England, discovering a passion for art. She studied in London, at the Westminster School of Art and married Walter Cuthbert in 1913. The couple road-tripped around Scotland as a holiday, and then took residence there. Having married into a strictly religious family and suffering bouts of ill-health, Wood ceased her art activities for a number of years. She trained as an actress and appeared on radio and later television where she read Scottish stories on the BBC children's TV programme, Jackanory under the name, *'Auntie Gwen'*. In 1923 she produced illustrations and poems for her first book *'The Baby In The Glass'*, and illustrated for the children's magazine '*Little Dots*'.

In 1927 she left her job, her home and her husband in Dundee and adopted her mother's maiden name, Wood, as a symbol of the new path she'd decided her life must take; her commitment to her art and to Scotland. The following year, Wood was involved in the birth of the National Party of Scotland, which would merge with the Scottish Party to become the Scottish National Party in 1934. Wood worked hard to promote the cause of Scottish nationalism; she became an effective public speaker and toured Scotland speaking at public meetings. In 1957 alone she gave seventy-three speeches.

Wood was a firm believer that cultural nationalism was just as important as political and economic nationalism. In consequence, she founded '*Scottish Watch*' in 1931, a youth organisation that encouraged its members to learn about Scottish culture. At its height, Scottish Watch was more popular in Scotland than the Boy Scouts. The Daily Record gave a free page to their activities every week as the newspaper was somewhat more nationalist then than in later years.

She also preferred direct action to negotiation and compromise. In 1932 she led a group of nationalists into Stirling Castle to take down the union flag and replace it with a lion rampant. She pulled down the lightning conductor from the statue of the Duke of Sutherland hoping that a bolt of lightening might finish the job as he'd been responsible for removing the inhabitants of the Highland glens to the colonies and she had the Union Flag placed under the carpet on the stairs of her Edinburgh home so that she could tread on it every day. At an SNP meeting when an activist was expelled, Wood declared, 'Ye'd expel Wallace!' and began to leave. Another member agreed and emptied a jug of water over the chairman. She established numerous groups, including the Scottish Patriots and made a nuisance of herself, serving time in prison for her many protests. Aged 80, she embarked on a 'fast unto death' in an effort to persuade the Conservative government to honour its election promise to publish a Green Paper on plans for a Scottish Assembly. Wood ended her week-long fast after then Labour MP Jim Sillars made a personal appeal to her on Scottish Television. During her fast she had sustained herself only with water. Michael Hirst, national vice-chairman of the Scottish Young Conservatives, lamented that the government had yielded to Wood's 'publicity-seeking stunts'.

It was revealed decades later that, in 1933, Special Branch had unsurprisingly prepared a report on her activity. It reported that Wood was chairperson of the Democratic Scottish Self-Government Organisation (DSSO) whose aims were 'to achieve complete separation of Scotland from England and to set up an independent Parliament with sovereignty vested in the Scottish people'. Special Branch explained, 'the DSSO had said that these aims could not be achieved except by direct action and not via The Westminster Parliament where the English outnumber the Scottish representatives by seven to one'.

In all she wrote ten books, the last being her autobiography, '*Yours Sincerely, for Scotland*', remaining active into her late-eighties. She died in Edinburgh on 30 June 1981, aged 88.

A memorial plaque was placed in Old Calton Cemetery in 2021.

'A RAT RACE IS FOR RATS'.

James (Jimmy) Reid. Trades Unionist and Journalist (1932 - 2010)

James 'Jimmy' Reid, was born in 1932, in Govan, Glasgow, a hub of shipbuilding activity; his upbringing deeply influencing his political and social outlook. Raised in a working-class family, he came face to face with the economic challenges and social inequalities that helped shape his engagement with the labour movement. The son of a shipyard worker father, Reid left St Gerards Secondary school at fourteen and served a very brief stint in a stockbroker's office. He attended the then Royal Technical College (now the University of Strathclyde), where his political consciousness continued to develop. Initially drawn to the Communist Party of Great Britain, Reid's involvement in the party was rooted in its advocacy for workers' rights and its criticism of capitalist exploitation. However, he remained pragmatic, recognising the limits of ideological purity in the face of real-world challenges.

The watershed moment of Reid's career came in 1971 when the Heath government announced plans to close the Clyde's shipyards, threatening over 6,000 jobs. Known for his exceptional oratorical skills and strategic acumen, Reid, alongside his fellow shop-stewards Jimmy Airlie and Sammy Barr, led a "work-in" rather than a strike. The work-in was a peaceful and highly effective form of protest where workers continued to perform their jobs, demonstrating the viability of the yards and their refusal to be idle in the face of government indifference. This approach contrasted with more confrontational methods and succeeded in garnering public sympathy and widespread support.

Reid's philosophy during the work-in was encapsulated in his insistence on discipline and dignity. Perhaps one of his defining moments was when he addressed the workers outlining that there would be "no hooliganism, no vandalism and no bevvying." He understood the power of perception and sought to present the workers as responsible and orderly, thereby winning favour with the public and the media. The eventual success of the campaign led to government intervention and investment, preserving many of the jobs previously thought doomed. This experience consolidated Jimmy Reid's place as a highly respected leader of the labour movement and proved how determined, yet peaceful activism could lead to significant change.

Following the work-in, Reid's political journey saw him distance himself from the Communist Party as he became increasingly disillusioned with Soviet policies, notably its aggressive suppression of dissent in Eastern Europe. In search of a more pragmatic approach to socialism, he joined the Labour Party in 1975, aligning himself with a broader vision for socialism in Britain.

In addition to trade unionism, Reid's voice resonated in journalism and broadcasting. He wrote prolifically for a variety of newspapers, providing commentary on political, social, and economic issues. His pieces often highlighted his intellectual flair and passion for social justice. Perhaps one of his most notable contributions to public discourse was his rectorial address given at the University of Glasgow in 1972, famously titled "A Rat Race is for Rats." The speech criticised societal values predicated on selfishness and greed and proposed a collective ethos anchored in shared prosperity and human well-being. The address remains one of the most acclaimed speeches in recent Scottish history, appreciated for its eloquence and insight. Indeed, it was printed in its entirety by the New York Times, which viewed it as the most inspiring speech since Lincoln's Gettysburg Address.

Reid's influence extended beyond the labour movement, touching broader socio-political debates. He championed causes that included social housing, education reform, and anti-nuclear campaigns.

Reid's uncomfortable association with Labour came to an abrupt conclusion after Tony Blair took over as leader in 1994. He retired to Rothesay on the Isle of Bute and continued to write and comment. In 2005 he announced that he had joined the Scottish National Party. His legacy is his commitment to the principles of equality, justice, and fairness. His eloquence and innovative approaches to industrial action left an indelible mark on Scottish society.

He died on August 10, 2010.

SELECTED QUOTES

Rose Reilly

“I even started drinking espresso, but nearly spat it out, I thought it tasted like poison. But everything Italians did, so did I; I embraced their way of life.”

“I had always a Scottish heart beating under an Italian jersey.”

“I didn’t say anything at all about the SFA. I can only speak for myself but when I got *sine died* I was in Italy, there was no communication. I didn’t even know until my friend Elsie told me.”

Lord Kelvin

“Radio has no future. X-rays are clearly a hoax. The aeroplane is scientifically impossible.”

“If you cannot measure it, then it is not science.”

“In science there is only physics; all the rest is stamp collecting.”

“Large increases in cost with questionable increases in performance can be tolerated only in race horses and women.”

Alex Salmond

“For me as leader my time is nearly over but for Scotland the campaign continues and the dream will never die.”

“If I’ve got any small role in this matter, it’s to say to Scots Americans: under no circumstances make Donald Trump President of the United States of America.”

“The rocks will melt with the sun before tuition fees are introduced in Scotland.”

Wendy Wood

"And there in confident arrogance, the Union Jack; the flag of our bondage, flew on the flagstaff of the Castle. A sudden anger flamed up in me…It was only a minute before the 'Jack' was at my feet and the gold and scarlet 'Lion' flag of Scotland was streaming out on a momentary wind."

"There is no place where Sunday is more real than among the hills. If I went up silent, Came down singing…and that is Sunday in the hills".

Jimmy Reid

"A rat race is for rats. We're not rats. We're human beings. Reject the insidious pressures in society that would blunt your critical faculties to all that is happening around you, that would caution silence in the face of injustice lest you jeopardise your chances of promotion and self-advancement."

"The strength of a society is measured by how it treats its weakest members."

"There will be no hooliganism. There will be no vandalism. There will be no bevvying ... because the world is watching us."

"From the very depth of my being, I challenge the right of any man or any group of men, in business or in government, to tell a fellow human being that he or she is expendable."

"When New Labour came to power, we got a right-wing Conservative government. I came to realise that voting Labour wasn't in Scotland's interests any more. Any doubt I had about that was cast aside for ever when I saw Gordon Brown cosying up to Margaret Thatcher in Downing Street."

VISIONARY TOWN PLANNER

Sir Robert Grieve. Polymath (1910 - 1995)

Bob Grieve was born in 1910 in Maryhill, Glasgow in a tenement, one of six children, to Peter Grieve and his wife, Catherine Boyle. Grieve's father, was a Clydeside boilermaker who did little with his family other than provide a weekly wage packet. His mother, Catherine, however, was radically socialist, well read and a caring and faithful Roman Catholic. Grieve was born at a time of significant social and economic change. He attended North Kelvinside School his academic and professional trajectory suggesting a rigorous foundation in planning, geography and public administration although details are slight.

Grieve's formative years coincided with the interwar period when Scotland was experiencing industrial decline and urban challenges such as overcrowding and poor housing conditions. These issues likely influenced his later dedication to urban and regional planning. He pursued studies that equipped him with the technical expertise and broad intellectual scope needed for his later roles in shaping Scotland's built environment.

One of Grieve's earliest major contributions was his involvement in regional planning, where he advocated for a more systematic approach to urban development. He championed the idea that town planning should not only address immediate infrastructure needs but also consider long-term social, economic, and environmental sustainability.

Grieve was a key figure in the Clyde Valley Regional Plan (1946–1949), a blueprint for the post-war redevelopment of the Glasgow region. One of Grieve's most significant contributions to Scotland's urban landscape was his role in the New Towns movement. He was a leading advocate for the development of Cumbernauld, a planned town designed to ease the population pressures on Glasgow. The town was conceived as a modern, self-sufficient urban centre with carefully integrated residential, commercial, and industrial zones.

Cumbernauld, which began development in the 1950s, was hailed as a pioneering example of modernist urban design. Its distinctive town centre, which placed pedestrian pathways above road networks, was considered innovative at the time. While aspects of the design were later criticised, the principles behind Cumbernauld; planned growth, efficient land use and improved quality of life, reflected Grieve's vision for a more organised and functional urban Scotland.

Beyond individual projects, Grieve had a lasting impact on Scottish national planning policy. He became the first Chairman of the Highlands and Islands Development Board in 1965, a position that allowed him to shape economic and infrastructure strategies for Scotland's rural regions. The HIDB aimed to revitalise the economically struggling Highlands, which had suffered from population decline and industrial stagnation.

Under Grieve's leadership, the HIDB initiated policies to promote tourism, improve transport infrastructure, and support local industries such as fishing, agriculture, and crafts. His approach was holistic. Rather than simply focusing on economic development, he sought to integrate social and cultural factors into planning decisions. His work contributed to the long-term resilience of Highland communities, many of which continue to benefit from the policies he helped implement.

In addition to his work as a planner and administrator, Grieve was an influential academic. He held a professorship at the University of Strathclyde where he contributed to the intellectual foundation of Scottish planning studies. His writings on urban and regional development helped establish planning as a serious academic discipline in Scotland.

Grieve also wrote extensively on Scotland's geography, economy, and culture. His publications reflected his deep appreciation for the Scottish landscape and its role in shaping national identity. His work often blended technical analysis with broader philosophical reflections on the relationship between people and place, demonstrating his polymathic ability to bridge multiple disciplines.

Sir Robert Grieve's influence on Scottish planning and development remains profound. His advocacy for regional planning, economic regeneration and sustainable development laid the foundation for many policies that continue to shape Scotland's built environment today.

Grieve's holistic approach to planning combining economics, infrastructure, social policy, and cultural awareness, set him apart as a true polymath. He was not just an administrator or planner; he was a thinker who saw the bigger picture, ensuring that Scotland's development was approached with both pragmatism and vision.

THE KING OF SKIFFLE.

Anthony James 'Lonnie' Donegan MBE. Musician. (1931 - 2002)

Lonnie Donegan was born in Glasgow's Bridgeton, the son of Mary Deighan and Peter Donegan, a professional violinist with the Scottish National Orchestra, before quitting music to join the Merchant Navy. When Donegan was two years old, the family moved to East Ham in the London Borough of Newham, some eight miles east of London's city centre. Donegan was evacuated to Cheshire in the north of England to escape the blitz in World War Two where he attended St. Ambrose College.

He was first bitten by the jazz bug around the age of fifteen when he and a fellow Boy Scout visited the Bruce Grove Ballroom to see the Freddy Randall Jazz Band perform a Sunday afternoon session. He bought his first guitar for thirty shillings and over the next few years he sought out every blues record he could afford along with his other love, traditional jazz.

In his later teens, he formed the Anthony Donegan Jazz Band, soon abbreviated to the Tony Donegan Jazz Band which he financed through his job as a part-time deliveryman for a photographer. In his spare time, he performed alongside other fans of jazz such as trombonist Chris Barber. This came to an end when Donegan was called up for National Service in 1949 but he soon found himself drumming in an armed forces jazz band, the Wolverines while in the army at Southampton. A posting to Vienna in Austria brought him into contact with American soldiers, access to stateside records and the American Forces Network radio station.

Just before his discharge he attended a gig at London's Caxton Hall where he listened to the legendary blues singer and guitarist Lonnie Johnson. Donegan was hugely impressed and immediately adopted the stage name of Lonnie.

Donegan sang and played guitar and banjo in the Chris Barber Band during a set devoted to 'Dixieland' music. He began playing with two other band members during the intervals, to provide what posters referred to as a 'skiffle' break playing folk and blues songs by artists such as Woody Guthrie. In 1954 he recorded a speeded-up version of '*Rock Island Line*' written and recorded earlier by Huddie William Ledbetter better known by his stage name Lead Belly. With '*John Henry*' on the flip side, it was a hit in 1956 and inspired the creation of a full album, *An Englishman Sings American Folk Songs*, released in America in the early 1960s. It was the first debut record to go gold in the UK, and reached the Top Ten in the United States. Donegan had somehow synthesised American southern blues with simple acoustic instruments such as the acoustic guitar, washtub bass, and washboard rhythm - all instruments within the financial reach of young people. The new style was called 'skiffle' and captivated an entire generation of post-war youth in the UK inspiring groups such as the Beatles; ironically in doing so, bringing about his fall from the chart success as these new beat groups rose in popularity. Paul McCartney said, "He was the first person we had heard of from Britain to get to the coveted No.1 spot in the charts, and we studied his records avidly. We all bought guitars to be in a skiffle group. He was the man."

Despite dozens of hits during the sixties, his lack of chart success in the seventies saw him begin to play the American cabaret circuit where, performing at Lake Tahoe, he had his first heart attack in 1976. He had a quadruple bypass surgery and returned to popularity briefly in 1978 when pop star Adam Faith persuaded luminaries as Ronnie Wood, Rory Gallagher, Brian May, Elton John and Ringo Starr to record Donegan's early songs with him on an album entitled *'Putting On The Style'*. He played at the Glastonbury Festival in 1999, and was made a Member of the British Empire in 2000. Around the same time, he married for the third time, became a father for the seventh time, moved to the Spanish resort of Malaga and suffered more heart problems, resulting in yet further bypass surgery.

Lonnie Donegan died on 3 November 2002, aged 71 after having a heart attack mid-way through a UK tour. Mark Knopfler released a tribute to Lonnie Donegan entitled 'Donegan's Gone' on his 2004 album, Shangri-La and said he was one of his greatest influences. Lonnie Donegan was known as King of the Skiffle and was instrumental in the establishment of pop and rock music as it developed in the sixties onward.

THE IONA COMMUNITY

George Fielden MacLeod, Baron MacLeod of Fuinary. Clergyman and Activist (1895 - 1991)

Born in 1895 in Glasgow, George MacLeod hailed from a distinguished and affluent family. His father, Sir John MacLeod, was a Conservative Member of Parliament, and his mother, Edith Fielden, came from a wealthy background. MacLeod received his early education at Winchester College, a prestigious independent school in England, before pursuing studies at Oriel College, Oxford. Initially, he embarked on a path toward a legal career, studying law at the University of Edinburgh. However, the outbreak of World War One in 1914 profoundly altered his trajectory.

During World War One, MacLeod served as a lieutenant in the Argyll and Sutherland Highlanders, experiencing the harrowing realities of trench warfare on the Western Front. He was awarded the Military Cross for bravery, but the war's brutality deeply affected him, prompting a spiritual awakening and a re-evaluation of his life's purpose. This period marked the beginning of his transition from law to theology.

After the war, MacLeod pursued theological studies and was ordained as a minister in the Church of Scotland in 1924. He began his ministry at St. Cuthbert's Church in Edinburgh, where his dynamic preaching style and commitment to social justice quickly garnered attention. Despite his initial success, MacLeod felt a growing disconnect between the Church and the working-class communities it sought to serve. This realisation led him to seek a more direct engagement with those marginalised by society.

In 1930, MacLeod took up the position of minister at Govan Old Parish Church in Glasgow, a parish characterised by significant poverty and unemployment. Witnessing the social and economic hardships faced by his congregants, he became increasingly critical of the Church's detachment from everyday struggles. In response, MacLeod founded the Iona Community in 1938, envisioning it as a movement that would bridge the gap between faith and practical action. The community began with the restoration of the medieval Iona Abbey on the Isle of Iona, symbolising spiritual renewal and communal living. This initiative attracted individuals from diverse backgrounds, all committed to living out their faith through social justice, peace initiatives, and community engagement.

MacLeod's theology was deeply rooted in the belief that Christianity should be actively engaged in addressing societal issues. He emphasised the importance of community, reconciliation, and the Church's role in advocating for the marginalised. His perspectives often challenged established norms within the Church of Scotland, positioning him as both a reformer and a prophet. MacLeod's commitment to social justice led him to participate in various peace movements and he was an outspoken critic of nuclear armament during the Cold War.

In 1957, MacLeod's contributions were recognised when he was elected Moderator of the General Assembly of the Church of Scotland, perhaps the highest honour within the Church. His tenure as Moderator allowed him to further advocate for the Church's active involvement in social issues and to promote the principles embodied by the Iona Community. In 1967, he was elevated to the peerage as Baron MacLeod of Fuinary, acknowledging his significant contributions to religious and social life in Scotland.

George MacLeod's legacy continues through the ongoing work of the Iona Community, which remains active in promoting social justice, peace, and reconciliation. The community's programs and initiatives reflect MacLeod's vision of a Church deeply connected to the practical realities of the world. His writings and sermons are still studied for their profound insights into the relationship between faith and action. MacLeod's life serves as a testament to the transformative power of aligning spiritual beliefs with tangible efforts to improve society.

In summary, George MacLeod's life was characterised by a relentless pursuit of a faith that engages directly with the world's challenges. His establishment of the Iona Community stands as a lasting symbol of the potential for religious communities to effect meaningful social change. Through his visionary leadership, MacLeod not only revitalised a historic site of Christian pilgrimage but also reinvigorated the Church's commitment to social justice, leaving an indelible mark on Scottish religious and social history.

A CHAMPION OF THE SCOTTISH WORKING CLASS

David Kirkwood, 1st Baron Kirkwood. Politician (1872 - 1955)

David Kirkwood was born in 1872, in Shettleston, Glasgow, into a working-class family. He was educated at Parkhead Public School, but left school at the age of fourteen to become an apprentice engineer, experiencing first hand the harsh conditions of industrial labour. Like many young men of his generation, he worked long hours in the shipyards and factories of Glasgow, where exploitation, poor wages, and unsafe working environments were common.

Kirkwood's early experiences in the workplace shaped his political consciousness. He became involved in trade union activities, fighting for better wages and conditions for workers. His skills as an orator and organiser quickly set him apart, and he became an influential figure within the Amalgamated Society of Engineers, one of Britain's most powerful trade unions at the time.

Kirkwood is most closely associated with the Red Clydeside movement, a period of radical socialist agitation centred in Glasgow during and after World War One. The movement, driven by workers, trade unionists, and socialist politicians, sought to challenge the capitalist system and demand better rights for the working class.

During the war, Kirkwood worked as an engineer in the munitions industry. He played a leading role in the Clyde Workers' Committee, a group that campaigned against wage restrictions and poor conditions in wartime factories. The British government, fearing socialist uprisings like those seen in Russia, viewed the Red Clydesiders as a major threat and attempted to suppress their activities.

One of the defining moments of Kirkwood's career came on January 31, 1919, during the Battle of George Square in Glasgow. Thousands of workers gathered in the square to demand a 40-hour work-week, a demand driven by the desire to prevent mass unemployment after the war. The government responded by sending in police and even calling upon the British Army, fearing a potential revolution.

Kirkwood was at the forefront of the demonstration and was knocked unconscious by police before being arrested. Along with several other leaders of the Red Clydeside movement, he was imprisoned, accused of inciting unrest. Though eventually released, the experience hardened his belief in the need for radical change and strengthened his reputation as a fearless champion of the working class.

Following his involvement in Red Clydeside, Kirkwood transitioned into mainstream politics. In 1922, he was elected Labour MP for Dumbarton Burgh, marking the beginning of a parliamentary career that lasted until 1951.

As an MP, Kirkwood continued to fight for the rights of workers, advocating for better wages, social housing, and improved welfare provisions. However, his time in Parliament also revealed tensions within the Labour movement. While he remained a socialist at heart, he sometimes clashed with more left-wing colleagues who believed he had become too willing to compromise.

One of Kirkwood's major contributions was his push for public housing reforms. Recognising the dire state of working-class housing in Scotland, he championed policies that led to the construction of affordable homes for thousands of Glaswegians. He also worked on policies related to unemployment benefits and healthcare, laying the groundwork for later reforms that would eventually lead to the creation of the welfare state. Kirkwood was a supporter of Home Rule for Scotland. In 1935, fellow MP, Gilbert McAllister said that Kirkwood, 'courteous to all men but bowing to none, divides his affections among porridge and politics, the Bible and Burns, Scottish Home Rule and Socialism, his family and his people in Clydebank'. Kirkwood retired from Parliament in 1951, ending nearly three decades as an MP and was created Baron Kirkwood of Bearsden. He remained a respected figure within the Labour movement though some on the left criticised him for abandoning his roots. His memoir, *'My Life of Revolt'*, published in 1935, offers valuable insight into his journey from engineering workshops to the heart of British politics. The book captures his belief in socialism as a force for positive change and his conviction that the struggles of ordinary people could shape history.

Kirkwood died in 1955, at the age of 82. Though he passed away at a time when British politics was moving in new directions, his legacy lived on.

THE MAN WHO REPATRIATED THE STONE

Ian Hamilton QC. Advocate and Nationalist (1925 - 2022)

Ian Hamilton was born in 1925, in Paisley, Renfrewshire, the son of a tailor, John Hamilton and his wife Martha Hamilton. He attended the John Neilston School in Paisley then Allan Glen's School in Glasgow before going on to the University of Glasgow to study law, after having served in the Royal Air Force.

It was at university that Hamilton joined the Scottish National Party (SNP), which would come to influence much of his life's work. He became involved in student politics and developed a strong conviction that Scotland deserved self-governance, a belief that would define his most famous act of protest.

In 1950, Hamilton, along with three fellow Scottish nationalists - Kay Matheson, Gavin Vernon, and Alan Stuart - executed one of the most audacious nationalist acts of the 20th century: the removal and repatriation of the Stone of Destiny from Westminster Abbey. The Stone, a symbol of Scottish monarchy and nationhood, had been taken to England by King Edward I in 1296 and placed beneath the Coronation Chair, where English - and later British - monarchs were crowned to demonstrate their overlordship of Scotland. To Hamilton and his compatriots, the stone's return to Scotland was not just a stunt, but a symbolic act of reclamation and defiance against centuries of subjugation.

The group succeeded in removing the three hundred and thirty-six pound stone from the Abbey on Christmas Day, sparking a nationwide manhunt and fierce debate. The act captivated the public, and though the stone was eventually returned by Hamilton to Arbroath Abbey and reinstated in Westminster Abbey. The event thrust the question of Scottish autonomy into the national spotlight. Interestingly, none of the group was prosecuted - perhaps to avoid further public sympathy - and the event became legendary in Scottish nationalist history.

Hamilton's legal career developed alongside his activism. He was called to the Scottish Bar in 1953 but when first admitted to the bar as a young advocate, Hamilton refused to swear allegiance to Queen Elisabeth 11 arguing that she could only be referred to as 'Queen Elizabeth' (without her regnal number) in Scotland as the regnal numbers counted Queen Elizabeth 1, who had not ruled over Scotland or any of the subsequent united kingdoms which it has entered into. He lost, but eventually became a Queen's Counsel (QC), gaining respect for his sharp intellect, rhetorical skill, and strong sense of justice. Though he maintained a successful legal practice, Hamilton remained a vocal political commentator and cultural figure, never losing sight of his nationalist ideals. He was deeply interested in Scottish law and its preservation as a distinct legal system within the United Kingdom.

Despite his early association with the SNP, Hamilton never tied himself permanently to any political party, preferring instead to operate as an independent voice. Over the decades, he remained committed to constitutional reform and frequently spoke out in favour of devolution and independence. In the run-up to the 1997 referendum on Scottish devolution, Hamilton was an enthusiastic advocate for the re-establishment of the Scottish Parliament, seeing it as a step toward full sovereignty.

Aside from his legal and political work, Hamilton was also an accomplished writer. He authored several books and essays, including *'Stone of Destiny'*, which provided a first-hand account of the 1950 operation. He also wrote two autobiographical works, that are also in part polemical, *'A Touch of Treason'* in 1990 and *'A Touch More Treason'* in 1994. His writing combined clarity, wit and a deep sense of national pride. He also blogged regularly in his later years, commenting on politics, law, and current affairs, often with a mix of insight and dry humor.

Hamilton's life and work were also dramatised in the 2008 film *'Stone of Destiny'*, which brought the story of the Stone's retrieval to a new generation, reinforcing Hamilton's place in the national imagination as a determined idealist willing to take bold action for his beliefs.

Ian Hamilton passed away in North Connel on October 3, 2022, at the age of 97. His death was widely mourned in Scotland, with tributes highlighting his commitment to justice, his unshakeable belief in the Scottish cause, and his distinctive place in modern Scottish history. He remains an enduring symbol of principled activism and legal brilliance; someone who bridged the gap between courtroom advocacy and street-level protest.

A FIERY AND ACTIVIST POLITICIAN

Thomas (Tommy) Sheridan. Politician and Activist. (1964 -)

Tommy Sheridan was born in Glasgow's Govan in 1964. He and his family, mum Alice, dad Tommy, and older sisters Lynn and Carol, moved to the south-side housing scheme of Pollok in 1966 where he was raised and attended St Monicas Primary School and Lourdes Secondary school. Sheridan's father was a factory worker in Hillington's Rolls Royce while his mother was a cleaner, barmaid and later a trade union organiser for the TGWU. His mother Alice introduced young Tommy to politics and by the age of sixteen had joined the Labour Party inspired by Tony Benn and his socialist ideals.

Encouraged by his mother to stay on at school, Sheridan chose to attend Stirling University in 1981 and graduated with a Joint Honours Degree in Economics and Politics. During the 'civil war without bullets' which the 1984/85 miner's strike represented, Sheridan was elected picket bus organiser and was subsequently arrested on three occasions whilst showing solidarity with the NUM across Central Scotland.

Returning to Pollok in the mid-1980s, Sheridan helped to build the grassroots opposition to Thatcher's poll tax and became an accomplished public speaker and housing scheme organiser. He had joined the Militant wing of the Labour Party and was a keen reader of Marx and Red Clydesider John Maclean. By 1989 he was the elected chairman of both the all-Scottish Anti-Poll Tax Federation and the All-Britain Group which went on to organise mass demonstrations and mass civil disobedience in the form of non-payment which resulted in multiple confrontations with the police, sheriff officers and the courts. Approximately one million Scots refused to pay and over fourteen million in England and Wales followed the lead of the Scots. The poll tax crumbled as it became uncollectible and Thatcher went down along with her flagship policy.

In October 1991 in Glasgow's Turnbull Street, Labour's Strathclyde Regional Council gave the green light to sheriff officers, Abernethy

McIntyre to conduct a warrant sale of the household goods of a single parent woman from Greenock. Sheridan and several hundred others physically intervened to prevent it taking place. The Warrant Sale was called off under police instructions and the crowd cheered but as Sheridan ripped up the court interdict issued the day before banning him from interfering in the public sale, he was charged with contempt of court and incitement to riot. The latter charge was dropped when it was discovered an undercover police officer threw a punch which started the disorder. Sheridan was tried in Edinburgh's High Court and sentenced to six months in Saughton Prison.

Whilst serving his prison sentence in April 1992, he stood for Westminster as a Scottish Militant Labour candidate. Sheridan had been expelled from Labour in 1991, became a fierce advocate of an independent socialist Scotland and came second in the Glasgow Pollok constituency with 20% of the vote which shocked the Labour establishment. Within a month he stood again for election from prison when he competed for the Glasgow Pollok ward and created political history in Scotland being the first politician elected from a prison cell. He was elected in May but didn't take up his seat until he was released in July 1992. He was re-elected in 1995 and 1999.

In 1999 Sheridan led the newly formed SSP into the Scottish Parliament elections and won 7.2% of the votes across Glasgow to secure election as a List MSP. He went on to introduce the Parliament's first successful Private Members Bill, the Abolition of Poindings and Warrant Sales. He also introduced the Free and Healthy School Meals Bill, but it was blocked by Labour, Liberal and Conservatives. By 2003 he led the SSP to over 15% of the votes in Glasgow and 6 MSPs across Scotland.

Political infighting and tabloid newspaper targeting of Sheridan combined to cause a massive split within the SSP by 2006 and many blame him personally for the demise of the party. High profile court cases in 2006 and 2010 resulted in close jury decisions initially in his favour but subsequently against him. By an 8-6 verdict he was found guilty of perjury and sentenced to three years imprisonment in January 2011. Sheridan persists in protesting his innocence and continues to divide opinion. He studied for and secured Law and Social Work degrees but was blacklisted from employment with Glasgow City Council in 2024. He joined the ALBA party as a founder member in 2021. His commitment to an independent socialist Scotland remains firm. Tommy Sheridan remains a fiery and charismatic figure. He has been a prominent voice for working-class politics, anti-poll tax campaigns and socialist ideals throughout his career. His political journey has been marked by both notable achievements and significant controversies, making him one of the most divisive but respected figures in Scottish political history.

A SCOTTISH RADICAL AND MARTYR

William (Willie) McRae. Lawyer and Political Activist (1923 - 1985)

William (Willie) McRae was born on May 18, 1923, in Carron, near Falkirk. He was educated at the University of Glasgow, where he studied law and went on to serve in the Royal Indian Navy during World War Two. McRae later returned to Scotland and became a respected solicitor, developing a career marked by legal prowess and passionate political engagement.

Although he never held elected office, McRae was deeply involved in the Scottish National Party (SNP). He stood for Parliament as an SNP candidate, contesting seats including Ross and Cromarty, but was never elected. Despite this, his influence within the party as their Legal Adviser and within the Scottish Nationalist movement in general, was substantial. He served on the SNP's National Executive and was known for his articulate and impassioned speeches advocating Scottish self-governance.

McRae's political activism extended beyond conventional campaigning. He was a vocal critic of the British government's nuclear policy and a committed environmentalist. One of his most significant campaigns was his opposition to the UK Atomic Energy Authority's proposal to dump nuclear waste from Japan and from elsewhere in the world in the Mullwhacher hills above the town of Ayr. Almost single-handedly he defeated them.

As a lawyer, McRae was known for his defence work and his advocacy on behalf of civil liberties. He was involved in several high-profile cases and was admired for his tenacity and commitment to justice. His passion for Scottish culture and heritage also shaped his public persona - he was deeply immersed in Gaelic traditions and often spoke out about preserving Scotland's linguistic and cultural identity. McRae was also alleged to have been involved in the dark underbelly of Scottish Nationalist politics; with the Dark Harvest Commandos, the

Scottish National Liberation Army and *Siol nan Gaidheal* (Seed of the Gael). He was opposed to the trafficking of drugs in Scotland's west coast sea lochs. He was witnessed by a local police Constable leaving Glasgow for his holiday home in Dornie in the Highlands patting his briefcase saying, "I've got them (The Thatcher Government) this time." Friends spoke of his access to details of judicial molestation of children at the highest levels and he proposed to write this up and reveal all after the weekend. A police witness testified to him having been followed from Glasgow on April 5th by two cars belonging to Special Branch. McRae's life came to a tragic and controversial end the following day as he drove north from Glasgow. He was found fatally injured in his car near the village of Dornie in the Scottish Highlands. Initially thought to be a car crash, it was later revealed that McRae had been shot in the head with a revolver. The gun, belonging to McRae, a Smith & Wesson .22 caliber, was found some distance from the car, (police evidence citing four different locations) while McRae, in a coma, was strapped immovable to his seat. His papers and watch lay neatly piled on a rock nearby. Before the gun was discovered, the Fiscal concluded almost instantly that McRae had taken his own life. However, several aspects of the case have led to widespread speculation and disbelief. No fingerprints were found on the gun, no powder burns were on his hand, his brother (a GP) and nurse who discovered the bullet wound, each indicated that the entry point was on the nape of his neck. The Crown stated it was the temple. The Crown argued that he'd been depressed that day but four people who spoke with him stated he was ebullient. Of the six people who found him, (one a holidaying professional accident investigator with the Australian military) not one was interviewed by police who relied solely on the testimony of police officers after the fact. Two bottles of Islay Mist whisky (the only whisky he drank), purchased as he left Glasgow, were missing but a half empty bottle of Grouse whisky was found in the car which stank of whisky. It hadn't broken despite the car rolling. McRae was found to have no alcohol in his blood at the post-mortem. Donald Morrison, the police officer who helped McRae into his car as he left Glasgow placed the bottles of Islay Mist in the footwell of McRae's Volvo. They would have had his fingerprints on them and would have proved the accuracy of his evidence. McRae's associates claimed he had been receiving threats. His home, his office and his holiday home had been broken into several times but nothing was stolen and the bulging briefcase he always carried - allegedly containing critical documents - was recovered by police after his death but was found by his brother to contain nothing untoward. The mysterious circumstances surrounding McRae's death have fuelled enduring suspicions of murder orchestrated by intelligence agencies. Despite several petitions and appeals for an enquiry, no such investigation has been granted and McRae remains a symbol of resistance and martyrdom for many.

A SCOTTISH LITERARY AND ARTISTIC ICON

Alasdair Gray. Poet, Painter and Author
(1934 - 2019)

Born in 1934, in Riddrie, Glasgow, Gray grew up in a working-class family, an experience that shaped his lifelong political and artistic sensibilities. Gray's father, Alexander, had been wounded in the First World War. He worked for many years in a factory making boxes, often went hillwalking and helped found the Scottish Youth Hostels Association. Gray's mother was Amy (née Fleming), whose parents had moved to Scotland from Lincolnshire because her father had been blacklisted in England for Trades Union membership.

During World War Two, Gray was evacuated to Perthshire but returned to Glasgow and later attended the Glasgow School of Art from 1952 to 1957. While there, he studied mural painting and became deeply immersed in both visual and literary arts. This dual passion for writing and painting would define his entire career with his books featuring his own distinctive illustrations and typography.

Gray's early artistic career involved various mural commissions, many of which have since been lost or destroyed, though some, such as his work in Òran Mór and Hillhead Subway Station, remain intact. His artistic influences ranged from medieval illuminated manuscripts to socialist realism, and his paintings often depicted working-class Glaswegians in dreamlike or mythical settings.

Gray worked as a teacher, muralist, and playwright before publishing his magnum opus, *'Lanark'*, at the age of forty-six. The novel, which took nearly thirty years to complete, was an experimental, semi-autobiographical work that blended social realism with dystopian fantasy. Structured in a nonlinear way, with elements of metafiction and self-referential humor, Lanark has been widely regarded as a Scottish masterpiece, drawing comparisons to Joyce's *'Ulysses'* and Kafka's *'The Trial'*.

Upon its publication in 1981, Lanark was immediately recognised as a landmark in Scottish literature. Gray's unique fusion of art and text, as well as his satirical take on Scottish identity and the struggles of artists, resonated with readers and critics alike. The book's famous epigraph, 'Work as if you live in the early days of a better nation' became a widely quoted slogan, particularly within Scottish political movements.

After Lanark, Gray remained a prolific writer, producing novels, short stories, plays, essays, and poetry. His works often explored themes of socialism, Scottish independence, and the power of storytelling. Notable novels include *'Janine', 'Poor Things', 'A History Maker'* and *'Old Men in Love'*.

Gray also produced several collections of short stories, including *'Unlikely Stories, Mostly'* and *'Ten Tales Tall & True'*. His nonfiction work, *'Why Scots Should Rule Scotland'* in 1992, was a passionate argument for Scottish independence, reflecting his lifelong support for the cause. Gray's contributions extended beyond literature. As a visual artist, he designed his own book covers and provided intricate illustrations for many of his works. His murals, found in places like the Ubiquitous Chip restaurant and the Òran Mór arts venue in Glasgow, remain key elements of his artistic legacy. His style - often surreal, symbolic, and infused with political messages - reflected his belief that art should be accessible and socially engaged. Politically, Gray was a vocal supporter of Scottish nationalism and socialism. His belief in self-governance and social justice permeated both his writing and public statements. Though sometimes controversial - his comments on English influence in Scotland drew criticism - he remained a steadfast advocate for Scottish culture and identity.

Alasdair Gray's influence on Scottish literature and art is profound. Writers such as Irvine Welsh, Ali Smith, and James Kelman have cited him as an inspiration and his stylistic innovations helped pave the way for a new wave of Scottish fiction that challenged traditional forms and themes. His blending of text and image also influenced contemporary book design and illustrated fiction. He was a true polymath. Gray's commitment to Glasgow as both a setting and a subject in his works helped cement the city's literary and artistic identity. His ability to merge political thought, fantasy, and working-class realism continues to make his works relevant to contemporary readers.

When Gray passed away on December 29, 2019, one day after his 85th birthday, tributes poured in from across the literary and artistic world. The then First Minister of Scotland, Nicola Sturgeon, described him as "one of the brightest intellectual and creative lights Scotland has known in modern times."

A BANK FOR THE WORKING CLASS.

Reverend Henry Duncan. Theologian and banker. (1774 - 1846)

Henry Duncan was born in 1774 in the manse in the village of Lochrutton four miles west of Dumfries; in times past, 'the Great Road to Ireland', where his father was minister of the Church of Scotland. In his childhood he was educated in Dumfries but in his teens he studied at St. Andrews University before moving to Liverpool to begin a career in Heywoods Bank. After three years, somewhat disillusioned, he left the city and undertook further study in divinity in both Edinburgh and Glasgow.

Through both sides of his family it was said that he was connected to one hundred and fifty clerics. Whether true or not, he followed in the footsteps of his father and grandfather and aged twenty-four, he received his licence as a preacher.

In 1799 he was offered three pulpits; one in Ireland, one in nearby Lochmaben and also in his home parish of Ruthwell. He chose Ruthwell although it was the poorest and offered the smallest stipend, remaining there for almost fifty years. His main concern was trying to help the poor although he had many strings to his bow. Duncan tended a farm behind his manse as well as a garden. In addition he was a talented artist with a focus on drawing. He also founded two newspapers, wrote essays under the title 'The Cottage Fireside' and was fascinated by geological science.

The Reverend William Buckland, Reader in Mineralogy and Geology at the University of Oxford, responded to Duncan's enquiries on what he considered to be a very important paleontological find following the first ever UK discovery of the fossil footmarks of four legged vertebrate animals which Duncan unearthed in the red sandstone near Lochmaben. In 1828 Duncan presented a paper to the Royal Society of Edinburgh describing his find. The original fossils can still be seen at Dumfries Museum.

Ruthwell was not only a very poor parish, but subject to periodical visits of extreme destitution; and for a small population of just over a thousand people, the fund for the poor he collected at the church door, amounted annually to only about twenty-five pounds. Duncan's philosophy centred upon a 'desire to foster a spirit of independence among the lower orders by cherishing the principles of provident economy through the establishment of friendly societies.' He researched the problem and drew upon his experience with the Heywoods bank before coming across a complicated paper written by John Bone from London which proposed the abolition of poor rates in England. Duncan viewed these proposals as too complex and decided instead to advance the establishment of savings banks throughout the country, which he published in his Dumfries Journal.

Appreciating that this would be regarded as a mere theory until it was verified by practical example, he proceeded to establish one of these banks in his own impoverished parish. From a £25 fund for the poor, the Ruthwell Parish Savings Bank opened for business in 1810 and secured increasing deposits over the course of four years of £151; £176; £241 and £922. It became the first economical bank for the savings of its working-class membership. As his success was reported in many of the leading newspapers of the day, his ideas were replicated, first throughout Scotland and then England. In 1815, Duncan's essay '*On the Nature and Advantages of Parish Banks; together with a Corrected Copy of the Rules and Regulations of the Parent Institution in Ruthwell',* saw his ideas spread throughout Europe and the rest of the world. Throughout his stewardship of the Trustee Savings Bank, Duncan received no remuneration or reward beyond the esteem of those who appreciated his work. Although Dr. Duncan and the Ruthwell Savings Bank were hugely influential, the Bank itself was not a great success. By 1875 only twenty-nine accounts remained, and these were transferred to Annan Savings Bank.

In 1839 Duncan became Moderator of the General Assembly of the Church of Scotland and became one of the founding members of the Free Church of Scotland at 'The Great Disruption' in 1843.

He died in 1846 while conducting a religious service in the cottage of an elder in his parish.

The headquarters of the TSB (a descendant of the original Trustee Savings Bank) at 120 George Street, Edinburgh, EH2 4LH, is named Henry Duncan House.

SPYMASTER AND DETECTIVE

Allan Pinkerton. Detective
(1819 - 1884)

Pinkerton was born in Glasgow's Gorbals in 1819. His father was a policeman.

He left school at the age of ten after his father's death but read widely and was largely self-educated. His early employment was as a cooper and in his spare time, he devoted himself to the Scottish Chartist Movement, a working-class movement for political reform in the United Kingdom that demanded an extension of the franchise, an end to property qualifications, annual parliaments elected by secret ballots, a more equal distribution of seats and the payment of MPs. Pinkerton was not raised in a religious upbringing, and was a lifelong atheist. As a Chartist, he had to go into hiding to avoid arrest and hearing of an American township called Dundee, fifty miles northwest of Chicago on the Fox River in Illinois, Pinkerton emigrated and built a cabin where he started a cooperage.

Having married Joan Carfrae a singer from Uddingston, near Glasgow on March 13, 1842, they remained married until his death. He sent for his wife, then living in Chicago, when their cabin was complete. As early as 1844, Pinkerton worked for the Chicago abolitionist leaders, and his Dundee home was a stop on the Underground Railroad - an organised network of secret routes and safe houses for enslaved African Americans escaping their captors in the south.

When looking for trees near his cabin to manufacture barrel staves, he came across a band of counterfeiters and informed the local sheriff who arrested them. In 1849, this led to Pinkerton being appointed the first police detective in Chicago.The following year he partnered with Chicago attorney Edward Rucker in forming the North-Western Police Agency, which later became Pinkerton & Co, and finally Pinkerton National Detective Agency, still in existence today as Pinkerton Consulting and Investigations.

During the early part of the American Civil War, Pinkerton served as head of the Union Intelligence Service and saw off an alleged plot to assassinate President-elect Abraham Lincoln. His agents often worked undercover as Confederate soldiers and sympathisers to gather (allegedly unreliable) military intelligence which he then provided to the Union. The company provided an array of private detective services—specialising in the capture of train robbers and counterfeiters and in providing private security services for a variety of industries.

Pinkerton's agency solved a series of train robberies during the 1850s, and he soon had all the business the fledgling company could handle. He never seemed to be afraid of danger. In many cases he personally chased down and arrested dangerous criminals. As a staunch abolitionist, he attended the secret meetings held by abolitionists such as John Brown and Frederick Douglass.

By the 1870s, Pinkerton's growing agency had accumulated an extensive collection of criminal dossiers and mug shots that became a model for other police forces. While Pinkerton was very pro-worker, his company was often hired by industrialists to provide intelligence on union organising efforts, his guards and agents gained notoriety as strikebreakers - a very far cry from Allan Pinkerton's origins as a member of the Chartist Movement in Scotland. That said, much of this repute came after his death.

As he aged he developed several ailments including malaria and suffered a mild stroke when he was in his sixties. However, the most widespread story is that Pinkerton, who had been a Union spy and had spent his life personally chasing many of the most dangerous outlaws in the country was walking his wife's poodle one day and died when he tripped over the dog, fell to the ground, and severely bit his own tongue. He died of a gangrene infection of the tongue a few days later.

Allan Pinkerton is buried in Graceland Cemetery, Chicago.

THE DEPICTION OF REAL LIFE

Dr. John Grierson CBE. Documentarian (1898 - 1972)

Grierson was born in the old schoolhouse in Deanston, near Doune to schoolmaster Robert Morrison Grierson from Boddam near Aberdeen and Jane Anthony, a teacher from Ayrshire. The family moved to Cambusbarron near Stirling in 1900, when the children were still young, after Grierson's father was appointed headmaster of Cambusbarron school. Grierson was raised in a family that valued education and social responsibility. His early exposure to issues of social justice influenced his later work in promoting documentaries as a means of addressing societal problems. After serving in World War One, Grierson studied at the University of Glasgow and later at the University of Chicago, where he became interested in mass communication and its effects on society.

During his time in the United States, Grierson encountered the work of American journalists and filmmakers, including Robert Flaherty, whose 1922 film *'Nanook of the North'* had a profound impact on him. While Grierson admired Flaherty's pioneering ethnographic approach, he believed that documentaries should go beyond mere observation to actively engage with social issues. This belief became the cornerstone of his documentary philosophy.

Grierson is credited with coining the term "documentary" in a 1926 review of Flaherty's film Moana, describing it as having 'documentary value' for its depiction of real life. His use of the term marked a shift in how non-fiction films were understood, framing them as creative interpretations of reality rather than simple recordings. For Grierson, documentaries were not just about capturing life as it happened - they were a means of exploring and explaining social phenomena, with the goal of informing and educating the public.

Grierson believed that film had the potential to serve as a tool for social good. His view was rooted in a democratic ethos: documentaries could bridge the gap between policymakers and the general public, fostering greater awareness and empathy for the challenges faced by different communities. This perspective would guide his work throughout his career.

In 1927, Grierson returned to Britain and began working for the Empire Marketing Board, a government agency tasked with promoting British trade and industry. Recognising the power of film as a communication tool, he founded the EMB Film Unit in 1929, where he produced films that highlighted the lives of ordinary people while promoting national unity and economic progress.

One of Grierson's most influential films during this period was *'Drifters'* (1929), which depicted the harsh and often dangerous lives of North Sea herring fishermen. Combining hard reality visuals with a clear social message, *'Drifters'* demonstrated Grierson's belief that documentaries should evoke both emotional and intellectual responses. The film was well-received, establishing Grierson as a leading figure in British cinema.

After the EMB was dissolved in 1933, Grierson moved to the General Post Office Film Unit, where he continued to develop innovative documentaries. Under his leadership, the Film Unit produced classics such as *'Night Mail'* (1936), directed by Harry Watt and Basil Wright. Featuring W.H. Auden's poetic narration and Benjamin Britten's musical score, *'Night Mail'* captured the efficiency and dedication of Britain's postal service, blending artistry with social commentary. By combining factual content with creative storytelling, he demonstrated that documentaries could be both informative and engaging, reaching a wide audience while addressing important social issues.

Grierson's influence extended far beyond Britain. In the late 1930s, he traveled to Canada, where he played a key role in establishing the National Film Board of Canada. As the NFB's first commissioner, Grierson helped to develop a thriving documentary tradition in Canada, producing films that celebrated the country's culture and explored its social challenges. His work at the NFB laid the foundation for Canada's reputation as a global leader in documentary filmmaking.

In recognition of his contributions to cinema and public service, Grierson was awarded the title of Commander of the Order of the British Empire. His legacy lives on not only in the films he created but also in the countless filmmakers he inspired, ensuring that the documentary remains a vital and dynamic form of storytelling.

THE MASTER OF POLITICAL SATIRE

Armando Iannucci. Satirist, Writer, Director, Producer. (1963 -)

Born in Clarkston near Glasgow in 1963, Armando Iannucci was raised in a family of Italian descent. His father, also called Armando, was from Naples while his mother was born in Glasgow from an Italian family. Before emigrating, Iannucci's father wrote for an anti-fascist newspaper as a teenager and joined the Italian partizans at age seventeen. He moved to Scotland in 1950 and ran a pizza factory in Springburn in Glasgow

Iannucci studied English literature at Oxford University where he developed a love for comedy and writing. His early influences included British satirical shows such as '*That Was the Week That Was*' and the works of *'Monty Python'*.

Iannucci's first major break in comedy came in radio, where he worked on BBC Radio 4's *'On the Hour'*, a satirical news show that parodied the self-importance and absurdity of broadcast journalism. This project led to '*The Day Today*' in 1994, a television adaptation that became a cult classic. The show introduced audiences to the character of Alan Partridge, played by Steve Coogan, a bumbling yet self-important broadcaster who would go on to star in numerous spin-offs and become one of Britain's most enduring comic figures.

In 1990, he married Rachel Jones, whom he met when she designed the lighting for his one-man show at Oxford. They have two sons and one daughter and currently live in Hertfordshire.

Iannucci's early work focused on media satire, his most significant contribution to comedy came with the series *'The Thick of It'* in 2005, before returning to the screen in 2007 with new characters forming the opposition party added to the cast. The show switched channels to BBC Two for its third series in 2009. A fourth series about a coalition government was broadcast in 2012 with the last episode transmitted on 27 October 2012. The show blended fly-on-the-wall documentary techniques with rapid-fire, profanity-laden dialogue, creating a chaotic and brutally realistic depiction of Westminster politics. At the heart of the show was Malcolm Tucker, played by Peter Capaldi, a foul-mouthed, aggressive spin doctor widely believed to be inspired by real-life political figures such as Alastair Campbell. Tucker's character epitomised the cynical, power-driven nature of modern politics, and his relentless tirades became a defining feature of the show. Although the Iannuccis and Capaldi families knew each other well at a parental level, he and Peter Capaldi did not know each other in childhood.

'*The Thick of It*' was praised for its authenticity, with many politicians admitting that it captured the inner workings of government better than most serious dramas. It won multiple BAFTAs and became a landmark in political comedy.

Following the success of *'The Thick of It',* Iannucci was invited to develop a political satire for American audiences. This led to *'Veep'* which ran from 2012 until 2019, an HBO series starring Julia Louis-Dreyfus as Selina Meyer, an ambitious but often hapless U.S. Vice President.

'Veep' retained Iannucci's signature style, fast-paced dialogue, brutal insults, and political manoeuvring and was a massive success, winning multiple Emmy Awards, including six consecutive wins for Louis-Dreyfus as Outstanding Lead Actress in a Comedy Series.

In 2017, Iannucci made his most ambitious foray into film with *'The Death of Stalin',* a dark political comedy based on the power struggle following the death of Soviet leader Joseph Stalin in 1953. The film starred Steve Buscemi, Michael Palin and Jeffrey Tambor and combined historical events with Iannucci's signature comedic style. The film was praised for balancing humour with the horrors of Stalinist rule, highlighting the paranoia and incompetence of totalitarian regimes. It was both a critical and commercial success, winning awards and earning a strong following. In 2020, Iannucci took on a more traditional literary adaptation with *'The Personal History of David Copperfield'*. This fresh take on Charles Dickens' classic novel featured Dev Patel in the title role and was praised for its humour, diverse casting, and inventive storytelling. The film marked a departure from his usual political focus, showcasing his versatility as a filmmaker.

Armando Iannucci continues to leave a lasting mark on political satire, shaping how audiences perceive politics and media. His work has influenced countless writers and comedians, proving that comedy can be both entertaining and insightful.

SELECTED QUOTES

Sir Robert Grieve

"The design for the British National Oil Corporation headquarters in St Vincent Street, Glasgow, was strongly opposed by us and to a greater or lesser extent by all the voluntary amenity bodies who studied it. The chairman of BNOC wrote to the effect that he and his corporation are as well able to assess design quality as we are. We think this opinion to be no more pertinent than any opinions we might have on how to run an oil company."

Lonnie Donegan

"In Britain, we were separated from our folk music tradition centuries ago and were imbued with the idea that music was for the upper classes. You had to be very clever to play music. When I came along with the old three chords, people began to think that if I could do it, so could they."

Tommy Sheridan

"Ask yourself constantly, am I treating my fellow citizens as I should treat my mum?"

"Look at Cuba: a whole generation raised without the 'me, myself, I ethic'; people who prioritise family, friendship, solidarity. One day Scotland could be like that."

"I got a six month's prison sentence in Saughton Jail for ripping up that court order ordering me not to interfere with a poll tax warrant against a poor single parent in Greenock. It was worth it. We stopped the warrant sale and sank Thatcher and her poll tax. Job done!"

Alasdair Gray

"Work as if you live in the early days of a better nation."

"Glasgow is still full of churches built in the last century. Half of them have been turned into warehouses."

"Everyone should have a cosy shell around them, a good coat with money in the pockets. I must be a Socialist."

Alan Pinkerton

"We never sleep!"

"In the end the law will follow the wrong-doer to a bitter fate and dishonour and punishment will be the portion of those who sin."

Dr John Grierson

"I look on cinema as a pulpit and use it as a propagandist."

"We believe that the cinema's capacity for getting around, for observing and selecting from life itself can be exploited in a new and vital art form."

Armando Iannucci

"Never underestimate the intelligence of the audience; make good programmes, and they will come."

"I refuse to work evenings or weekends. If a script sees my character meeting for dinner, I put a line through the word and write, 'lunch'."

NUA-BHÀRDACHD GHÀIDHLIG

Sorley MacLean. Gaelic Poet (1911 - 1996)

Sorley Maclean was born in Osgaig, a small village on the Isle of Skye where he went to school.

As well as running a small croft, Sorley's father, Malcolm MacLean, had a tailoring business. His mother Christina's family also came from Skye and together they had seven children of whom Sorley was the second oldest son. Each family was notable for its knowledge and practice of Gaelic song and language.

The family income was severely hit by the Great Depression of the 1930s and their poverty had a significant effect on MacLean's early life. He studied English literature, not Gaelic, at Edinburgh University because it offered better career prospects and there encountered and found an affinity with the work of Hugh MacDairmid, Ezra Pound and other modernist poets. Despite this influence, he adopted Gaelic as the medium most appropriate for his poetry although he translated much of his work into English in order to open it up to a wider public than those just conversant with the Gaelic language.

MacLean was raised in the Free Presbyterian Church, dominant in the Gaelic-speaking areas. At a very early age he rejected its doctrines in favour of socialism and was a Marxist by the late 1930s when he believed that the Soviet Union and the Red Army were the only agents that could defeat Fascism. His heroes were Scottish Trades Union leader executed for leading the Irish Easter Rising, James Connolly and Scottish pacifist and socialist, John MacLean.

After attaining his first class degree, he trained as a teacher in order to support his family rather than going to Oxford or Cambridge to undertake research. Instead, he returned to Skye as a teacher, moved to the Isle of Mull and then back to Edinburgh in 1939 just as the Second World War started.

In 1940 he enrolled in the army and was wounded three times in the North African campaign. At the Battle of El Alamein, many of the bones in his feet were broken, ending his war. Following his convalescence, he returned to teaching English at Boroughmuir in Edinburgh. While teaching there he met Renee Cameron and married her on 24 July 1946 in Inverness. They had three daughters and six grandchildren. Shortly thereafter he became headmaster of Plockton Secondary School in Wester Ross.

For the greater part of his life he remained a Dominic and his work was largely unknown outside Gaelic circles until the 1970s when his poems were included in a poetry collection called '*Four Points of a Saltire*'. He then appeared at the Cambridge Poetry Festival promoting his name in England as well as Scotland and Ireland where he had become something of a cult figure thanks to a fan base that included Irish poet Seamus Heaney. Most of MacLean's poetry was produced in his twenties and thirties. It is often said that what Hugh MacDairmid did for the Scots language, Sorley MacLean did for Gaelic, sparking a Gaelic renaissance in Scottish literature. Moreover, he was instrumental in preserving and promoting the teaching of Gaelic in Scottish schools.

MacLean's poetry is characterised by its emotional perspective, intellectual depth and linguistic rigour. His work often reflected on the Highland Clearances, a period of significant upheaval in Scotland, and explored the complexities of Gaelic identity in modern Scotland. His poems are drawn from nature and Gaelic mythology and he made use of traditional Gaelic poetic forms alongside more modern free-verse structures. From the early 1970s, Sorley MacLean was in demand internationally as a reader of his own poetry. His readings were described as deeply moving even by listeners who did not speak Gaelic. In later years he published little favouring 'quality and authenticity over quantity.' MacLean was writer in residence at Edinburgh University from 1973 to 1975 and was *Filidh* at *Sabhal Mòr Ostaig,* the Gaelic college on Skye from 1975 to 1976.

Sorely MacLean is now regarded as one of the greatest Scottish poets of the twentieth Century. In later life he wrote less poetry, instead becoming a scholar of Highland history and genealogy as well as becoming and authority on the Gaelic language. He died after a short illness in 1996 in Raigmore Hospital Inverness, aged eighty-five.

BRITAIN'S FIRST LABOUR PRIME MINISTER

James Ramsay MacDonald (1886 - 1937)

Ramsay MacDonald was born on October 12, 1866, in Lossiemouth, into a working-class family. His mother was a housemaid, and his father was a farm labourer. Growing up in poverty, MacDonald had limited formal education but was ambitious and intelligent. He worked as a schoolteacher and later moved to London, where he became involved in socialist politics.

In the 1890s, MacDonald joined the Independent Labour Party (ILP), an early socialist movement advocating for workers' rights and social reforms. He worked as a journalist and political organiser, gaining a reputation as a skilled speaker and writer. By 1900, he was instrumental in forming the Labour Representation Committee (LRC), which later evolved into the Labour Party.

MacDonald was elected as an MP for Leicester in 1906, when the Labour Party won twenty-nine seats in Parliament. He quickly rose to prominence due to his intelligence, diplomatic skills and ability to appeal to both radical and moderate elements within the party. In 1911, he became Leader of the Labour Party, succeeding Keir Hardie.

However, MacDonald's leadership faced a major test during World War One when he opposed Britain's involvement in the war, arguing that it was a conflict driven by imperialism rather than democracy. His anti-war stance was unpopular and he resigned as Labour leader in 1914. He was vilified by the press, labeled as unpatriotic, and lost his parliamentary seat in the 1918 election.

Despite his temporary fall from grace, MacDonald remained influential in Labour politics. He returned to Parliament in 1922, and with the collapse of the Liberal Party, Labour became the main opposition to the Conservatives. In 1924, the Conservatives lost their majority, and Labour, with support from the Liberals, formed its first government, with MacDonald as Britain's first Labour Prime Minister.

His first term in office lasted less than a year but was significant. MacDonald sought to prove that Labour could govern responsibly, focusing on moderate social reforms, housing programs, and international diplomacy. However, his government fell when he was accused of being sympathetic to communism after recognising the Soviet Union. The 'Zinoviev Letter' scandal, an MI5 forged document published by the press, indubitably contributed to Labour's defeat in the 1924 general election.

In 1929, Labour won the most seats in Parliament, and MacDonald became Prime Minister for a second time. However, this period coincided with the Great Depression, which severely affected Britain's economy. As unemployment soared, MacDonald faced a crisis: should he maintain welfare spending to support workers or cut spending to protect Britain's financial stability?

MacDonald, along with Chancellor of the Exchequer Philip Snowden, chose to implement spending cuts, including reductions in unemployment benefits. This decision angered much of the Labour Party, which viewed it as a betrayal of socialist principles. When his own party refused to support the cuts, MacDonald formed a National Government in 1931 with Conservative and Liberal support.

MacDonald's decision to work with the Conservatives was seen as a betrayal by many in Labour, leading to his expulsion from the party. In the 1931 election, the National Government won a landslide victory, but MacDonald's personal support was weak. He remained Prime Minister but was increasingly sidelined, with real power shifting to the Conservatives under Stanley Baldwin. By 1935, MacDonald was politically isolated and in declining health. He resigned as Prime Minister and was replaced by Baldwin. He continued in Parliament but lost his seat in the 1935 election.

Ramsay MacDonald died on November 9, 1937, while on a sea voyage. On one hand, MacDonald was a trailblazer: the first Labour Prime Minister, a key figure in making Labour a major political force, and an advocate for social justice and international peace. On the other hand, his decision to join the National Government is seen as a betrayal of Labour's principles. Many on the left view him as someone who abandoned the working class to side with the political establishment.

THE MAN WHO DISCOVERED PENICILLIN

Sir Alexander Fleming. Doctor and Scientist (1881 - 1955)

Alexander Fleming was born in 1881, at Lochfield Farm near Darvel, in Ayrshire. He was the third of four children in a modest farming family. His early education took place at Loudoun Moor School and later at Kilmarnock Academy before he moved to London at the age of fourteen to attend the Royal Polytechnic Institution.

Fleming's career in medicine began somewhat by chance. After working in a shipping office, he inherited a small sum of money from an uncle, which enabled him to study medicine at St. Mary's Hospital Medical School in London. He excelled in his studies and graduated with distinction in 1906. His early research focused on immunology and bacterial infections, which laid the groundwork for his later discoveries.

After qualifying as a doctor, Fleming joined St. Mary's Hospital as an assistant bacteriologist under Sir Almroth Wright, a pioneer in vaccine therapy. During World War One, Fleming served in the Royal Army Medical Corps, working in field hospitals where he observed firsthand the limitations of antiseptics in treating infected wounds. He noted that many soldiers died not from their injuries but from bacterial infections that antiseptics failed to cure.

Fleming's war experience convinced him that more effective treatments for bacterial infections were needed. He returned to St. Mary's after the war and continued his research on antibacterial substances. In 1921, he discovered lysozyme, an enzyme found in bodily fluids like tears and saliva that could kill some bacteria. Though lysozyme was not powerful enough to treat serious infections, it was an important step in understanding how the body naturally fights bacteria.

Fleming's most significant discovery occurred in September 1928, when he returned to his laboratory after a vacation. He noticed that a petri dish containing Staphylococcus bacteria had been contaminated with a mysterious mould. Around the mould, the bacteria had been destroyed, while the rest of the dish remained covered in bacterial growth.

Fleming identified the mould as a strain of Penicillium notatum and realised that it produced a substance that killed bacteria. He named this substance Penicillin. Over the next several months, he conducted experiments to test its effectiveness against various bacteria. He found that penicillin was remarkably potent against many harmful bacteria, including those that caused scarlet fever, pneumonia, diphtheria and meningitis.

Despite its promise, penicillin posed major challenges. It was difficult to extract and purify, and Fleming lacked the resources to develop it into a usable drug. In 1929, he published his findings in the British Journal of Experimental Pathology, but his discovery received little immediate attention.

Although Fleming had identified penicillin's antibacterial properties, its potential remained largely untapped for over a decade. It was not until the early 1940s that a team of scientists at the University of Oxford, led by Howard Florey and Ernst Boris Chain, found a way to purify and mass-produce penicillin. With the outbreak of World War II, the need for an effective treatment for battlefield infections became urgent, leading to large-scale production efforts in Britain and the United States.

By 1944, penicillin was being used to treat wounded soldiers and civilians, proving to be a medical breakthrough. It became known as the 'miracle drug', drastically reducing deaths from infections that had once been fatal.

Fleming's contributions were finally recognised on a global scale. In 1945, he was awarded the Nobel Prize in Physiology or Medicine, along with Florey and Chain, for the discovery and development of penicillin. He was also knighted by King George VI in 1944, becoming Sir Alexander Fleming. Fleming remained active in research and public health advocacy until his death. He warned against the misuse of antibiotics, predicting the rise of antibiotic resistance; a problem that today remains critical in modern medicine. The discovery of penicillin marked a turning point in medical history. Before antibiotics, bacterial infections such as tuberculosis, syphilis, and strep throat were often fatal. Thanks to penicillin and later antibiotics, conditions that once carried high mortality rates became easily treatable. Fleming passed away on March 11, 1955, from a heart attack in London. He was buried in St. Paul's Cathedral, a rare honour reflecting his immense contribution to science and humanity.

A LIFE-LONG COMMUNIST AND MILITANT

Michael 'Mick' McGahey. Trades Unionist (1925 - 1999)

Mick McGahey was born in 1925, in the Lanarkshire mining town of Shotts. His father, John McGahey, was a miner and a founding member of the Communist Party of Great Britain who actively participated in the 1926 General Strike, an event that highlighted the tensions between labour and government. This familial backdrop of political activism and labour involvement profoundly influenced Mick's upbringing. The family relocated to Cambuslang in search of employment where Mick attended school before entering the workforce. At the tender age of fourteen, he began working at the Gateside Colliery, marking the start of a twenty-five year career as a miner.

McGahey's commitment to workers' rights became evident early in his mining career. By eighteen, he was elected chairman of his local union branch, showcasing his leadership abilities and dedication to his peers. His ascent within the National Union of Mineworkers was steady; in 1958, he secured a position on the Scottish Executive of the NUM, and by 1967, he had risen to President of the Scottish Area.

His influence wasn't confined to union activities alone. In 1971, McGahey was elected to the Executive Committee of the CPGB, reflecting his deep-seated belief in communist principles and their application to labour rights.

The early 1970s were a period of significant industrial action for British miners. McGahey played a pivotal role in the miners' strikes of 1972 and 1974, which were primarily industrial disputes but had became politicised due to the policies of Prime Minister Edward Heath. McGahey's militant stance often put him at odds with more moderate union leaders. For instance, he criticised then NUM President Joe Gormley for his cautious approach, coining the term '*ballotitis*' to describe an over-reliance on ballots. Despite his prominence, McGahey never ascended to the national presidency of the NUM. He was the logical person to succeed Joe Gormley as president of the NUM, but Gormley refused to retire until McGahey was 55 years of age, by which time he was prevented by the union rules from standing for election.

The miners' strike of 1984 –1985 was one of the most significant industrial disputes in British history. McGahey, serving as the National Vice-President of the NUM during this period, was a staunch opponent of holding a national ballot, believing that regional autonomy was paramount. He viewed the appointment of Ian MacGregor as chair of the National Coal Board as a direct threat, describing it as a "declaration of war" against miners. When MI5 was ordered to put McGahey under twenty-four hour surveillance, the best spy-catchers at the security service's disposal were put on the case. According to the book about the history of MI5, *'Defence of the Realm'*, it states that despite using the most sophisticated listening techniques, MI5 were stumped because they couldn't decipher hard-drinking McGahey's thick, expletive-littered West of Scotland accent. The book also stated that McGahey was kept under surveillance over a 15-year period. Despite his militant reputation, McGahey was also a voice of reflection. Post-strike, he expressed regret over the aggressive picketing strategies employed in Nottinghamshire, acknowledging that such actions alienated fellow miners and sowed division within the labour movement. He emphasised the importance of unity and was a proponent of reconciling with the breakaway Union of Democratic Mineworkers, a stance that sometimes put him at odds with other NUM leaders.

Beyond the UK, McGahey was a fervent internationalist. He led discussions on global labour issues, notably concerning Chile and South Africa and spearheaded delegations to foster connections with workers in Eastern Europe. His advocacy for peace and disarmament further underscored his commitment to global solidarity. A self-educated man, McGahey drew inspiration from thinkers like Karl Marx and cultural figures such as Robert Burns. His profound understanding of working-class struggles made him a natural successor to Scottish socialist icons like Willie Gallacher and John Maclean.

In 1954, McGahey married Catherine Young, and together they had two daughters and a son. A lifelong heavy smoker, he suffered from chronic emphysema and pneumoconiosis in his later years, leading to his death on January 30, 1999. His legacy is commemorated through various memorials. A notable tribute stands in Cambuslang, featuring mine workings, symbolising his dedication to the mining community and in 2006, a memorial in Bonnyrigg was unveiled to mark the 10th anniversary of his address at the Midlothian TUC Worker's Memorial Day event.

RON CULLEY

THE MAN WHO POWERED THE HIGHLANDS

Thomas (Tom) Johnston CH.PC.FRSE Politician (1881 - 1965)

Tom Johnston was born in Kirkintilloch near Glasgow in 1881, the son of David Johnston, a grocer, and his wife, Mary Blackwood, both conservative Presbyterians. He was educated locally at Lairdslaw Public School then at nearby Lenzie Academy where he received a classical education. He left school and became a clerk in an iron-founding business and then in an insurance office before attending the University of Glasgow to study Moral Philosophy and Political Economy although he didn't graduate. While there, he became involved in politics, campaigning unsuccessfully for Keir Hardie, the first leader of the Labour Party, to be made the Rector of the University. In 1906 he helped launch the socialist paper, '*Forward*', and he became associated with the Independent Labour Party and Red Clydesiders. In 1909 he published a book, '*Our Scots Noble Families*', which aimed to discredit the landed aristocracy and contributed to Johnston becoming one of the intellectual dynamos of the Red Clydeside movement. When World War One began, the by now Kirkintilloch Labour councillor led the anti-war movement with his publication '*Forward*'. It was briefly suppressed in 1916 by the British Government and only reopened when Johnston promised not to do anti-war items. Two years prior, in 1914 at the outbreak of World War One, he married Margaret Cochrane. They were married for over fifty years.

Johnston went on to become the Labour Member of Parliament for Stirling and Clackmannan West from 1922 to 1924, 1929 to 1931 and 1935 to 1945 and MP for Dundee from 1924 to 1929. He was first appointed to Government as the Lord Privy Seal in 1931, before serving as Secretary of State for Scotland in Winston Churchill's Coalition Government from February 1941 to May 1945.

Johnston had long been a supporter of limited devolution and, with Churchill largely occupied running the war, he was given a fairly free hand in Scotland. During the war Johnston worked to form a Scottish Council of State and a Scottish Council of Industry although his most enduring contribution resulted from his formation of the North of Scotland Hydro-Electric Board in 1943. At the time, only one percent of the Highland population enjoyed mains electricity outside sizeable settlements. The role of the North of Scotland Hydro-Electric Board was to harness the vast potential for hydro-electric power in the Highlands, partly for the direct benefit of residents, but also to provide power for energy-hungry industries like aluminium smelting and to help safeguard the energy needs of the UK.

There was a strategy behind Johnston's initiatives. He set up an all-powerful and all-party Council of State and by using its authority, successfully resisted key building workers from Scotland being conscripted to the armed forces. Johnston argued that that helped local authorities, the Special Housing Association and private builders to complete 36,200 houses, in addition to carrying out repairs on 75,000 houses damaged by bombing. He further argued, "It enabled us to secure the erection of Civil Defence hostels in such a manner as would enable their rapid conversion after the war to separate dwelling houses. It gave us labour too for the restoration and rehabilitation in suitable cases of dwellings previously condemned, and for the conversion of empty shops and offices into dwelling houses." He also created a nascent Scottish National Health Service by "using hospital beds earmarked for Civil Defence casualties to accommodate ordinary patients who could not afford specialist services". Although Aneurin Bevan gets all the credit for the creation of the NHS, it is worth recalling that it was Johnston with Ernest Brown, Minister of Health, who were responsible for the original White Paper outlining a National Health Service approved by the War Cabinet on February 9, 1944 and that key elements of it had existed for decades in Scotland.

Johnston retired from active politics in 1945 when he was still only 64. He went on to serve as the Chairman of the Hydro Board which he had set up during the war, then helped to transform Scotland's economy as head of the Scottish Tourist Board and for good measure ran the Forestry Commission too.

He died at his home in Milngavie on September 5, 1965, his latter years being blighted by a number of small strokes. Many argue he was the best Secretary of State for Scotland ever appointed to the role.

FROM BUSBY TO BRAZIL

Thomas Donohoe. Footballing Missionary (1863 - 1925)

Donohoe was the son of Irish parents, who had come to Scotland after *An Gorta Mor,* The Great Famine. A tall man, well over six feet and part of a family of seven children, he was brought up in the village of Busby in Renfrewshire, where he, his father and his brothers all were employed at the local dye-works. He played his football in the local leagues.

In 1890 aged 27, Donohoe married in Glasgow; to Elizabeth Montague known as Eliza, from the Gorbals, who was also employed at the Busby dye-works.

Struggling with a growing family and a meagre income, Donohoe sought opportunities outside Scotland. With Scottish technical skills in demand as Latin America attempted to industrialise, he found a job as a master dyer at a new textile factory in Brazil. So, in May 1894, he set sail from Southampton to Rio, leaving behind his wife and two young sons.

Bangu consisted of little more than a Hamlet sitting beside the textile factory when Donohoe arrived but he soon settled among the small British expat community in the village. Though content with his employment he missed his football. There were no teams in the neighbourhood, no equipment to be bought in the shops, and no knowledge of the game whatsoever existed among the locals. So Donohoe wrote to his wife Eliza and setting out his priorities, asked her to join him and to bring a football, as well as their children.

Not long after her arrival, in September 1894, the first football match in Brazil took place in the field beside the textile factory. Attempts to build a league were thwarted when one of the managers of the textile factory, who believed football would lead to degeneracy among his workers frustrated these efforts. By the time the factory owners relented, in 1904, a Sao Paulo league was already in its third season allowing another Scot,

Charles Miller, to claim that although a 'kick-about' had most certainly taken place by Donohoe some eight months prior to his arrival, he'd brought a copy of the rules and had managed to fashion a league.

However, Donahue taught the game and had formed local competitions with other migrant groups and workplaces. From these humble beginnings the game went on to become the premier sport of Brazil with Donohoe playing a central role.

Today, football has become a hugely essential part of Brazilian culture and the local Bangu football team, Bangu Atlético, take great pride in the contribution that Thomas Donohoe made to Brazilian football all those years ago. So much so that they commissioned a five metre statue of him which was unveiled outside their stadium in Rio to mark the 2014 World Cup, the final of which was hosted in Rio De Janeiro.

Inside Bangu's local museum are replicas of Donohoe's football and boots. On its walls are hundreds of black and white photos chronicling the town's history, including an image of Bangu Atletico Clube's line-up from 1905, which features Francisco Carregal, the first black man to play for a Brazilian football club.

East Renfrewshire Council also marked his contribution with a bust of the great man in a car par outside the Cartvale pub. Pelé, the Brazilian football legend, credits Donohoe with introducing football to Brazil in a 2016 interview with a Scottish newspaper.

In 2015, in the Rio de Janeiro International Short Film Festival, a Portuguese movie about Bangu and Thomas Donohoe called "*Bola Para Seu Danau*" ("Ball For Your Danau") won the *Curta Rio* Award. "*Seu Danau*" was Donohoe's Brazilian nickname.

Donohoe only played four matches for Bangu A.C. because he was forty-one years old when the club was founded. Thomas Donohoe made a contribution, via his church, towards the building of the Christ the Redeemer Statue in Rio de Janeiro. His wife also made a donation.

THE GENIUS BEHIND ELECTROMAGNETISM

James Clerk Maxwell. Einstein's Inspiration (1831 - 1879)

James Clerk Maxwell was born in 1831 in Edinburgh, to a wealthy family. His father, John Clerk Maxwell, was a lawyer and his mother, Frances Cay, was well-educated and encouraged his intellectual curiosity. Unfortunately, his mother passed away when Maxwell was only eight years old, leaving his father and tutors to guide his education.

Maxwell displayed an early interest in geometry and mathematics, creating complex mechanical models as a child. At the age of ten, he attended the Edinburgh Academy where he quickly gained a reputation as a prodigy. By the time he was fourteen, he had written his first scientific paper on ovals, a topic in geometry, which was later presented to the Royal Society of Edinburgh.

In 1847, Maxwell entered the University of Edinburgh, where he continued his studies in mathematics and physics. At eighteen, he transferred to the University of Cambridge, where he excelled in theoretical physics. He graduated in 1854 with top honours and soon began his academic career.

Maxwell's most significant contribution to science was his formulation of electromagnetic field theory. Building on the work of Michael Faraday, André-Marie Ampère and others, he developed a set of four fundamental equations - now known as Maxwell's equations - that describe the relationship between electric and magnetic fields. These equations demonstrated that electric and magnetic fields were not separate forces but rather interdependent phenomena forming a single electromagnetic field.

One of Maxwell's key discoveries was that electromagnetic waves travel at the speed of light, leading him to propose that light itself is an electromagnetic wave. This insight unified the theories of electricity, magnetism and optics, fundamentally altering the study of physics and leading to the development of wireless communication, including radio, television, and radar.

Maxwell's equations were later refined and simplified by Oliver Heaviside, but their impact remains foundational in modern physics and engineering.

Maxwell made pioneering contributions to thermodynamics and statistical mechanics, particularly in his work on the kinetic theory of gases. He proposed that gases consist of countless molecules moving in random directions with their speeds following a statistical distribution.

This idea, later refined with Ludwig Boltzmann, led to the Maxwell-Boltzmann distribution, which describes the probability of molecules having different velocities at a given temperature. This work played a crucial role in understanding heat, pressure, and energy transfer in gases, laying the groundwork for quantum mechanics and statistical physics.

In addition to electromagnetism and thermodynamics, Maxwell was a pioneer in the study of colour perception. He conducted experiments on how the human eye perceives colour and demonstrated that all visible colours could be created by combining three primary colours; red, green, and blue. In 1861, he produced the first-ever colour photograph by taking three separate black-and-white photographs through red, green, and blue filters, then projecting them together. This work formed the basis for modern colour photography and digital screens.

In 1871, Maxwell was appointed the first Cavendish Professor of Physics at the University of Cambridge where he helped establish the Cavendish Laboratory, one of the world's leading centres for experimental physics. Under his leadership, the laboratory became instrumental in future discoveries, including the electron and the structure of the atom.

Despite his immense contributions, Maxwell remained relatively unknown compared to figures like Newton and Einstein although Albert Einstein once remarked that Maxwell's work was 'the most profound and the most fruitful that physics has experienced since the time of Newton.'

His work deeply influenced 20th-century physics, particularly in relativity and quantum mechanics. His equations directly inspired Einstein's special theory of relativity and his work on electromagnetism led to the development of wireless technology, including radio waves and radar. Tragically, Maxwell died of stomach cancer at the age of forty-eight in 1879. Although he passed away young, his scientific contributions transformed our understanding of the natural world and continue to shape modern technology and physics.

A DEFINING FIGURE IN SCOTTISH POLITICS

Margo Symington MacDonald. Politician and Activist. (1943 - 2014)

Margo MacDonald was born on April 19, 1943, in Hamilton, one of three siblings. Her mother, Jean, was a nurse, and her father, Robert Aitken was described as a very cruel man from whom her mother separated when Margo was twelve years old. She was educated at local Hamilton Academy and trained as a teacher of physical education at Dunfermline College of Physical Education immediately after leaving school but it was her deep-rooted belief in Scottish independence that ultimately defined her public life. MacDonald's entry into politics came at a time when the independence movement was still in its formative years, struggling to gain mainstream acceptance.

She married her first husband, Peter MacDonald, in 1965 and they ran a pub in Blantyre together. The MacDonalds had two daughters, Petra and Zoe, before the marriage ended in divorce. Her second marriage was to politician and columnist Jim Sillars whom she married in 1981. Sillars went on to win the 1988 Glasgow Govan by-election for the SNP. Margo's daughter Petra MacDonald married Craig Reid of the Proclaimers.

Her first significant political breakthrough came in 1973 when she won a by-election in Glasgow Govan for the Scottish National Party (SNP). Her victory was a historic moment for the SNP, as it demonstrated that the party could win parliamentary seats under the first-past-the-post system. This victory sent shockwaves through the UK political establishment, showing that Scottish nationalism was becoming a potent force. However, she lost the seat in the 1974 general election, highlighting the challenges the SNP faced in sustaining electoral success at that time. Despite this setback, she remained a dedicated advocate for independence and worked tirelessly to build support for the cause.

MacDonald remained involved with the SNP for many years, becoming one of its most recognised figures. However, her relationship with the party was not always smooth. She often found herself at odds with the party leadership, particularly on issues of strategy and policy direction.

One of the key points of contention between MacDonald and the SNP leadership was her strong belief in left-wing, socialist policies. She was deeply committed to social justice and felt that the SNP should take a more radical approach to addressing inequality. Over time, these differences led to tensions between her and party leaders.

By the late 1990s, with the establishment of the Scottish Parliament, MacDonald re-entered frontline politics. She was elected as an SNP MSP in 1999 but left the party in 2003, choosing instead to serve as an independent MSP. This decision marked the beginning of a new phase in her political career, one in which she became one of Holyrood's most respected and outspoken independent voices. As an independent MSP, MacDonald was free to advocate for issues she believed in without the constraints of party politics. She became a leading advocate for various social issues, including improving public healthcare, fighting for the rights of disabled people, and promoting progressive tax policies.

One of her most controversial and high-profile campaigns was her support for the legalisation of assisted dying. MacDonald introduced bills in the Scottish Parliament advocating for the right of terminally ill individuals to end their own lives with medical assistance. This was a highly divisive issue, with strong opposition from religious groups and some politicians. However, MacDonald argued passionately that individuals should have the right to die with dignity. Although her proposals were ultimately rejected by the Scottish Parliament, they sparked an important national debate on the subject, and her work laid the foundation for ongoing discussions about assisted dying in Scotland.

Throughout her career, MacDonald remained steadfast in her belief that Scotland should be an independent nation. She supported the 2014 Scottish independence referendum and played a crucial role in shaping the debate.

Margo MacDonald was diagnosed with Parkinson's disease in 1996, but she refused to let the illness define her. Despite the physical challenges she faced, she continued to serve as an MSP until her passing. She remained active in politics, campaigning, debating, and engaging with the public even as her condition worsened.She died on April 4, 2014, at the age of 70. Her death was met with widespread tributes from across the political spectrum. First Minister Alex Salmond described her as a "true force of nature" and praised her lifelong dedication to the people of Scotland. Other political figures, including those who had often disagreed with her, acknowledged her contribution to Scottish politics and her unwavering commitment to justice and fairness.

A VISIONARY OF ART AND DESIGN

Charles Rennie Mackintosh, Artist and Architect. (1868 - 1928)

Charles Rennie Mackintosh was born at 70 Parson Street, Glasgow in 1868, the fourth of eleven children and second son of William McIntosh, a superintendent and chief clerk of the City of Glasgow Police. His wife Margaret Mackintosh (née Rennie) grew up in the Townhead area of the city. Macintosh attended Reid's public school and then the equally prestigious Allan Glen's school from 1880 to 1883. From a young age, he showed an aptitude for drawing and design. He attended the Glasgow School of Art, where he trained as an architect while also developing his skills in decorative design. While there, he formed a close working relationship with fellow students Margaret Macdonald, and Herbert MacNair. Together, they became instrumental in developing what would later be called the '*Glasgow Style*' which combined organic forms, geometric patterns, and a restrained colour palette, reflecting a modern yet highly decorative approach to design.

Mackintosh's architectural career was defined by his innovative use of space, light, and materials. One of his most famous projects was The Glasgow School of Art, designed between 1897 and 1909. The building remains one of his most celebrated works, showcasing his ability to blend function with artistic expression. He also designed The Hill House located in Helensburgh, Scotland. This residence was commissioned by publisher Walter Blackie and reflected Mackintosh's ability to create a cohesive living environment. He designed not only the building but also the furniture and interior details, ensuring that every element contributed to the overall aesthetic.

His work extended beyond Scotland, as seen in the House for an Art Lover, a then unrealised design created in 1901 for a competition held by a German magazine. Although it was not built during his lifetime, the design was later reconstructed in Bellahouston Park, Glasgow in the 1990s.

Mackintosh's design philosophy extended beyond architecture into interiors, furniture, and decorative arts. His furniture pieces, often characterised by tall, slender proportions and geometric shapes, remain highly sought after today. One of his most famous designs is the high-backed chair, which features a distinctive elongated back and minimalist structure. These chairs were not just functional pieces but also sculptural statements that defined the spaces they inhabited. His interiors often included stylised floral motifs, stained glass, and elegant woodwork. Mackintosh and his wife, Margaret Macdonald, collaborated on several projects, blending his structural precision with her delicate, organic designs. Together, they created harmonious spaces that blurred the line between architecture and art.

One of the most significant influences on Mackintosh's work was Japanese art and design. The late 19th century saw a growing fascination with Japanese aesthetics in Europe, known as *Japonisme*. Mackintosh admired the simplicity, asymmetry, and natural motifs found in Japanese design. These elements can be seen in his use of clean lines, open spaces and an emphasis on craftsmanship.

His restrained approach to decoration, where every element had a purpose, contrasted with the more elaborate styles of the Victorian era. This minimalist aesthetic set the foundation for later modernist movements.

Despite his immense talent, Mackintosh struggled professionally in his later years. By the 1910s, tastes were shifting toward new forms of modernism, and his style was seen as outdated. Economic difficulties and a lack of commissions forced him to move away from architecture.

In 1914, Mackintosh and his wife relocated to England, where he focused on painting rather than design. He developed a distinctive watercolour style, capturing landscapes and floral motifs with precision and sensitivity. Many of these works were created during his time in France, where he lived for a period in the 1920s.

Unfortunately, his later years were marked by financial hardship and declining health. He was diagnosed with cancer and passed away in 1928, at the age of sixty.

Today, his legacy lives on through preserved buildings, exhibitions, and reproductions of his furniture. The Glasgow School of Art, despite suffering fire damage in recent years, remains an iconic representation of his architectural vision. Additionally, The Hill House and other surviving works continue to attract visitors from around the world. He is now regarded as a pioneer who bridged tradition and modernity. His visionary designs continue to inspire and influence the world of art and design.

FLOWER OF SCOTLAND...

Roy Murdoch Buchanan Williamson. Musician. (1936 - 1990)

Roy Williamson was a singer/songwriter, who was born in Edinburgh's New Town. His father, Archie, was a celebrated advocate while his mother, Agnes was a talented pianist who frequently took her two sons, Robert and Roy to musical events. Both brothers attended a Rudolph Steiner school in Edinburgh but were then sent to Edinburgh Academy Primary School as it was thought safer during the war years. In 1944, his forty-five year old father took his own life when Roy was only eight years old. Young Roy was advised only that this death had been 'sudden' and it wasn't until his mother died in 1970 that he learned the cause of his father's death had been coal gas poisoning, at the time, the most common form of suicide.

Archie's suicide had a profound effect on Williamson's mother and she was sent to a psychiatric hospital for a few months while the brothers were cared for by relatives in Aberdeen. He spent some of his school life at the prestigious Gordonstoun School in Moray and developed a love of painting, ships and sailing. His life-long asthmatic condition scuppered his ambition to join the navy.

His mother was eventually declared fit and she returned to the family home in Edinburgh but continued to be fragile throughout her life.

Although his first love was the sea, Williamson went to Art School following a period teaching at Moray Sea School where his thalassophile instincts governed his subsequent artistic endeavour.

It was at Art School where he met both his life-long musical partner, Ronnie Browne as well as his first wife, Violet Thomson. Both Browne and Williamson were rugby players; Roy for Edinburgh Wanderers on the wing and Ronnie for Boroughmuir.

The advent of foreign holidays had become more common and inspired by his interest in guitar, Williamson went to Spain on vacation where he became engrossed in the flamenco style of guitar-playing.

Returning home, he formed the 'Corrie Folk Trio' with Bill Smith and Ron Cruikshank. The Trio's first performance was in the Waverley Bar on St Mary's Street, Edinburgh. After a few weeks Ron Cruikshank left and was replaced by Ronnie Browne subsequently adding female Northern Irish singer Paddie Bell to become the 'Corrie Folk Trio and Paddie Bell'. When a couple of years later both Bill Smith and Paddie Bell moved on due to 'musical differences', 'The Corries' were born. Over time, Williamson had become a most accomplished and celebrated musician and played a host of instruments on stage while singing harmony to Ronnie Browne's more mellifluous voice. Deciding one day that the group's van was becoming over-filled with a range of instruments, Williamson (a noted craftsman) designed and built two 'Combolins'. The first, played by Browne was a guitar/mandolin instrument with bass strings, while Williamson played one which had thirteen sympathetic strings designed as if a drone similar to the Indian sitar. Williamson chose the wood for the instruments from antique hardwood furniture as well as premium-grade spruce and featured his artistic embellishments in silver and mother of pearl. Initially difficult to master these complex instruments, they eventually became a permanent feature of the Corries' repertoire.

On television, on stage and on recordings, the Corries became huge stars in Scotland and further afield; their collection of songs reflecting the history of Scotland as well as a few humorous songs usually penned for them by fellow folkie, Bill Hill. The Corries' rise to fame somewhat coincided with a rise in Scottish Nationalism (which both members supported) and their repertoire was built around Scottish battles long past, Highland myths and legends and ancient Scottish love songs. Acknowledging the thistle as the flower of Scotland, one of its most recognisable symbols and Scotland's national emblem, Roy Williamson wrote '*Flower of Scotland*' in the mid-sixties. The song, whose lyrics refer to the Wars of Scottish Independence, urges contemporary Scots to rise again as an independent nation and remember the day their ancestors deterred Edward's English invaders. It was first heard in a 1967 BBC television series, where it did not yet include the uplifting third verse '*But we can still rise now and be a nation again!*' In July 2006, the RSNO conducted an online poll in which voters could choose a national anthem from one of five candidates. '*Flower of Scotland*' came out the winner with 41% of the votes. Williamson died of a brain tumour in 1990. His funeral was held in Edinburgh at the Mortonhall Crematorium.

THE FATHER OF SCOTTISH MOUNTAIN RESCUE

Hamish MacInnes. Mountaineer (1930 - 2020)

Born on July 7, 1930, in Gatehouse of Fleet, Galloway, MacInnes developed an early fascination with the outdoors. His father's surname was McInnes, but Hamish, (according to his obituary in *The Times*) 'later adopted the more distinctive Scottish spelling of the family name'. He was the youngest child amongst five siblings. He had three sisters and a brother who was eighteen years older than Hamish. By the age of 16, he had already climbed the Matterhorn, showcasing a natural aptitude for mountaineering. His adventurous spirit led him to New Zealand in the early 1950s, where he achieved several first ascents, including the notable Bowie Ridge on Mount Cook and the Southwest Ridge of Nazomi above the Hooker Glacier.

MacInnes was not only a climber but also an inventor who revolutionised mountaineering equipment. He designed the first all-metal ice axe, moving away from the traditional wooden shafts, which significantly improved durability and performance. Additionally, he invented a hammer with inclined picks for Scottish winter work in the early 1960s and developed the MacInnes stretcher, a lightweight, foldable alloy stretcher that became a standard in mountain rescue operations worldwide. These innovations have been credited with saving countless lives in mountainous terrains.

Recognising the need for organised mountain rescue services, MacInnes played a pivotal role in establishing and leading the Glencoe Mountain Rescue Team from 1961. He authored the *'International Mountain Rescue Handbook'* in 1972, which remains a definitive guide in the field. His commitment to safety extended to co-founding the Search and Rescue Dog Association in Scotland in 1965, enhancing search capabilities in challenging terrains.

Beyond his practical contributions, MacInnes was a prolific author, sharing his extensive knowledge through numerous books on mountaineering and safety. His expertise also led him to the film industry, where he worked as a safety advisor and climbing consultant on movies such as '*The Eiger Sanction*' and '*The Mission*'. Notably, he contributed to the production of '*Monty Python and the Holy Grail*', building the iconic '*Bridge of Death*', and forging a lasting friendship with Michael Palin.

MacInnes's lifelong dedication to mountaineering and rescue operations earned him several honours, including the British Empire Medal in 1962 and an Officer of the Order of the British Empire (OBE) in 1979. He also received an Honorary Doctorate from Herriot-Watt University in 1992, the University of Stirling in 1997 and the University of Dundee in 2004. In 2007 he was awarded honorary fellowship of the Royal Geographical Society. He was inducted into the Scottish Sports Hall of Fame in 2003 and received the Scottish Award for Excellence in Mountain Culture in 2008. In 2016 he was presented with the Chancellor's Medal from the University of the Highlands and Islands.His innovative equipment designs, foundational rescue techniques, and extensive writings have left a lasting legacy in the mountaineering community. His life and contributions were further celebrated in the 2018 documentary '*Final Ascent: The Legend of Hamish MacInnes*', which chronicled his remarkable journey and enduring impact on mountain safety and exploration.

MacInnes lived in Glen Coe from 1959 until 1998, where he resided at '*Allt Na Reigh*', a cottage within the glen that was subsequently purchased by media personality, Jimmy Savile. MacInnes later said that he was hoodwinked by Savile and asked that the house, which was believed to have been the scene of some of the sexual offences for which Savile subsequently became infamous, not be demolished. However, after his death, a friend of MacInnes told the BBC that MacInnes *would* have wanted the house knocked down to remove the stain from the landscape. In June 2024, the house's current owners were granted planning permission to demolish it and replace it with a new residence, to be named Hamish House in MacInnes' honour.

In 2014, MacInnes suffered a urinary tract infection which, initially undiagnosed, rendered him severely confused and suffering from delirium. He was sectioned into Belford psychiatric hospital in the Scottish Highlands. From there he made multiple attempts to escape, including scaling up the outside of the hospital to stand on its roof. After around five years the infection was diagnosed and treated. MacInnes recovered, though he lost memories of his adventuring career that he sought to rebuild by reading his accounts of them. He died on 22 November 2020, aged 90, at his home in Glen Coe.

THE COMMUNIST PARLIAMENTARIAN

William (Willie) Gallacher (1881 - 1965)

Born on December 25, 1881, in Paisley, Gallacher was the son of an Irish father and a Scottish mother. His father died when he was seven years old, and one of his earliest ambitions was to earn enough money so that his mother would no longer have to work as a washerwoman. With his sisters, he finally achieved that goal at the age of nineteen, but his mother died shortly afterwards at the age of fifty-four. After completing his elementary education, he worked as a brass fitter, experiencing firsthand the challenges faced by the working class. His early exposure to labour hardships ignited his interest in politics, leading him to join the Independent Labour Party (ILP) in 1905. However, disillusioned with the ILP's reformist approach, Gallacher shifted to the more radical British Socialist Party (BSP), where he collaborated with notable socialists like John Maclean and John R. Campbell. The 'weakness for alcohol' shown by his father and elder brother and the suffering that it caused his mother, led him to become involved with the Temperance Movement in his mid-adolescence. However, later in life, he left the Movement but remained a lifelong Teetotaller.

During World War One, Glasgow became a hub for labour unrest, a period known as Red Clydeside. Gallacher emerged as a prominent leader, co-founding the Clyde Workers' Committee (CWC) to oppose the Munitions of War Act 1915, which restricted workers' rights. As chairman of the CWC, he advocated for workers' autonomy and was arrested in 1916 for publishing anti-war sentiments in 'The Worker', resulting in a six-month imprisonment.

In January 1919, Gallacher played a key role in organising strikes demanding a forty-hour workweek. The protests escalated into what became known as 'Bloody Friday', leading to violent clashes with the police. Gallacher was arrested again, charged with incitement to riot, and sentenced to five months in prison

Gallacher's experiences during Red Clydeside deepened his commitment to communist ideals. In 1920, he attended the Third International in Moscow, where he met Vladimir Lenin. This encounter solidified his belief in the necessity of a unified communist party in Britain. Upon returning, Gallacher was instrumental in founding the Communist Party of Great Britain, aiming to represent the working class and promote socialist policies.

Gallacher contested multiple parliamentary elections before achieving success. His persistence paid off in the 1935 general election when he was elected as the Member of Parliament for West Fife, becoming one of the few communists to hold a seat in the House of Commons. He retained this position until 1950.

As an MP, Gallacher was a vocal advocate for workers' rights and international solidarity. In 1936, he, along with other leftist figures, urged the British government to support the Spanish Republic against Franco's fascist forces during the Spanish Civil War.

The onset of World War Two and the subsequent Nazi-Soviet Pact in 1939 created divisions within the CPGB. Gallacher initially supported Britain's declaration of war against Germany, a stance that led to tensions within the party. However, following Germany's invasion of the Soviet Union in 1941, the CPGB fully endorsed the war effort, aligning with Gallacher's position.

In the 1945 general election, Gallacher was re-elected, joined by fellow communist Phil Piratin. However, the advent of the Cold War and growing anti-communist sentiments led to his defeat in the 1950 election, marking the end of communist representation in the British Parliament.

After his parliamentary career, Gallacher continued to be active in the CPGB, serving as its president from 1956 to 1963. He authored several works, including *'The Case for Communism'* in 1949 and his autobiography *'The Chosen Few'* in 1940, detailing his political journey and advocating for communist principles.

Gallacher passed away on August 12, 1965 in his hometown of Paisley. His life remains a testament to unwavering dedication to workers' rights and the pursuit of social justice. As a central figure in Red Clydeside and a pioneering communist MP, his contributions have left an indelible mark on British political history.

SELECTED QUOTES

Ramsay MacDonald

"Golf is to me what his Sabine farm was to the poet Horace - a solace and an inspiration."

"The man who saves time by galloping loses it by missing his way; the shepherd who hurries his flock to get them home spends the night on the mountain looking for the lost; economy does not consist in haste, but in certainty."

Sir Alexander Fleming

"One sometimes finds what one is not looking for. When I woke up just after dawn on Sept. 28, 1928, I certainly didn't plan to revolutionise all medicine by discovering the world's first antibiotic, or bacteria killer. But I guess that was exactly what I did."

"Penicillin sat on a shelf for ten years while I was called a quack."

"Suggested remedy for the common cold: A good gulp of whisky at bedtime. It's not very scientific, but it helps."

Mick McGahey

"They'll stop chasing you when you stop running."

"Give the other side the roughest ride of their lives but always make sure they have the bus fare home"

Roy Williamson

"Those days are gone now and in the past they must remain but we can still rise now and be a nation again"

"It's cracking, man! It's like having little brains on the end of your fingertips. It's almost as if they can think for themselves." (On playing guitar shortly after his first brain operation.)

Hamish MacInnes

"Only too often it is a fight for life: there is nothing more satisfying than the successful evacuation of a critically injured person on a highly technical rescue, where a single mistake could result in the death of the casualty. It is, on a grand scale, a game of chance in which nature holds most of the cards".

Willie Gallacher

"Hello!" (When introduced to Lenin)

"I immediately felt that I was talking, not to some faraway great man hedged around with an impassable barrier of airs, but to Lenin, the great Party comrade who had a warm smile and cheery word for every proletarian fighter".

A VISIONARY IN NUTRITION AND GLOBAL FOOD SECURITY

Sir John Boyd Orr. Physician and Nutritionist (1880 - 1971)

John Boyd Orr was born in1880, in Kilmaurs, Ayrshire, into a religious and socially conscious family. His father, a quarry owner, was deeply involved in local charitable work, instilling in his son a strong sense of duty toward the less fortunate.

Orr's early education took place in a small village school before he won a scholarship to Kilmarnock Academy. Later, he attended the University of Glasgow, where he studied biological sciences, eventually earning a medical degree. During his studies, he worked as a teacher, using his earnings to fund his education, and developed a keen interest in nutrition and its impact on health.

Orr's medical career initially led him to general practice, but his passion for scientific research in nutrition took precedence. In 1914, he joined the Rowett Research Institute in Aberdeen, where he focused on the relationship between diet and health. His studies revealed the stark contrasts in nutritional intake between the rich and the poor, reinforcing his belief that diet played a fundamental role in overall well-being

His research on human and animal nutrition had significant implications. He discovered that poor nutrition was a leading cause of disease and reduced life expectancy and he championed the idea that governments should intervene to ensure adequate food supplies for all citizens. His findings influenced policies on school meals, child nutrition, and wartime rationing in Britain.

During World War One, Orr served as a medical officer and was exposed to the devastating effects of malnutrition among soldiers. This experience further strengthened his resolve to work toward food security, leading him to expand his research to address global hunger and poverty.

Known as Popeye to his family, Boyd Orr married Elizabeth Pearson Callum, whom he had met as a teenager in West Kilbride in 1915. They had three children.

After years of groundbreaking research, Orr became the first Director-General of the Food and Agriculture Organisation in 1945, shortly after the establishment of the United Nations. His vision for the FAO was ambitious; he sought to create a global food system that ensured equitable distribution of resources and eradicated hunger. He strongly advocated an international food policy based on scientific principles, calling for wealthier nations to contribute to a worldwide food reserve that could be used in times of crisis.

Orr proposed the idea of a 'World Food Board' which would regulate food supplies and prices to prevent famine and malnutrition. However, his radical ideas faced resistance from powerful countries that feared losing control over their national food policies. Despite political opposition, his influence led to several improvements in international food security efforts and his work laid the foundation for later global food programs.

For his relentless dedication to alleviating hunger, Orr was awarded the Nobel Peace Prize in 1949. The Nobel Committee recognised his scientific contributions and his broader vision of a world where food was a fundamental human right. Unlike many peace laureates, he was honoured not for diplomacy or conflict resolution but for his work in nutrition and public health; insisting that peace was impossible without food security.

After receiving the Nobel Prize, Orr used the prize money to establish charitable organisations aimed at addressing poverty and malnutrition. He continued to advocate better global food policies and sought to bridge the gap between scientific research and political action.

In his later years, Orr remained active in public discourse, writing extensively on nutrition, agriculture, and global inequalities. He was knighted in 1935 and later made Baron Boyd Orr of Brechin in 1949, recognising his contributions to science and public health.

His efforts earned him the Nobel Peace Prize in 1949, recognising his commitment to addressing global malnutrition and advocating for a more equitable food system (and in the process making Kilmarnock Academy one of only two schools in Scotland (the other being Hawick High School) to have had two Nobel Prize Winners on their books)

John Boyd Orr passed away on June 25, 1971, leaving behind a legacy that continues to shape discussions on food security and nutrition policy.

EXECUTED AS A A MARTYR TO THE CAUSE

James Connolly. Republican, Socialist and Trades Union Leader (1868 - 12 May 1916)

James Connolly was born in Edinburgh's Cowgate, known locally as 'Little Ireland'. He was the third son of Mary McGinn and John Connolly, an impoverished manure carter, whose job was keeping the city's streets clean. Each of them were Irish immigrants. His Catholic father hailed from County Monaghan, a province of Ulster bordering the North of Ireland, and his mother, a Protestant and domestic servant, came from the Unionist town of Ballymena in coastal County Antrim in the North of Ireland.

Connolly attended St. Patrick's School in the Cowgate but was substantially self-taught and aged ten, left school to work for the Edinburgh Evening News as a printers' devil, cleaning ink off rollers and running errands for the printers. When aged fourteen, he joined the British Army serving in Ireland for seven years. - an experience which left him with a deep dislike of British policies in Ireland and especially of the role of the British Army. In 1889 he left the army (some reports say he deserted) and returned to Scotland, settling in Dundee. While in Dublin, the year before, Connolly had met Lillie Reynolds, and in 1890, she followed him to Scotland where, with special dispensation by the Catholic Bishop of Dunkeld they were married in St John the Baptist Church, Perth. Following their marriage, they moved to Edinburgh and lived at 22 West Port in the Grassmarket area, close to the Cowgate where Connolly had grown up. He worked as a labourer and then as a manure carter with Edinburgh Corporation and together they had seven children (six daughters and one son), with six of them reaching adulthood. Owing to her better education, Lillie helped improve her husband's speeches and writing. He was active in the Independent Labour Party groupings alongside Kier Hardie and read voraciously, studying history and literature, even managing to teach himself some German and French to read Marxist classics in their original languages. He became involved in Scottish Socialist organisations but with a young family he needed to earn a living. The Dublin Socialist Club was looking for a secretary and so he and his family moved to Dublin where Connolly founded the Irish Socialist Republican Party. As organiser for the party, Connolly led the movement in Ireland towards a revolutionary platform and campaigned against British imperial interests, organising a demonstration against Jubilee celebrations in Dublin, which ultimately resulted in his first stint in an Irish prison. Connolly was a founding editor of '*The Socialist'*, and the far-left American Socialist Labour Party invited him to tour America in an attempt to appeal to the huge numbers of Irish migrant workers in their cities. The acclaim with which his words were received by Irish workers persuaded the American Socialist Labour Party to bring Connolly to America full-time and he emigrated in 1902, aged thirty-four. On his arrival in the United States, Connolly found work as a salesman for insurance companies. But by 1905, and after being elected to the national executive of the Socialist Labour Party, he became an organiser for the Industrial Workers of the World. However, in 1909 he he was persuaded by James Larkin of the Irish Transport and General Workers' Union to return to Ireland and to continue his remarkable writings.

In 1914, as WW1 commenced, Connolly assumed the presidency of the Irish Neutrality League and the following year he revived his old title, *Workers' Republic* wherein his editorials continued to urge Irish resistance. On Easter Monday 14 April 1916, Connolly prepared mobilisation orders for the Irish Citizens' Army, a small Trades Union militia and ten days later, on Easter Monday, with Connolly commissioned by the Military Council of the Irish Republican Brotherhood, a secret, oath-bound fraternal organisation, as Commandant of the Dublin Districts, Patrick Pearce, President and Commander-in-Chief, read the *Proclamation of the Irish Republic* from the steps of the General Post Office. In the four day British military bombardment that followed, Connolly led men on to the streets and supervised the construction of barricades. He was twice wounded. On Friday 29 April, carried on a stretcher, he was among the last to evacuate the GPO. Pearse issued the order for the Irish Volunteer fighters, now under constant British bombardment, to lay down their arms. Connolly was among sixteen republican prisoners executed for their role in the Rising. Unable to stand because of his combat injury, Connolly was placed before a firing squad tied to a chair. His body was placed, without rite or coffin, with those of his comrades in a common grave at the Arbour Hill military cemetery, located at the rear of the National Museum of Ireland.

Throughout his life he was to speak with a Scottish accent. Dublin's Connolly Station and Connolly Hospital in Blanchardstown were named in his honour. A plaque with his image has been placed in his memory in Edinburgh's Cowgate.

'HE TOOK US TO WAR ON A FICTION...'

Sir Anthony Charles Lynton (Tony) Blair KG. Politician (1953 -)

Tony Blair was born in 1953 at the Queen Mary Maternity Home in Edinburgh, the second son of Leo and Hazel Blair. His father was the illegitimate son of two entertainers and was adopted as a baby by a Glasgow shipyard worker named James Blair and his wife, Mary. Tony Blair's mother was the daughter of George Corscadden, a butcher and Orangeman who moved to Glasgow in 1916 and was from a family of Protestant farmers in County Donegal, Ireland and were themselves descended from Ulster-Scots settlers whose surname was originally Garscadden, now part of Glasgow. While staying in Edinburgh, the family resided in the Willowbrae area of Edinburgh where his father worked as a junior tax inspector whilst studying for a law degree from Edinburgh University.

When only nineteen months old, Blair and his family moved from Edinburgh to Adelaide in Australia where his father, Leo had secured a lecturing position in its university. The family returned to the United Kingdom in 1958 and lived for a while with Blair's grandmother and her husband at their home in Stepps on the outskirts of Glasgow.

When Blair was but five years old, his father accepted a job as a lecturer at Durham University and moved the family there. Blair attended Durham's Chorister School, a fee-paying boarding and day public school and was then sent to spend his school term-time boarding at fee-paying Fettes College in Edinburgh from 1966 to 1971. Blair left Fettes College at the age of eighteen and next spent a gap year in London working as a rock music promoter before entering St John's College, Oxford from which he graduated with a second class honours degree in Jurisprudence. He served a barrister pupillage at Lincoln's Inn where he was called to the Bar and where he met his future wife, Cherie Booth. Blair joined the Labour Party shortly after graduating from Oxford in 1975, aligning himself with the soft left of the party and stood unsuccessfully as a candidate for Hackney Council elections in 1982. When the 1983 General Election was called, Blair secured the nomination for Sedgefield and, at the age of thirty, he was elected as their MP despite the party's overall thumping defeat. Blair rose rapidly through the Labour ranks and held positions such as as Shadow Assistant Treasury spokesman, Shadow Trade and Industry spokesman on the City of London and, under the leadership of John Smith, Shadow Home Secretary. When John Smith died suddenly of a heart attack on 12 May 1994, Blair was elected Leader of the Labour Party and it was rumoured that Blair promised to give Gordon Brown control of economic policy in return for Brown not standing against him in the leadership election.

He was elected Prime Minister in 1997 having persuaded the party to ditch its socialist Clause Four which was generally understood to mean wholesale nationalisation of major industries and to call the party, 'New Labour'. When Blair became Prime Minister aged 43, he was the youngest person to reach that office since Lord Liverpool in 1812. With victories in 1997, 2001, and 2005, Blair was the Labour Party's longest-serving prime minister and the first person to lead the party to three consecutive general election victories. While he was given credit for the Good Friday Agreement which ended the Troubles in Northern Ireland, he was also heavily criticised as during his first six years in office he ordered British troops into combat five times, more than any other prime minister in British history, for siding with US President George Bush in invading Iraq and for misleading the House of Commons in doing so.

In 2011, Blair became godfather to one of right-wing newspaper baron and friend Rupert Murdoch's children but he and Murdoch later ended their friendship after Murdoch discovered his wife, Wendy Deng's written notes charting her allegedly adulterous relationship with Blair.

Gordon Brown, who considered himself the senior of the two, understood always that Blair would give way to him and in June 2007, Blair officially resigned as prime minister after ten years in office, when he was officially confirmed as Middle East Envoy for the United Nations, the European Union, the United States and Russia. Blair originally indicated that he would retain his parliamentary seat after his resignation as prime minister. However, on being confirmed for the Middle East role, he resigned from the Commons by taking up 'an office of profit'. Upon resigning, he formed Tony Blair Associates providing advice on a commercial and *pro bono* basis, on political and economic trends and governmental reform. He was a controversial politician but it's hard to argue he wasn't radical.

BANNOCKBURN

King Robert the Bruce. King of Scotland (1274 - 1329)

Robert the Bruce was born on July 11, 1274, into a noble family with claims to the Scottish throne. His grandfather, Robert *de Brus*, had once been a contender for the crown and the family was deeply entwined in the politics of Scotland and England. His mother, Marjorie, was descended from the Scottish royal line, which bolstered his legitimate claim.

The late 13th century was a tumultuous time for Scotland. Following the death of King Alexander III in 1286 and the subsequent demise of his heir, Margaret, Maid of Norway, Scotland faced a succession crisis. This led to the involvement of King Edward I of England, who sought to dominate Scotland. In 1296, Edward invaded, initiating a period of English occupation and resistance.

Initially, Robert the Bruce was involved in the Scottish resistance against English rule but also displayed pragmatism, at times aligning with Edward I when it suited his interests. This dual allegiance reflected the complex political landscape of the time, where loyalties shifted and were based upon survival and opportunity.

The turning point came after the death of William Wallace, another iconic figure of Scottish resistance, in 1305. With Wallace gone, the mantle of leadership fell to Bruce and others vying for influence. In 1306, Bruce took a decisive and controversial step by murdering his rival, John Comyn, at Greyfriars Church in Dumfries. This act eliminated a key competitor and paved the way for his coronation as King of Scots at Scone on March 25, 1306.

Bruce's early reign was fraught with challenges. His murder of Comyn and subsequent coronation provoked a swift response from Edward I, who viewed Bruce as a rebel. The English king sent forces to suppress Bruce's claim, leading to a series of defeats and a period of exile for the Scottish king. Bruce's family suffered greatly during this time; his wife, daughter, and sisters were captured and imprisoned, and his brothers were executed.

Despite these setbacks, Bruce persevered. His resilience and strategic acumen gradually turned the tide in his favour. He adopted guerrilla tactics, focusing on small, decisive battles and targeting castles held by the English. This strategy eroded English control and rallied Scottish nobles to his cause. The death of Edward I in 1307 and the accession of his less capable son, Edward II, provided Bruce with a crucial advantage. The new king's lack of military prowess and political acumen allowed Bruce to consolidate his power.

The pivotal moment of Bruce's reign came in 1314 at the Battle of Bannockburn, near Stirling. Facing a numerically superior English force led by Edward II, Bruce's army employed effective tactics and superior knowledge of the terrain to secure a decisive victory. Bannockburn was not only a military triumph but also a symbolic affirmation of Scotland's right to self-rule. The victory at Bannockburn solidified Bruce's position as king and emboldened the Scottish cause. Over the next several years, Bruce continued to push for recognition of Scotland's independence. In 1320, the Declaration of Arbroath was sent to Pope John XXII, asserting Scotland's sovereignty and Bruce's rightful kingship. This document, signed by Scottish nobles, is considered a foundational text in Scotland's national identity. In 1328, after years of negotiation and intermittent conflict, the Treaty of Edinburgh-Northampton was signed. This treaty formally recognised Robert the Bruce as the King of Scots and acknowledged Scotland's independence from England. The following year, Bruce died on June 7, 1329, in Cardross, probably of leprosy or another debilitating illness. He was succeeded by his son, David II.

Robert the Bruce's legacy is profound. He is remembered not only as a warrior king who achieved Scotland's independence but also as a symbol of perseverance and national pride. His life and reign are commemorated in Scottish culture and his story continues to inspire the fight for self-determination. Robert the Bruce's reign was a defining period in Scottish history. His leadership during the First War of Scottish Independence transformed Scotland from a nation on the brink of subjugation into a proud, independent kingdom. His victory at Bannockburn and the subsequent recognition of Scottish independence marked a turning point in the nation's history, securing his legacy as one of Scotland's greatest kings.

A LIFE OF COMPASSION AND SERVICE

William Quarrier. Social Carer and Philanthropist (1829 - 1903)

William Quarrier was born in Greenock, in 1829. His early life was marked by hardship. His father died when he was just a boy, and his mother struggled to provide for the family. By the age of six, Quarrier was already working as a shoeshine boy to help support his household. This firsthand experience of poverty had a profound impact on him, shaping his values and inspiring his lifelong commitment to helping the poor and marginalised.

Despite these challenges, Quarrier was determined to improve his situation. He was apprenticed to a shoemaker and eventually established his own successful business in Glasgow. At seventeen he began work as a shoemaker after training as an apprentice. At this stage, he became a devout Christian. Quarrier attended Blackfriars Street Church and later Adelaide Place Baptist Church where he served as a deacon. He soon owned a chain of shops and married Isabella Hunter, the daughter of his first employer. Quarrier fathered four children: Isabella, Agnes, Frank and Mary Quarrier.

By his thirties, he had become financially comfortable and well-respected in the city. But rather than retreat into a life of comfort, Quarrier turned his attention to philanthropy.

Quarrier's Christian faith was central to his life and work. A devout member of the United Presbyterian Church, he believed strongly in the Christian duty to care for the poor and suffering. In the 1860s, he began organising support for destitute children in Glasgow. He started small, distributing food and clothing and placing children in foster homes. But his vision grew rapidly.

In 1871, Quarrier opened the first of his 'Orphan Homes of Scotland' in Bridge of Weir, Renfrewshire. Unlike the typical institutional orphanages of the time, Quarrier's homes were designed to be small and family-like. They were organised as a children's village with cottages, each run by a house parent, providing a more nurturing and homely environment.

Over the years, the village expanded to include more than 40 homes, a school, a church, a fire station and even a hospital. Children received an education, vocational training, and moral instruction. Quarrier's goal was not just to shelter them but to prepare them for productive, independent lives.

One of the more controversial aspects of Quarrier's work was the emigration of children to Canada. Like other philanthropic organisations of the era, the Orphan Homes of Scotland participated in the British child migration movement. From the late 19th century into the early 20th, thousands of children were sent from the UK to Canada, where it was believed they would have better opportunities. Quarrier genuinely believed that emigration offered a brighter future for children who would otherwise face limited prospects in industrial Scotland. However, modern perspectives have questioned the ethics and outcomes of these programs, with some child migrants later reporting hardship and abuse. While Quarrier's intentions were rooted in compassion, this aspect of his legacy remains complex and debated.

William Quarrier remained actively involved in the management of the homes until his death in 1903. He and his wife Isabella appear to have been loved and respected by the children they helped, often being referred to as 'father' and 'mother' by those in their care. At the time of his death, more than 7,000 children had passed through the Orphan Homes of Scotland. After his passing, the work he began continued under the leadership of his family and trustees. The organisation eventually became known simply as 'Quarriers' and evolved to meet the changing needs of society. Today, Quarriers is a leading Scottish social care charity, providing services not only to children but also to adults with disabilities, families in crisis, and people affected by homelessness and addiction.

William Quarrier's life story is a powerful example of how personal hardship can be transformed into a force for good. From a poverty-stricken child in Greenock to the founder of one of Scotland's most enduring charitable institutions, Quarrier dedicated his life to lifting others out of misery. His work, driven by Christian faith and a belief in the potential of every child, continues to influence social care more than a century later. Though some aspects of his legacy are viewed through a more critical lens today, his overall impact remains one of hope, kindness, and transformative compassion.

William Quarrier died on 16 October 1903. He is buried alongside his wife in the Mount Zion Church cemetery at Quarrier's Village.

THE MASTER OF ADVENTURE AND ESPIONAGE

John Buchan, Baron Tweedsmuir. Author and Politician (1875 - 1940)

John Buchan was born in 1875, into a strict Calvinist family at 18–20 York Place, a double villa now named after him, in Perth. He was the first child of John Buchan – a Free Church of Scotland minister – and Helen Jane Buchan. His upbringing was deeply rooted in religious and moral values. The family moved to Fife and later to Glasgow, where Buchan attended Hutchesons' Grammar School.

He excelled academically and went on to study at the University of Glasgow before securing a scholarship to Oxford's Brasenose College. At Oxford, he studied classics and developed a passion for literature and history. He became involved in student journalism and began writing fiction, laying the foundation for his literary career. He was also elected as the president of the Oxford Union and initially worked as a lawyer and a journalist while continuing to write. His early novels, such as '*Sir Quixote of the Moors*' written in 1895 and *'John Burnet of Barns'* in 1898, were historical romances inspired by Sir Walter Scott. However, it was his experiences outside of literature that helped shape the themes of espionage and adventure that would define his later works.

In 1901, he joined the British government's administration in South Africa after the Second Anglo-Boer War. His time there gave him first-hand insight into imperial politics and diplomacy which would influence his later writing. He returned to Britain and became a publisher while continuing to write novels, essays, and biographies. With the outbreak of the First World War, Buchan began writing a history of the war for Nelson's, the publishers, which was to extend to twenty-four volumes by the end of the conflict. He worked in the Foreign Office and for a time was a war correspondent in France for The Times of London in 1915. His most famous work, *'The Thirty-Nine Steps'*, was published in 1915 during World War One. Written while he was recovering from illness, the novel introduced Richard Hannay, a resourceful, adventurous individual who finds himself caught in a web of espionage and political intrigue. The novel's fast-paced narrative, chase sequences, and themes of conspiracy set the template for modern spy fiction.

The story revolves around Hannay, who is drawn into a dangerous plot after an American spy is murdered in his apartment. Pursued across Scotland by both enemy agents and the police, he must uncover a secret that could change the course of the war. The novel's blend of suspense, action, and patriotism made it an instant success.

Hannay would return in several sequels, including *'Greenmantle'*, *'Mr. Standfast'*, another Richard Hannay novel, *'The Three Hostages'* and *'The Island of Sheep'* in 1936, Hannay's final adventure. While best known for his thrillers, Buchan was a prolific writer across multiple genres. He wrote biographies of historical figures such as Sir Walter Scott, Oliver Cromwell and Augustus Caesar, showcasing his deep historical knowledge. His historical novels, including Witch Wood, explored Scotland's religious conflicts.

Buchan's influence on spy fiction cannot be overstated. His work laid the groundwork for authors like Ian Fleming, Eric Ambler, and John le Carré, shaping the modern espionage thriller genre.

Buchan's success as a writer did not keep him away from public life. He was deeply involved in British politics and governance.

During World War I, he worked for the War Propaganda Bureau, producing material that promoted the British war effort. He later became Director of Information, a role in which he managed wartime propaganda. His writing skills proved invaluable in shaping public opinion during the conflict.

After the war, he continued to write while also entering politics. In 1927, he was elected as a Conservative MP for the Scottish Universities seat, serving until 1935. During this time, he balanced political duties with his literary career, producing historical works, biographies, and novels.

In 1935, he was appointed as Governor General of Canada, representing King George V in the country. Elevated to the peerage as Baron Tweedsmuir, he embraced his new role enthusiastically, traveling extensively and promoting Canadian unity. His tenure lasted until his death in 1940 when he died after suffering a stroke while in office as Governor General of Canada. His legacy, however, endures.

A CHAMPION OF ETHICAL FOREIGN POLICY

Robin Finlayson Cook. Politician (1946 - 2005)

Robert Cook was born in1946, in Bellshill. Raised in a politically engaged family, the only son of Peter, a chemistry teacher, and Christina Cook he developed a passion for debate and socialist ideals from an early age. Cook attended the University of Edinburgh, where he studied English Literature and later became involved in student politics. His academic background contributed to his reputation as one of the most articulate and well-read politicians of his time.

Cook's political career began in local government, but he quickly rose through the ranks of the Labour Party. He was elected as the Member of Parliament for Edinburgh Central in 1974 at the age of 28. He later represented Livingston from 1983 until his death in 2005. His early years in Parliament were marked by his formidable debating skills, which earned him respect across party lines.

During the 1980s and early 1990s, Cook played a significant role in modernising the Labour Party, moving it toward the centre-left. He served in key opposition roles, including Shadow Health Secretary and Shadow Trade and Industry Secretary. His ability to master complex policy issues and present them persuasively made him one of Labour's most effective communicators.

One of Cook's most notable contributions in opposition was his scrutiny of the Conservative government's privatisation policies, particularly in the health sector. His arguments against inefficiencies and injustices in privatised healthcare services resonated with many, reinforcing his reputation as a politician driven by principles rather than political expediency.

Following Labour's landslide victory in 1997, Cook was appointed Foreign Secretary in Tony Blair's government. He immediately made headlines by declaring that British foreign policy would have an ethical dimension. This approach sought to balance national interests with moral considerations, such as human rights, democracy, and international law.

His tenure as Foreign Secretary was marked by several key issues: he sought to restrict arms sales to regimes with poor human rights records, including Indonesia and Saudi Arabia. However, his efforts were often constrained by economic and diplomatic pressures. He supported British interventions to prevent human rights abuses, particularly in Sierra Leone, where the UK played a key role in stabilising the country. He also backed NATO's intervention in Kosovo in 1999, arguing that stopping ethnic cleansing was a moral imperative. He was also a strong pro-European and worked to improve Britain's relationship with the European Union. He championed greater cooperation and was a vocal advocate for EU enlargement. Despite these achievements, Cook faced internal tensions within the government. His ethical foreign policy often clashed with realpolitik considerations, particularly in arms trade policies. In 2001, following Labour's re-election, Blair moved him to the role of Leader of the House of Commons - a demotion that reflected the growing divide between the two men.

Cook's most defining political moment came in 2003 when he resigned from the Cabinet in protest against the Iraq War. His resignation speech in the House of Commons was widely praised as one of the most powerful parliamentary speeches in modern British history, the first speech ever to have received a standing ovation in the history of the House. He argued that the case for war had not been proven and criticised Blair's decision to follow the U.S. into conflict without broader international support. His decision was later vindicated as public opinion turned against the war. After leaving the Cabinet, Cook wrote a widely acclaimed column for The Guardian where he provided sharp critiques of government policies. Tragically, Cook's life was cut short on August 6, 2005, when he allegedly died of a heart attack while hiking in Scotland. Many questions remain unanswered regarding the controversial circumstances of his death which followed his anti-government comments about Iraq but also his quote, "How can we let the Scottish people suffer another Tory government hell-bent on union destruction and driving down living standards? I am seriously considering leading all Scottish Labour MP's over the burning bridge to join with the SNP and declare UDI". Robin Cook was widely mourned across the political spectrum, with tributes highlighting his integrity, intellect and unwavering commitment to principle. His political career was defined by his commitment to ethics, integrity, and intellectual rigour; his principled resignation over the Iraq War cementing his legacy as one of the few politicians willing to stand against the tide for what he believed was right. In an era where political pragmatism often overshadows principle, Cook remained an enduring symbol of honesty and moral courage in public life.

THE FLYING SCOTSMAN

Grahame Obree. Cyclist (1965 -)

Graeme Obree was born in 1965, in Nuneaton, England, but was raised in Scotland and considers himself Scottish. As a child, he struggled with bullying, which led him to find solace in cycling. He began to develop a passion for speed and endurance, cycling long distances on his own. His interest in cycling extended beyond just riding - he was also fascinated by the mechanics of the sport. This mechanical curiosity would later shape his reputation as an innovator.

Obree was not part of a traditional cycling program; he trained alone and had an unconventional approach to his craft. His background was not in professional sports science or coaching but in hands-on mechanics, which led him to develop unique ideas that would eventually revolutionise time-trial cycling.

One of Obree's most significant contributions to cycling was his homemade bicycle, which he called *'Old Faithful'*. Built with parts from a washing machine, the bike was designed with an aggressive aerodynamic position that allowed him to reduce wind resistance and increase efficiency. Obree's unorthodox riding position, with his arms tucked under his chest and his body as compact as possible was unlike anything seen before.

His motivation for designing *'Old Faithful'* was simple: he wanted to break the world hour record which measures how far a cyclist can ride in one hour in a velodrome. The record at the time was held by Francesco Moser, an Italian cyclist who had set it using advanced technology and support from a team of experts. Obree, by contrast, was an independent thinker with limited financial resources, making his achievement all the more remarkable.

On July 17, 1993, at the Vikingskipet Velodrome in Norway, Graeme Obree attempted to break the world hour record. His first effort was unsuccessful, but he returned the next day and succeeded, covering 32.07 miles in one hour. This was a monumental achievement, given that he had built his bike himself and trained using his own methods.

However, his glory was short-lived. Just six days later, the legendary Spanish cyclist Miguel Indurain, who had won multiple Tour de France titles, reclaimed the record. But Obree was undeterred. He returned to the track in April 1994 and took the record back, this time setting a new distance of 32.75 miles.

Despite his success, Obree faced constant battles with cycling's governing body, the *Union Cycliste Internationale*. The UCI was skeptical of his riding position and bike design, and they introduced rules specifically to outlaw his innovations. When he attempted to compete in the 1994 World Championships, his riding position was banned just hours before the race, forcing him to adapt on the spot.

Not one to back down, Obree developed a new aerodynamic position known as the "Superman" position, in which his arms were stretched forward, creating an even more streamlined posture. This position was also eventually banned, highlighting the cycling world's resistance to innovation.

Beyond the physical and technical challenges, Obree faced significant personal struggles. He has been open about his battles with depression which nearly led him to take his own life on multiple occasions. His struggles were exacerbated by the pressures of professional cycling and the resistance he faced from the sport's governing bodies.

Later in life, Obree publicly came out as gay, which he described as another personal challenge he had to overcome. His openness about mental health and his identity has made him an inspiration not just for cyclists but for anyone facing similar struggles.

After retiring from professional cycling, Obree continued to pursue innovative ideas. He turned his attention to human-powered vehicles and attempted to set a new speed record on a recumbent bicycle. His passion for engineering and speed has never waned.

Obree has also shared his story in books and documentaries, most notably in his autobiography, *'The Flying Scotsman'*, which was later adapted into a film. His story is one of resilience, innovation, and determination.

SELECTED QUOTES

James Connolly

"If you remove the English Army tomorrow and hoist the green flag over Dublin Castle, unless you set about the organisation of the Socialist Republic your efforts will be in vain. England will still rule you."

"The Irish people will only be free, when they own everything from the plough to the stars"

"We believe in constitutional action in normal times; we believe in revolutionary action in exceptional times."

Tony Blair

"I believe Mrs. Thatcher's emphasis on enterprise was right."

"A day like today is not a day for soundbites, we can leave those at home, but I feel the hand of history upon our shoulder with respect to this, I really do."

John Buchan

"There may be peace without joy, and joy without peace, but the two combined make happiness."

"An atheist is a man who has no invisible means of support."

"Without humour you cannot run a sweetie-shop, let alone a nation."

William Quarrier

"In connection with the work, it must be remembered that we never call on anyone for money nor do we send out collectors or resort to bazaars or entertainments to raise it. The work is the Lord's and we commit everything to Him in prayer realising that we are only instruments and can be dispensed with when He who employs us sees fit to call us aside."

Graeme Obree

"Cycling is escapism. Now I can just go out and ride a bike. I still like to go hard, I still like to feel my lungs burning, but that's just because of how I feel right now, not because of some potential future achievement. There's no element of 'futurism'. When I'm cycling now, I'm in the present."

"My biggest fear isn't crashing this bike at eighty-five mph and losing my skin - it's sitting in a chair at ninety and thinking 'I wish I'd done more'".

"People gave me a hard time, particularly for my alcoholism. I've since been diagnosed as manic depressive, but fortunately doctors have been able to help me with drugs."

Robin Cook.

"I have not been an extravagant supporter of the Scottish dimension but I have changed my mind."

"There were no international terrorists in Iraq until we went in. It was we who gave the perfect conditions in which Al Qaeda could thrive."

"I may not have succeeded in halting the war, but I did secure the right of parliament to decide on war."

King Robert the Bruce (Attrib.)

"If at first you don't succeed try, try and try again"

"Historians in England will say I am a liar. But history is written by those who have hanged heroes"

"I have broken my good battle-axe." (Upon burying it in the head of English Knight Henry *de Bohun* just before the commencement of the Battle of Bannockburn)

THE PIONEER OF THE OIL INDUSTRY

James 'Paraffin' Young (1811 - 1883)

James Young was born in 1811 in Shuttle Street in the Drygate area of Glasgow into a working-class family. His father was a carpenter, and Young showed an early aptitude for mechanics and science. Despite his modest background, he pursued education through self-study and night classes while working as an apprentice. His natural curiosity and talent for chemistry led him to attend Anderson's University (now part of the University of Strathclyde), where he studied under the renowned chemist Thomas Graham.

Graham, who later became known for his work on colloids and dialysis, recognised Young's potential and hired him as an assistant. Young's exposure to cutting-edge chemical research during this time played a crucial role in shaping his career.

In 1838 he married Mary Young from Paisley and in 1839 they moved to Lancashire where working as an assistant to Graham, he gained employment in the chemical industry. It was in Manchester, while working at the chemical firm of Tennant, Clow & Co. that Young made his groundbreaking discovery.

In the early 1840s, Young was employed at a plant that manufactured lubricating oils from animal fats. However, he became intrigued by the natural seepage of oil from a coal mine in Derbyshire. Conducting experiments, he found that by heating certain types of coal, he could extract a crude oil that, when distilled, produced useful products such as lubricants and a lighter, cleaner-burning fuel that could replace whale oil in lamps.

Young's discovery was revolutionary. Up until then, most people relied on whale oil, tallow, or other animal-based substances for lighting, but these were expensive and often impure. His method of distilling paraffin oil from coal was a major breakthrough, offering an abundant and more affordable alternative.

In 1850, Young patented his method of extracting oil from coal and established the world's first commercial oil refinery in Bathgate, West

Lothian. His company, Young's Paraffin Light and Mineral Oil Company, became a major industrial enterprise. The refinery produced various petroleum products, including lamp oil, lubricants, and waxes, and it set the blueprint for later petroleum refining processes.

Young's method, known as "destructive distillation," involved heating shale or bituminous coal in a controlled environment to break it down into oils, waxes, and gases. The resulting liquid was then refined into different products. This process, though later replaced by crude oil refining, marked the first systematic approach to petroleum processing on an industrial scale.

Young's work laid the foundation for the global oil industry. Though his process initially relied on coal, his techniques were later adapted for crude petroleum refining when oil fields were discovered in North America and Russia. The large-scale production of paraffin oil allowed for widespread, affordable lighting, dramatically improving living conditions in urban areas.

By the 1860s, Young's company was thriving, and he was recognised as one of the leading industrialists of his time. However, as petroleum extraction became more widespread, his process was gradually replaced by refining crude oil, which was more abundant and cost-effective. Nonetheless, Young's contributions to the oil industry remained highly influential, and he is often credited as the pioneer of modern petroleum refining.

Young's success attracted competitors who sought to replicate his process. He was involved in a series of legal battles to defend his patents. In 1864, he sued companies in the United States that were using similar refining methods. The case was significant because it helped establish legal precedents in patent law concerning the petroleum industry. Despite facing challenges, Young's business continued to flourish, and he eventually retired with considerable wealth. He used his fortune to support scientific research and education, funding various institutions and scholarships. He maintained a keen interest in science and industry until his death.

James Young died on May 13, 1883, at the age of 71, leaving behind a legacy as a pioneer of the oil industry. His innovative refining techniques played a crucial role in shaping the modern energy sector, and his impact is still felt today.

THE FATHER OF THE AMERICAN NAVY

John Paul Jones (1747 - 1792)

John Paul Jones was born John Paul on July 6, 1747, in Kirkcudbrightshire. His father was a gardener, and the young John Paul had little formal education. However, he was drawn to the sea from an early age and began his maritime career at the age of thirteen as an apprentice aboard the merchant ship *Friendship*. His early years at sea were formative, providing him with the experience and knowledge that would later serve him well in naval combat.

By the time he was in his early twenties, he had become a skilled seaman, working on merchant and slave ships. However, his career took a turn in 1773 when he was accused of murdering a mutinous sailor in self-defence. Fearing legal retribution, he fled to the American colonies and adopted the surname 'Jones' to obscure his past.

When the American Revolution broke out in 1775, Jones saw an opportunity to make a name for himself in the nascent American navy. With his vast maritime experience, he quickly gained the attention of the Continental Congress and was commissioned as a lieutenant in the newly formed Continental Navy. His first command was aboard the *Alfred*, where he raised the first American naval flag, marking a symbolic moment in American naval history.

Jones' early naval campaigns were marked by audacity and innovation. He was instrumental in disrupting British shipping and commerce, striking at British vessels along the American coastline and the Caribbean. His successes earned him command of the *Ranger* in 1777, a ship that would play a crucial role in his most famous exploits.

John Paul Jones is perhaps best remembered for his daring raids along the British coast. In April 1778, he led a bold attack on the town of Whitehaven, England, a significant British port. The raid was intended to bring the war to British soil, causing panic and demonstrating American naval strength. Though the attack was only moderately successful, it proved that the British mainland was vulnerable, boosting American morale.

His greatest moment came in September 1779 while commanding the *Bonhomme Richard*, a French-built warship provided by America's ally, France. Jones engaged the British warship *HMS Serapis* off Flamborough Head in the North Sea. Outgunned and outmanned, Jones refused to surrender despite his ship suffering severe damage. When the British captain taunted him about surrendering, Jones famously replied, "I have not yet begun to fight!"

Despite the *Bonhomme Richard* eventually sinking, Jones and his crew captured *Serapis*, securing a crucial victory. This battle cemented his reputation as a fearless naval commander and proved that the Continental Navy could stand against the Royal Navy, the world's most powerful naval force at the time.

After the American Revolution, Jones struggled to find a role within the newly independent United States. Though he was honoured and recognised for his contributions, there was little opportunity for him in the peacetime navy. In 1788, he accepted an offer to serve as a rear admiral in the Russian Navy under Catherine the Great. He fought against the Ottoman Empire in the Russo-Turkish War, displaying the same bold tactics that had defined his career. However, political intrigue, his infelicitous behaviour and jealousy among Russian officers led to his early dismissal.

Jones spent his final years in France, where he lived in relative obscurity. He attempted to secure positions in various navies, but his health deteriorated, and he never returned to active duty. On July 18, 1792, John Paul Jones died in Paris at the age of forty-five. He was buried in a modest grave, largely forgotten for nearly a century.

John Paul Jones' contributions to naval warfare and American history were not fully recognised until the early 20th century. In 1905, President Theodore Roosevelt ordered that his remains be exhumed and reburied with full military honours at the U.S. Naval Academy in Annapolis, Maryland. Today, his crypt serves as a reminder of his enduring legacy. Jones' strategic innovations, emphasis on discipline, and refusal to surrender set the foundation for the United States Navy. His belief in a strong naval force influenced American military doctrine for generations. His famous words, "I have not yet begun to fight," continue to inspire naval officers and military personnel to this day. He is still referred to as the 'Father of the American Navy'.

'THE MOST IMPORTANT PHILOSOPHER EVER TO WRITE IN ENGLISH'

David Hume. Philosopher. (1711 - 1776)

Hume was christened David Home and born in a sandstone tenement building which overlooked Edinburgh's Lawnmarket on the Royal Mile, just down from Edinburgh Castle. He was the second of two sons born to Catherine and Joseph Home of Chirnside near Berwick. His father died just after David's second birthday and his mother, Catherine, who never remarried, raised the two brothers and their sister on her own.

Hume changed his family name's spelling in 1734, as the surname 'Home', pronounced 'Hume' in Scotland, was mispronounced when in England. He never married and lived partly at his family home in Berwickshire. At the age of eighteen, Hume made a philosophical discovery that inspired him to 'throw up every other pleasure or business to apply entirely to it'. From this inspiration, Hume set out to spend more than ten years reading and writing resulting in a psychological crisis in the young man which he attributed to a 'laziness of temper'. Hume's physician diagnosed him with the 'disease of the learned' and prescribed a course of bitters and anti-hysteric pills taken along with a pint of red wine every day. His health improved somewhat, but changed his physique from that of a lean and raw-boned man to being 'sturdy, robust and healthful-like.' Indeed, Hume would thereafter become well known for being obese and having a fondness for good port.

The psychological crisis eventually passed and Hume remained intent on articulating his thoughts. He moved to France, where he could live cheaply, and finally settled in La Flèche, a village in Anjou best known for its Jesuit college where Descartes had studied a century before. In 1734, when he was only 23, he began writing '*A Treatise of Human Nature*' and returned to England in 1737 to ready the book for publication. Hume was impeded in his attempts to begin an academic career by protests over his alleged atheism which cause him to complain that this first work, '*A Treatise of Human*

Nature', 'fell dead-born from the press' although it attracted enough of reaction to fuel his lifelong reputation as an atheist and a sceptic. However, he found literary success as an essayist, and as a librarian at Edinburgh University which enabled him to earn a living and provided access to books. The library was the largest in Scotland and boasted some 30,000 volumes. His time there was well spent and resulted in the huge success of his work, 'The History of England', a massive, six-volume opus which became a best-seller and was acclaimed as the standard text book for historians.

In 1748, *'An Enquiry concerning Human Understanding'* was published, covering the central ideas of book one of the '*Treatise'* and included material he had earlier excised. In 1751, he published *'An Enquiry concerning the Principles of Morals'*, which he described as 'incomparably the best' of all of his work.

In 1763, Hume accepted a position as private secretary to the British Ambassador to France whereupon, during his three-year stay in Paris, he became Secretary to the Embassy, and eventually its *chargé d'affaires*. Due to his position, his writings, wit and conversation, he became extremely popular with the Parisian elite, enjoying the conversation and company of famous European intellectuals and was known for his love of good food and wine, as well as his enjoyment of the attentions and affections of women. He returned to Edinburgh in 1769, building a house in Edinburgh's New Town where he spent his autumnal years quietly, succumbing to intestinal cancer in 1776.

Attention to Hume's philosophical works grew after the German philosopher Immanuel Kant credited Hume with awakening him from his 'dogmatic slumber.' According to a second German Philosopher, Arthur Schopenhauer, 'there is more to be learned from each page of David Hume than from the collected philosophical works of Hegel, Herbart and Schleiermacher taken together.' Albert Einstein in 1915, wrote that he was inspired by Hume's positivism when formulating his theory of special relativity. Charles Darwin counted Hume as a central influence.

Viewed by many as the most important philosopher ever to write in English, David Hume presented a positive view of human nature but a sceptical view of religion's usefulness. He was one of the central pillars of the Scottish Enlightenment and was of particular influence over the work of his friend, Adam Smith whose book, *'The Wealth of Nations'* became viewed as 'the Bible of Capitalism.'

THE STRUGGLE FOR SOCIALISM, REPUBLICANISM AND SCOTTISH INDEPENDENCE.

Donald Anderson. Historian and Political Activist. (1936 -)

Donald Anderson was born in Glasgow's Cowcaddens, moving to Firhill when aged eight. His father John (Jack) Anderson and mother, Mary (Molly) MacMillan divorced when he was eight years old and young Donald spent his later childhood years with his father and new Stepmother, Alice Waterton, in both Glasgow and Leeds where he finished his schooling. His father was in the Royal Navy and Anderson and his English stepmother did not get on particularly well in his father's absence. Leaving school aged fifteen, he worked as an apprenticed draftsman in Leeds, then took occupation as a boot and shoe surgical fitter until four years in uniform with National Service took him to the Middle East, Cyprus, Aqaba, Jordan and Bahrain serving as a chef with the Cameronian Scottish Rifles. Anderson was soon in trouble for selling goods supporting Scottish Independence and was often imprisoned or was placed on 'jankers' for his political efforts.

One of his Captains when in the Territorial Army was the Duke of Hamilton who shrugged his shoulders and appeared to ignore Anderson's removal of the Union flag and replacing it with Scottish colours, suggesting they had something in common politically. During his army tenure he often found himself in trouble as he was handy with his fists and took exception to English soldiers referring to him as a 'Porridge Wog' or 'Jock Wog'. Usually these altercations ended in his custody. One separate offence was 'donating' army food and clothing to members of the local Palestinian community which, he insists, taught him about the Highland Clearances - a subject he'd never been taught in school in Scotland. More popular with the local Arab community than with the Army's Special Investigations Branch, he was passed beer, Marxist writings and Scottish historical books through the prison bars by locals, further awakening his burgeoning interest in politics and deepening his respect for the indigenous community.

Demobbed, Anderson worked in a number of different fields; the merchant navy and Pilkington's among them, where as a union official, he led a six week strike. Some time later, he commenced classes at a number of colleges due to his then requirement to work 'Continental Shifts' occasioning the need variously to find classes morning, afternoon and evening to mesh with his employment duties. Subsequently he graduated in Politics and Economic History at the University of Strathclyde and followed this by qualifying as a teacher at Jordanhill College of Education.

Politically, Anderson was involved with a number of groups focussed upon Scottish Independence, Republicanism and Socialism. In 1969 he was arrested with several others alleging that he was involved in the robberies of post offices and bookmakers and of forming 'a secret army' with the intention of using the funds to advance the cause of Scottish Independence from the United Kingdom. The case against him was found not proven and he was released after having been remanded for twenty-four weeks (an extended period due to a pay freeze causing a slow-down in the justice system). This affected his teaching of History and Modern Studies (having been formally instructed not to teach *Scottish* History or *Scottish* Modern Studies) and Special Branch officers would periodically inspect the jotters of his pupils after-hours for evidence of sedition.

Arrested again in 1973 his case was again found not to be proven although others were convicted. Allegedly, Anderson was not uninvolved in the Scottish Liberation Army, the Scottish Citizens' Army of the Republic and the Army of the Provisional Government and experienced much surveillance from Special Branch; Anderson specifying humorously one occasion when he (with one lung) another colleague with one leg, a second colleague with one arm and a fourth with one eye were being tracked by a Special Branch helicopter.

During the early period of the Irish Troubles, Anderson led a delegation of four Scottish nationalist republicans to meet with Rory Ó Brádaigh, the Chief of Staff of the IRA, to ask that no action be taken by them in Scotland as Scots were as put-upon by England as was Ireland.

Their request was granted but although a press release was issued, only one newspaper carried the story. Only three bombings took place in Scotland during this time, all by the Ulster Defence Force which placed devices in Glasgow's Old Burnt Barns Pub, Derry Treanor's and the Clelland Bar on the accurate suspicion that money was being raised there for the Republican cause. Politically, Anderson engaged with the Scottish Socialists' Party but upon discovering that both covertly and overtly they had elements supporting Unionism, left and focussed upon his work with the Scottish Republican and Socialist Movement and the John Maclean Society.

He remains a connoisseur of good Scotch Malt Whisky.

JEBEDIAH CLIESBOTHAM

Sir Walter Scott. Author and Cultural Icon (1771 - 1832)

Walter Scott was born on 15 August 1771, in a third-floor apartment on College Wynd, a narrow alleyway leading from the Cowgate to the gates of the old University of Edinburgh He was the ninth child (six having died in infancy) born to parents, Walter Scott, a prominent solicitor and Anne Rutherford. A childhood bout of polio in 1773, a condition that would greatly affect his life and writing, left Scott lame. To aid his recovery, he was sent to his grandfather's farm in the Scottish Borders, where he developed a deep appreciation for Scottish folklore, ballads, and history. This rural upbringing would later influence much of his literary work.

Scott returned to attend the Royal High School of Edinburgh and later studied law at the University of Edinburgh. Although he qualified as an advocate in 1792 and pursued a legal career, his passion for literature and history soon led him in a different direction.

Scott's first major literary success came through poetry. Fascinated by traditional Scottish ballads, he published *'Minstrelsy of the Scottish Border',* a collection of old Scottish ballads that he had gathered and edited. The work gained significant attention and established Scott as a literary figure.

Building on this success, he published several narrative poems, including '*The Lay of the Last Minstrel* ' in 1805, '*Marmion*' in 1808 and *'The Lady of the Lake'* in1810. These works, written in a highly rhythmic and dramatic style, were immensely popular and solidified his reputation as one of the leading poets of his time. *'The Lady of the Lake'*, in particular, was a cultural phenomenon, inspiring operas, artworks, and even influencing fashion. However, Scott's dominance in poetry was eventually challenged by Lord Byron, whose works became the new literary sensation. Recognising this shift, Scott turned to prose fiction, where he would make his most lasting impact. In consequence, in 1814, Scott published

'Waverley', his first novel, anonymously. It was an instant success and is often considered the first true historical novel. The book, set during the Jacobite rising of 1745, combined historical events with fictional characters, a formula that would define Scott's style and influence generations of writers.

During the summers from 1804, Scott made his home at the large house of Ashestiel, on the south bank of the River Tweed, 6 miles north of Selkirk. When his lease on this property expired in 1811, he bought Cartley Hole Farm, downstream on the Tweed nearer Melrose. The farm had the disparaging nickname of 'Clarty Hole', and Scott renamed it "Abbotsford" .

Following '*Waverley*', Scott produced a series of novels that became known as the '*Waverley Novels',* each published anonymously using the pen name 'Jebediah Cliesbotham' until 1827. These included *'Guy Mannering'* in 1815, *'The Antiquary'* in 1816, *'Old Mortality'* in1816, *'Rob Roy'* in 1817), *'The Heart of Midlothian* in 1818, and *'The Bride of Lammermoor'* in 1819, among others. Each novel explored different periods of Scottish and English history, blending romance, adventure, and political intrigue.

One of his most famous novels, *'Ivanhoe'* written in 1820, marked a shift from Scottish themes to medieval England. The novel, set in the 12th century, popularised Robin Hood and Richard the Lionheart as heroic figures and was instrumental in shaping the modern perception of the Middle Ages. It also had a significant impact on Victorian medievalism and later historical fiction. Scott's novels were immensely popular across Europe and America, inspiring writers such as Alexandre Dumas, Victor Hugo, and Leo Tolstoy. His ability to bring historical events to life with vivid detail and compelling characters set a new standard for historical fiction.

Scott's later years were marked by financial difficulties. In 1825, a financial crisis led to the collapse of his publisher and his own business ventures, leaving him in massive debt. Instead of declaring bankruptcy, Scott chose to write his way out of debt, producing a series of novels and histories at a remarkable pace. Despite declining health, he worked tirelessly, publishing *'Woodstock'* in 1826, *'The Fair Maid of Perth* in 1828, and *'Count Robert of Paris'* in 1832, among others. Scott's financial struggles took a toll on his health, and he suffered a series of strokes. In 1832, he returned to his home, Abbotsford House, where he died on

September 21 at the age of 61. Beyond literature, Scott played a significant role in preserving and promoting Scottish culture. He was deeply involved in the rediscovery and restoration of Scotland's historical sites, including Edinburgh Castle and the Crown Jewels of Scotland. He also orchestrated King George IV's visit to Scotland in 1822, which helped revive interest in Scottish traditions such as tartan and kilts.

'DON'T PISS IN THE WATER SUPPLY!'

Alexander James (Alex) Harvey. Musician (1935 - 1982)

Alex Harvey was born and raised in the district of Kinning Park in Glasgow, an area closely associated with nearby Govan and Ibrox Stadium, home of Glasgow Rangers FC.

He worked in a number of jobs from carpentry, to waiting tables, to carving gravestones before finding success in music. After buying his first guitar, he began performing in skiffle groups such as the *'Clyde River Jazz Band'* and the *'Kansas City Skiffle Group'* before forming *'Alex Harvey and his Big Beat Band'*. In 1960, at Alloa Town Hall, they opened for pop star John Askew known professionally as *'Johnny Gentle and his Group'*...his 'Group' that night being the then *'Silver Beatles'* incorporating Lennon, McCartney, and Harrison along with Stuart Sutcliffe and Tommy Moore. Ringo had yet to join. Sutcliffe and Moore had yet to leave.

His band alternated between *'Alex Harvey's Big Soul Band'*, and *'Alex Harvey and his Big Beat Band'* spending considerable time touring in the United Kingdom and Germany. He also won a competition that sought 'Scotland's answer to Tommy Steele', then regarded as Britain's first teen idol and rock and roll star (although it's difficult to imagine Harvey singing, *'Little White Bull'*). Without a record deal, Harvey formed a psychedelic band called *'Big Moth'* but found no success as record companies viewed them as having no commercial potential so he joined the pit-band for the London West End musical *'Hair'*. He stayed for several years and led the band in the cast recording of the musical *'Hair Rave-up'* which also included a number of Harvey's own songs that hadn't been sung in the show.

Alex's brother Les, a guitarist with *'Stone The Crows'*, was killed whilst performing due to an un-earthed microphone.This tragedy prompted Harvey to undertake a new direction in rock and he recruited fellow Glaswegian band *'Tear Gas'* for an innovative musical redirection. In 1972, major artistes such as David Bowie (who lived with him for a while) and Alice Cooper were introducing theatricality into their acts and Harvey, in the fifteenth year of his career, decided to emulate and outdo them, so having joined forces with progressive rock band *'Tear Gas'* (whose members at the time were bassist Chris Glen, Ted McKenna on percussion, his cousin Hugh on keyboards and Zal Cleminson on guitar, with Harvey fronting the band), the *Sensational Alex Harvey Band* (often shortened to *SAHB)* were formed and went from strength to strength. In 1973 they played more UK gigs than any other band and supported the then mega-band *'Slade'* when few other bands wanted to be listened to in their shadow. By 1976, *SAHB* were the biggest-grossing touring band in the country. His theatricality proved enormously popular. At the Reading Festival, Harvey appeared on stage, dressed as Christ and tethered to a cross, shouting, 'I was framed!'. He played a street gangster in his song '*Framed*', a private eye in '*Man In The Jar*' and a superhero in '*Vambo*'. At every show he advised his audience, "Don't piss in the water supply!" The band had top forty hits in Britain with singles, '*Delilah*' a melodramatic and ostentatious cover version of the Tom Jones hit, which reached number seven in 1975, and also with '*The Boston Tea Party'* in June 1976. They produced a succession of highly regarded albums; '*The Blues', 'Roman Wall Blues', 'The Joker Is Wild', 'The Mafia Stole My Guitar'* and '*Soldier On The Wall'*. Popular songs included, '*Tomorrow Belongs To Me', 'There's No Lights On The Christmas Tree Mother, They're Burning Big Louie Tonight', 'Next'* and '*The Faith Healer'*. They toured constantly until 1976 when Harvey left the group at the height of its fame. The other band members continued as *SAHB* (somewhat bewilderingly without Harvey) and brought out another album, '*Fourplay*'. Harvey re-joined the group for a 1978 recording of the album, '*Rock Drill*' and toured the UK in Autumn 1981 with the last gig at Workington's Carnegie Theatre in November. After going solo, he released two more albums and went on tour with his new band from 1979. On 4 February 1982, returning from a tour in Belgium, Harvey died from a heart attack, one day before his 47th birthday. Harvey married twice; first to Mary Martin, with whom he had a son and secondly to Trudy, with whom he also had a son. Harvey was a Master Mason in Lodge Union, No. 332, based at 1543 Shettleston Road, Sandyhills in Glasgow. He was initiated on 22 June 1955 and was passed to the Second Degree in Freemasonry on 24 August 1955. He received his Third Degree on 16 November 1955 aged twenty.

'THE FIRST BLAST OF THE TRUMPET AGAINST THE MONSTROUS REGIMENT OF WOMEN'

John Knox. Theologian. (Circa 1514 - 1572)

Knox was the foremost leader of the Scottish Reformation, and was known for the austere moral tone of the Church of Scotland. He brought the Protestant Reformation to Scotland and was one of the key founders of the Scottish Presbyterian Church. Born in Haddington some time between 1514 and 1515. His father was a merchant so he would have grown up in some comfort although he was orphaned at an early age. Knox was ordained as a Catholic priest in 1536 in Edinburgh by the Bishop of Dunblane and was assigned to the parish of St. Andrews where he became the castle's priest, working as an ecclesiastical lawyer. While he was there, twenty-one French ships approached St Andrews in Fife, besieged the castle and forced the surrender of the garrison. Protestant nobles and others, including Knox, were taken prisoner and forced to row the French galleys.

While some of the nobles were sent to prisons in France, Knox remained a galley slave until released some two years later. Exiled from Scotland, Knox spent time in England working on his views of reform. In England, under the Protestant King Edward V1, he argued that the King, although of tender years, was blessed with wisdom whose dedication to the Protestant cause was invaluable. However, the King died prematurely in 1554 and was succeeded by the Catholic Queen Mary Tudor. The Scottish Realm at the time of Knox's existence was under the Stuarts and the Catholic Church whom Knox blamed for the squalid economic circumstances of the poor. Knox left England and moved to Geneva in Switzerland where he spent time under the tutelage of reformer John Calvin and was able to learn from what Knox described as 'the most perfect school of Christ'. He formed the view that a Protestant Reformation in Scotland was possible and decided to fight for a Scottish Protestant Reformation following an invitation to return to Scotland via a letter from his mother-in-law, Elizabeth Bowes. He returned, toured various parts of Scotland preaching the reformed doctrines and liturgy, and was welcomed by many of the nobility including the Earl of Mar.

Upon setting foot on Scottish soil, he argued that the power to improve matters lay with Mary Queen of Scots. This led to a fight to establish the Reformed Protestant Church in Scotland bringing about a Protestant Reformation which would alter the governance and belief systems in Scotland. He published *'The First Blast of the Trumpet Against the Monstrous Regiment of Women'* in 1558 within which he argued that the Scottish Kirk had been led by corrupt and foreign leaders and that the country needed reform and change for its own advancement and religious morality. Mary Queen of Scots was inevitably a hinderance to Knox's ambitions as she was strictly Catholic and criticised Knox's actions which she believed attacked her authority and beliefs. Although Mary remained Scotland's Queen, the power of the Scottish Protestants was gaining momentum. Mary summoned Knox to Holyrood on several occasions following reports of his preaching, leading initially to something of a stand-off. Knox was particularly critical of Mary's decision to marry Don Carlos, the Catholic son of Philip ll of Spain. Eventually, Mary asked her counsellors if Knox had not committed treasonable acts but the decision was not to punish Knox.

Both Knox and Mary married; Knox, following the demise of his first wife Marjory Bowes who died early in his Edinburgh ministry, following upon which aged fifty, he was betrothed to Margaret Stewart, then aged only seventeen and daughter of Andrew, Lord Stewart of Ochiltree. Mary also married - to Henry Stuart, Lord Darnley, against which union Knox preached. By the following year, 1566, Mary was looking at options for removing Darnley by divorce. Her hesitation was the risk of making her son illegitimate. Darnley was subsequently murdered, his body and that of his valet being discovered in the orchard of the Kirk o' Field church in Edinburgh. Almost immediately, Mary married the chief suspect, the Earl of Bothwell. She was forced to abdicate and was imprisoned in Lochleven Castle. Subsequently, Mary was sent to England under house arrest as Knox openly called for her execution.

Knox continued preaching through troubles times in Scotland and, as he became more enfeebled, continued to speak the word of God. He was notable not so much for the overthrow of Roman Catholicism in Scotland, but for ensuring the replacement of the established Christian religion with

Presbyterianism rather than Anglicanism and for establishing the presbyterian form of worship of Calvin, rather than Lutheranism or the Anglicanism of England. Knox died in Edinburgh in 1572. Although he has a statue at the highest point of the Glasgow Necropolis, his actual body lies in the ground behind St Giles' Cathedral in Edinburgh.

A simple plaque marks the spot under car park number twenty-three.

SELECTED QUOTES

James 'Paraffin' Young

"The art of engineering is the greatest of all the arts of mankind in that it uses science and art in the creation of useful objects and does so in the service of human kind in all of its aspects".

John Paul Jones

"I wish to have no connection with any ship that does not sail fast; for I intend to go in harm's way."

"I have not yet begun to fight!"

Donald Anderson

"I'm a Scot…no' a Brit!"

"And as for me being a wonderful man, not many people know this."

"Scottish teachers were taught little if any Scottish history in the Anglicised universities in Scotland which meant they could not pass much in that way onto their pupils."

"From time to time, Special Branch officers would come into my classroom after school hours and inspect the weans' jotters to make sure I wasn't preaching sedition!"

Alex Harvey

"Don't piss in the water supply."

"The machine scared me a bit because I don't really want to be a star."

"Music's got straight, really straight. It's exactly the way it was in 1956 when it was '*How Much Is That Doggie In The Window?*' and then Elvis came bustin' through and it was a breath of fresh air."

"I didn't realise I was singing in a Scottish accent. It was just the way it happened."

John Knox

"To promote a woman to bear rule, superiority, dominion, or empire above any realm, nation, or city, is repugnant to nature; contumely to God, a thing most contrary to his revealed will and approved ordinance; and finally, it is the subversion of good order, of all equity and justice."

"Woman in her greatest perfection was made to serve and obey man, not to rule and command him."

"We call her not a hoor...but she was brought up in the company of the wildest hoormongers. In the company of such men was our Queen brought up. What she was and is, her best self knows." (On Mary Queen of Scots.)

Sir Walter Scott

"Oh, what a tangled web we weave when first we practise to deceive!"

"All men who have turned out worth anything have had the chief hand in their own education."

"The race of mankind would perish did they cease to aid each other. We cannot exist without mutual help. All therefore that need aid have a right to ask it from their fellow-men; and no one who has the power of granting can refuse it without guilt."

"Of all vices, drinking is the most incompatible with greatness."

"If a farmer fills his barn with grain, he gets mice. If he leaves it empty, he gets actors."

'HE DIDN'T LIVE BY THE SAME RULES AS EVERYONE ELSE.'

Ivor Cutler. Poet and Entertainer. (1923 - 2006)

Ivor Cutler, born Isidore Cutler, grew up in the Glasgow area of Govan into a middle-class, Jewish family of Eastern European descent, his Grandparents having migrated from Poland and Belarus - other sources say Russia. His father, Jack Morris Cutler was a draper and jeweller.

Aged sixteen, Cutler was evacuated to the Scottish Borders town of Annan and a year later took a job as an apprentice fitter at Rolls-Royce. In 1941, he decided to prove wrong those who claimed that those of the Jewish faith were not fighting for their country in any number by enlisting and joining the airforce. He trained as a navigator but was dismissed for being too absent-minded and served out the rest of the war as a first aider and storeman with the Windsor Engineering Company before studying at Glasgow School of Art and becoming employed as a schoolteacher of music, art and poetry in Paisley. His views on corporal punishment resulted in him cutting up his leather belt (tawse) and giving it in pieces to his pupils

A.S.Neil, the famed Scottish educationalist, founded the progressive Summerhill School in Suffolk and young Cutler found himself attracted to the democratic, laissez-faire principles of the school. He lived in the grounds of the school teaching drama, married and had two children, although the marriage did not last. Cutler continued to teach until 1980 for the Inner London Education Authority - to the alleged chagrin of some parents, who found his unorthodox methods subversive.

In 1957, he began to perform songs and poems stating that for the first six years he wasn't any good. However, following an introduction to comedy impresario, Ned Sherrin who was impressed by Cutler's surrealistic humour and poetry, he was booked to appear on the '*Acker Bilk Show*' and '*Late Night Line-Up*' on television. There he was spotted by Beatle Paul McCartney who in 1967 was in the midst of casting his film,

'Magical Mystery Tour'. Cutler was cast as bus conductor, 'Buster Bloodvessel' who cautioned his passengers, "I am concerned for you to enjoy yourselves within the limits of British decency", before developing a passion for Ringo's large aunt Jessie.

Shortly thereafter, his 1967 record, '*Ludo*', was produced by Beatles' producer George Martin in Abbey Road recording sessions. Cutler's distinctive deep Scottish accent, coupled with the unusual breathiness of his foot-peddled harmonium, became the trademark of his songwriting style and performance as much as his offbeat lyrics. He became known for his regular performances on BBC radio, and in particular the numerous sessions recorded over three decades for influential radio presenters John Peel and Andy Kershaw. Due to the interest generated by his radio sessions, Cutler was also able to advance his recording career, making albums in the 1970s with Virgin, and later Creation Records.

He last appeared on stage at the Queen Elizabeth Hall in London in January 2004. The event was filmed and shown in a documentary about his life the following year, *'Ivor Cutler: Looking for Truth with a pin.'*

Cutler's books and radio series included such titles as *'Cockadoodle Don't', 'Life in a Scotch Sitting Room Volume 2', 'Many Flies Have Feathers', 'Jammy Smears'* and '*Gruts*'. In 1980 he was awarded the Pye Radio Award for Humour.

He was a long-standing member of the Noise Abatement Society and forbade his audience ever to whistle in appreciation at his work. He also had a life-long love of languages and taught himself Chinese, choosing the language above Japanese 'because the textbooks were cheaper' and was in the habit of frequenting Soho's Chinatown, where he could display his knowledge. He occasionally presented a stern demeanour with strangers, insisting on them addressing him as Mr. Cutler. He usually wore a fez or a beret of some description and seemed uncomfortable about his bald head, remarking, "*Sur le volcan ne pousse pas l'herbe*"…'Grass does not grow on a volcano!'

John Peel famously described him as a true maverick and that he was the only artist ever to have been played on Radios One, Two, Three and Four.

POET, FOLKLORIST AND POLITICAL ACTIVIST

Hamish Henderson. Intellectual, Soldier and Cultural Icon. (1919 - 2002)

Born in Blairgowrie, Perthshire in 1919, Henderson was raised by his mother after the death of his father. His early years were marked by financial hardship, but his intellectual abilities earned him a scholarship to Dulwich College in London. However, his mother died shortly before he was due to take up his place and he had to live in an orphanage while studying there. Later, he attended the University of Cambridge, where he studied modern languages. His linguistic skills would prove invaluable during World War II, but even before that, he showed an early interest in folk music and socialist politics, themes that would define much of his later life.

Henderson's experiences during World War II had a profound effect on him. He received a commission in the Intelligence Corps and was very effective as an interrogator due to his command of six European languages and his deep understanding of German culture. He was involved in the North African and Italian campaigns and played a significant role in negotiating the surrender of Italian forces in 1943. His poetry from this period, most notably *'Elegies for the Dead in Cyrenaica'* in 1948, captured the horrors of war with a lyrical intensity that resonated with readers and critics alike. The collection won the Somerset Maugham Award and is considered one of the most powerful poetic responses to World War II.

Politically, Henderson was deeply influenced by what he saw during the war. His experiences reinforced his commitment to socialism, anti-fascism and internationalism. He believed in the power of ordinary people to shape history and saw folk music as a means of expressing their struggles and aspirations becoming a leading figure in the Scottish folk revival, inspired by the work of American folklorists such as Alan Lomax. He dedicated himself to collecting and preserving Scotland's folk traditions and in the 1950s and 1960s, he traveled across Scotland, recording songs, stories, and oral histories from ordinary people. His work with the School of Scottish Studies at the University of Edinburgh helped create one of the most important archives of Scottish folk culture.

He was also an active songwriter, contributing songs that became anthems of political and social movements. One of his most famous compositions, *'Freedom Come-All-Ye'*, is often regarded as the unofficial Scottish National Anthem. Written in Scots, the song reflects Henderson's anti-imperialist stance and his hope for a more just and equal world.

Henderson's political activism was inseparable from his artistic work. He was a committed socialist and a strong advocate for Scottish independence. He saw folk music as a form of resistance, a way for ordinary people to assert their identities and challenge authority. Throughout his life, he supported causes ranging from nuclear disarmament to workers' rights and anti-apartheid campaigns.

During the 1950s and 1960s, Henderson was closely involved in Scotland's left-wing movements. He was a vocal supporter of the Campaign for Nuclear Disarmament and took part in anti-war protests. He also worked to preserve Scotland's cultural heritage at a time when it was under threat from modernisation and anglicisation.

His views often put him at odds with the political establishment, but he remained a respected and beloved figure. His ability to bring people together whether through song, poetry, or activism made him a powerful force for change. For many years he held court in Sandy Bell's pub in Edinburgh, the meeting place for local and visiting folk musicians. In his later years, Henderson continued to promote Scottish culture and radical politics. He remained active in the folk scene, mentoring younger musicians and poets. His contributions were increasingly recognised and he received numerous honours including an honorary doctorate from the University of Edinburgh in 1992.

Henderson's influence on Scottish culture is immense. His work in folklore helped preserve Scotland's oral traditions for future generations. His poetry and songs, particularly *'Elegies for the Dead in Cyrenaica'*, *'The 51st Highland Division's Farewell to Sicily'* and *'Freedom Come All Ye'* remain a major contribution to Scottish literature. His songs continue to be performed and adapted by musicians committed to social justice and Scottish identity.

When he died in 2002, Henderson left behind a legacy that continues to inspire. His vision of a Scotland rooted in its folk traditions but open to the world; socialist, internationalist, and fiercely independent continues to resonate strongly today. Hamish Henderson was one of Scotland's most influential cultural figures of the 20th century.

A MENSA ADVENTURER AND POLITICIAN

Rory James Nugent Stewart. Politician, Academic and Polyglot (1973 -)

Born in Hong Kong in 1973, Rory Stewart is the son of Brian Stewart, a senior British intelligence officer and diplomat with a Scottish heritage. The Stewart family comes from a long-standing Scottish lineage, tracing ancestry back to the Royal House of Stewart. Stewart was raised largely at the family's home, Broich House (built in 1770) in Crieff, Perthshire. This rural upbringing played an important role in grounding his sense of national identity, despite the international and privileged dimensions of his later life. His father, Brian Stewart, was born in Edinburgh and maintained strong ties to Scotland throughout his life. Rory Stewart has frequently referenced his father's influence, often reflecting on their time spent together in Scotland - walking in the hills, discussing politics, and contemplating history.

Educated at Eton and later at Balliol College, Oxford, Stewart's accent and style does not suggest a Scottish background, but he has never shied away from acknowledging and embracing his roots. As a teenager, he was a member of the Labour Party. During his gap year in 1991, he served a limited commission in the Black Watch for five months as second lieutenant. After graduating, Stewart joined the Foreign Office. In Indonesia, he served as the Political & Economic Second Secretary from 1997 to 1999. He was appointed at the age of twenty-six as the British Representative to Montenegro in the wake of the Kosovo Campaign. Following the 2003 invasion of Iraq, Stewart was appointed as the Coalition Provisional Authority Deputy Governorate Co-ordinator in Maysan and Deputy Governorate Co-ordinator/Senior Advisor in Chi Qar Province. He denies suggestions that he worked for MI6. In 2000, Stewart took leave from the Foreign Office to walk across Iran, Afghanistan, Pakistan, India, and Nepal; a remarkable feat that he chronicled in his widely acclaimed book *'The Places in Between'*, famously, walking across Afghanistan just after the fall of the Taliban in 2002, often alone and in conditions of real danger. His book won the *'Glenfiddich Spirit of Scotland Award'* and was short-listed for a Scottish Arts Council prize.

A member of MENSA, Stewart joined the Conservative party in summer 2009 despite never having voted for them and was selected as a candidate for Penrith and the Borders, edging Scotland, which seat he held from 2010 - 2019. In 2012, Stewart married Shoshana Clark, an American and former employee.

His political career was marked by an unusual independence and an often visible discomfort with Westminster's tribalism. Despite being a Conservative, he frequently positioned himself as a centrist and reformer, not shying away from criticising his own party. He held various junior ministerial roles, eventually serving as Secretary of State for International Development in 2019. After Prime Minister Theresa May resigned, Stewart stood as a candidate to be party leader stating at the outset that he would not serve under Boris Johnston. When Johnson became prime minister in July 2019, Stewart resigned from the cabinet. In 2019, Stewart had the Conservative Whip removed after voting to back a motion paving the way for a law seeking to delay the UK's exit date from the European Union. On 3 October 2019, Stewart announced he had resigned from the Conservative Party.

In 2021, Stewart and his family moved to Jordan for two years to work for the Turquoise Mountain Foundation, setting up a project to restore a Roman site near the Golan Heights to create employment in the area. During this time, Stewart was also travelling to Yale University for lecture commitments.

Stewart has been a member of the faculty of the John. F. Kennedy School of Government, Ryan Family Professor of Human Rights at Harvard University. He is presently a senior fellow at Yale University's Jackson Institute.

In 2022, Stewart joined forces with ex-Labour spin doctor, Alastair Campbell to launch *'The Rest Is Politics'*, a British podcast and television series which has become the leading political podcast in the United Kingdom. Campbell and Stewart generally discuss contemporary news and politics with a strong focus on UK politics, but also international developments, such as foreign elections and humanitarian catastrophes.

In 2023, he stated he had often considered standing for election to the Scottish Parliament, branding the idea 'very attractive'. He stated that he cared deeply about Scotland and that, "Scottish Conservatism has more in common with the way that I view the world" adding his father was, "A man for tartan trousers, bagpipes, the whole lot," and that he thought it was "fun being Scottish because it was a way of irritating the English".

THE BREAK-UP OF BRITAIN

Thomas (Tom) Cunningham Nairn. Political Theorist and Academic (1932 - 2023)

Tom Nairn was born in Freuchie in Fife, and was the son of a primary school headmaster. He attended Dunfermline High School and Edinburgh College of Art before graduating from the University of Edinburgh with an MA in Philosophy. The following year, he was awarded a British Council scholarship to study at the *Scuola Normale Superiore* in Pisa, Italy. This period was pivotal in shaping his intellectual trajectory as he immersed himself in Italian culture and engaged deeply with the works of Antonio Gramsci. Reflecting on this experience, Nairn noted that Italy's broader intellectual atmosphere allowed him to transcend the confines of orthodox Marxism prevalent in Britain at the time.

Throughout the 1960s, Nairn's career was marked by a blend of academic positions and unconventional roles. He studied at the University of Dijon (now the University of Burgundy), worked as a night watchman in warehouses and taught at various institutions, including the University of Birmingham from 1965 to 1966. His tenure at Hornsey College of Art in 1968 was particularly notable; during a period of student occupation, Nairn became actively involved, contributing to a major critique of the educational system. This involvement led to his dismissal, after which he spent three decades without a secure university position.

From 1972 to 1976, Nairn was associated with the Transnational Institute in Amsterdam. However, he resigned when his vision of transforming it into a pan-European think tank did not materialise. Subsequently, he worked intermittently as a journalist and television researcher, primarily for Channel 4 and Scottish Television in Glasgow. In the mid-1990s, he briefly joined the Central European University and later established a Master's course on Nationalism at the University of Edinburgh. In 2001, Nairn accepted an Innovation Professorship in Nationalism and Cultural Diversity at the Royal Melbourne Institute of Technology in Australia. He remained there until

January 2010, after which he returned to Europe, holding a fellowship at the Institute for Advanced Study at Durham University in 2009.

Nairn was a seminal figure in the British New Left. Alongside historian Perry Anderson, he developed the Nairn-Anderson thesis in the 1960s and 1970s which sought to explain Britain's unique development trajectory, contrasting it with continental Europe's movements toward anti-clericalism and republicanism post the 1789 French Revolution.

A staunch advocate for European integration, Nairn first presented his arguments in *'The Left Against Europe'* in 1973, challenging the prevailing leftist skepticism in the UK regarding European unity. He was also a fervent supporter of Scottish independence and devolution, criticising the Blair Labour government of the 1990s and 2000s for not granting sufficient powers to the Scottish Parliament and the Welsh Assembly. Nairn contended that Scotland's economic potential was stifled by the concentration of power in London and the archaic nature of the British state.

His seminal work, *'The Break-Up of Britain'* in 1977, offered a Marxist critique of the emergence of global nationalism. Nairn posited that imperialism by core countries spurred peripheral elites to mobilise their masses by crafting powerful myths rooted in local artifacts and events. These 'peripheral intelligentsias', influenced by romanticism and populism, sought to assert their distinct identities. His insights on nationalism gained renewed attention during Britain's protracted Brexit negotiations post-2016, especially concerning Scotland's desire to remain in the European Union.

Nairn's republican inclinations were evident in *'The Enchanted Glass' i*n 1988, one of the earliest modern critiques of the British monarchy from an abolitionist perspective. The book, which won the Saltire Society Scottish Book of the Year Award, employed the term *'Ukania'* to highlight the irrational and Ruritanian nature of the British constitutional monarchy. In 2009, Nairn was elected a fellow of the Academy of Social Sciences in Australia, recognising his significant contributions to political science and political economy. He spent his later years in Scotland with his long-term partner, Millicent Petrie, and had two stepchildren.

Tom Nairn passed away on 21 January 2023 at the age of ninety, leaving behind a legacy of profound scholarship that continues to shape discussions on nationalism, the monarchy and the British State. His extensive body of work has profoundly influenced contemporary political thought in Scotland and beyond.

THE BLACKSMITH AND THE BICYCLE

Kirkpatrick Macmillan. Inventor. (1812 - 1878)

Born in 1812, in Keir, Dumfries and Galloway, Macmillan was the son of Robert Macmillan, a blacksmith. Growing up in a rural setting, he apprenticed under his father, honing skills that would later play a crucial role in his inventive endeavours. The blacksmith trade not only provided him with technical proficiency but also a creative outlet to explore mechanical innovations.

The story of Macmillan's invention begins with his observation of the 'hobby horse', a two-wheeled, foot-propelled vehicle popular in the early 19th century. Dissatisfied with the need to push off the ground to gain momentum, Macmillan envisioned a machine that could be propelled without the rider's feet touching the ground. Utilising his blacksmithing expertise, he constructed a pedal-driven bicycle around 1839. This design featured iron-rimmed wooden wheels, with the larger rear wheel connected to pedals via connecting rods, allowing for continuous motion without ground contact. The machine was extremely heavy and the physical effort required to ride it must have been considerable. Nevertheless, Macmillan quickly mastered the art of riding it on the rough country roads, and was soon accustomed to making the fourteen-mile journey to Dumfries in less than an hour

In June 1842, Macmillan made a pioneer trip to Glasgow on his velocipede. He spent the night in Cumnock and next day continued his journey to Glasgow. All along the road folk fled in terror when they saw Macmillan and his wooden-iron steed in the distance. The news spread that the Prince of Darkness himself was approaching and when Kirkpatrick reached Glasgow a large crowd had gathered to see the strange arrival. As he rode into the Gorbals, however, Macmillan had the ill-luck to knock down a small child. The result was that a few days later, a police statement read, 'a gentleman who stated he came from Thornhill in Dumfriesshire, was placed at the Gorbals public bar, charged with riding a velocipede to the obstruction of the passage, and with having, by doing so, thrown over a child'.

The child who was thrown down had not sustained any injury, and under the circumstances the offender was fined only five shillings.

After this exciting trip to the city Macmillan cycled back home, where he lived quietly until his death in 1878. A tall, well-built, handsome looking man, the blacksmith-inventor was much respected far and wide. He was always willing to show his bicycle to anyone or to help neighbours construct one of their own. He practised dentistry in his spare time.

Regardless of any debate surrounding his invention, Macmillan's legacy endures, particularly in Scotland. A plaque on the family smithy in Courthill commemorates his contribution, reading, 'He builded better than he knew.' While the global recognition of Macmillan as the sole inventor of the pedal bicycle remains contentious, his story reflects the spirit of innovation characteristic of the 19th century; a period marked by rapid technological advancements and the reimagining of personal transportation.

He never thought of patenting his invention or trying to make any money out of it, but others who saw it were not slow to realise its potential and soon copies began to appear for sale. Gavin Dalzell of Lesmahagow copied his machine in 1846 and passed on the details to so many people that for more than fifty years he was generally regarded as the inventor of the bicycle. However, Macmillan was quite unconcerned with the fuss his invention had prompted, preferring to enjoy the quiet country life to which he was accustomed

Kirkpatrick Macmillan's tale is emblematic of the complexities inherent in attributing singular invention claims, especially in an era where documentation was sparse, and multiple innovators were concurrently developing similar technologies. Whether or not he was the first to create a pedal-driven bicycle, the narrative of a humble Scottish blacksmith contributing to a transformative mode of transport captures the imagination and highlights an often-overlooked figure in the annals of invention.

THE REBEL, TEACHER AND REVOLUTIONARY

Margaret Frances Skinnider. Activist and Trades Unionist (1892 - 1971)

Margaret Skinnider was born in 1892 in Coatbridge, to Irish parents. Though she grew up in Scotland, she was deeply connected to her Irish heritage and became actively involved in nationalist movements.

As a young woman, she trained as a teacher and worked in a Glasgow school. However, she was also drawn to activism. She joined the Glasgow branch of *Cumann na mBan*, the women's auxiliary of the Irish Volunteers and became involved in the fight for Irish independence. She was also a skilled markswoman, having practiced shooting while participating in activities organised by the Glasgow branch of the Irish Volunteers.

Her involvement with the Irish nationalist movement deepened through her friendship with prominent figures such as Countess Markievicz and James Connolly. Inspired by their vision of an independent Ireland, she decided to take an active role in the struggle.

In 1916, Skinnider traveled to Dublin to take part in the Easter Rising, the armed insurrection against British rule in Ireland. She smuggled ammunition and detonators from Scotland in her luggage, demonstrating her commitment to the cause.

During the rebellion, she fought alongside the Irish Citizen Army under James Connolly, primarily in St. Stephen's Green and in the Royal College of Surgeons. Unlike many women at the time who were restricted to non-combatant roles, Skinnider actively took up arms, sniping at British forces. In her later memoir, *Doing My Bit for Ireland* written in 1917, she described the experience of being a female combatant in a traditionally male-dominated struggle.

Her bravery came at a cost. While attempting to advance on British positions, she was shot three times, sustaining serious injuries. She was taken to the hospital, where she was treated for her wounds but she was ultimately unable to continue fighting.

After the defeat of the Rising, many rebels were arrested and executed, including Connolly and other leaders. Skinnider, still recovering, managed to avoid execution and later fled to the United States to continue advocating for Irish independence.

After recovering from her injuries, Skinnider worked to spread awareness about the Irish cause. She traveled to the United States where she gave lectures and raised funds for the Republican movement.

She returned to Ireland in 1917, resuming her activism and joining *Cumann na mBan*, where she played a key role in the Irish War of Independence from 1919 to1921. She worked as a courier, smuggled weapons and provided logistical support to the IRA.

After the Anglo-Irish Treaty of 1921 which led to the partition of Ireland, Skinnider opposed the agreement and sided with the Anti-Treaty forces in the Irish Civil War. Like many republicans, she was arrested and imprisoned by the Free State government.

Following her release, she remained active in politics and social issues, particularly in fighting for the rights of women in post-independence Ireland. She was a strong advocate for equal pay and the right of women to participate fully in Irish political and economic life.

Margaret Skinnider's dedication to women's rights did not end with the revolutionary period. She became deeply involved in trade unions and worked tirelessly to improve conditions for women workers in Ireland. She was an advocate for equal pay, a cause she championed through her work in the Irish National Teachers' Organisation.

At a time when Irish society was becoming increasingly conservative and patriarchal, Skinnider remained a vocal advocate for women's rights. Her contributions to the labour movement helped lay the groundwork for future feminist activism in Ireland.

Skinnider spent her later years working as a teacher while continuing to be active in political and labour movements. She became a leading figure in the INTO, serving as its president in the 1950s. Her work helped shape Irish labor policies, particularly concerning women's employment rights.

She remained a committed Republican and socialist throughout her life, though she saw Ireland become a divided state, with many of the revolutionary ideals she fought for left unrealised. Margaret Skinnider passed away in 1971, but her legacy lives on. She is now recognised as one of the most important female combatants in the 1916 Easter Rising.

THE INVENTION OF LOGARITHMS.

John Napier. Theologian and Mathematician (1550 - 1617)

John Napier (also spelled Neper),was born into a wealthy family in 1550 in Edinburgh. His father was Sir Archibald Napier. John was a highly intelligent child and was schooled in the University of St. Andrews when he was thirteen years old. While there, he lived in St Salvator's College where the Principal of the University took personal care of him.

Although there are few records to confirm his subsequent early travel, most historians reckon he travelled in Europe following the advice given by his uncle Adam Bothwell in a letter written to Napier's father in 1560, saying, *"I pray you, sir, to send John to schools either in France or Flanders for he can learn no good at home"*.

In 1571, Napier turned twenty-one and returned to Scotland. The following year he married Elizabeth Stirling, daughter of Scottish mathematician, James Stirling. The couple had two children before Elizabeth died in 1579. Napier later married Agnes Chisholm, with whom he had ten children. On the death of his father in 1608, Napier and his large family moved into Merchiston Castle, where he lived for the rest of his life.

Throughout his life, Napier had an interest in theology and developed strongly anti-papal views, going as far as to write that the Pope was the Antichrist. Initially, Napier's study of mathematics was only a hobby and he wrote that he *'often found it hard to find the time for the necessary calculations between working on theology'*.

However he is best known for his study of mathematics and originated the concept of logarithms as a mathematical device to aid calculations. Napier first made this discovery publicly known in 1614 in his book called *'A Description of the Wonderful Canon of Logarithms'*. He stated, "Seeing there is nothing that is so troublesome to mathematical practice than the multiplications, divisions, square and cubical extractions of great numbers which besides the tedious expense of time are subject to many slippery errors, I began, therefore, to consider how I might remove those hindrances."

His invention of logarithms allowed the expression of large ranges of numbers in a more manageable form. In researching this conundrum, he also advanced the notion of the decimal fraction by introducing the use of the decimal point. His suggestion that a simple point could be used to separate the whole number and fractional parts of a number soon became accepted practice throughout the world.

Napier was also known as "Marvellous Merchiston" for the many ingenious mechanisms he built to improve his crops and cattle. He approached agriculture in a scientific way and he experimented with, 'Improving and manuring of all sorts of field land with common salts whereby the same may bring forth in more abundance both of grass and corn of all sorts, far cheaper than by the common way of dunging used heretofore in Scotland'.

He also invented an apparatus to remove water from flooded coal pits and devices to survey and measure land. In addition, he described military devices that were similar to today's submarine, machine gun, and army tank.

Napier was occasionally viewed as dabbling in the occult and is thought to have experimented with alchemy and necromancy - the practice of communicating with the dead in order to foretell future events and discover hidden knowledge.

The development of logarithms is given credit as the most important factor in the general adoption of decimal arithmetic.

Edinburgh Napier University in Edinburgh is named after him. His birthplace, Merchiston Tower in Edinburgh, is now part of the facilities of the University.

'ON YONDER HILL THERE STOOD A COO, IT'S NO' THERE NOO...IT MUST HAVE SHIFTIT.'

William Topaz McGonagall. Poet and Tragedian. (1825/1830 - 1902)

McGonagall claimed throughout his life to have been born in Edinburgh although his Irish parents, Charles and Margaret in the 1841 Census recorded his birthplace as Ireland. McGonagall junior's claim may have been occasioned by the benefits conferred upon native-born Scots under the Poor Law of 1845. His biographer David Phillips consulted his census, marriage and death records and calculated 1825 as McGonagall's more likely birth date. For most of his life he lived in Dundee. In 1846, he married Jean King, a fellow mill worker from Stirling with whom he had five sons and two daughters.

He trained as a hand-loom weaver like his father and had a brief career on the stage but, aged fifty-two stated, "The most startling incident in my life was the time I discovered myself to be a poet, which was in the year 1877". He toured Scotland and was a man of apparent supreme self-confidence with apparently no insight as to the fact that his audience was more amused than impressed and regarded him affectionately as Scotland's worst poet who only seemed partially in on the joke. His self-belief in his own brilliance as a poet was unshakeable and he became a well-known personality in Scotland although his poetry readings were regularly attended by riotous audiences throwing rotten fruit and other projectiles sufficient to see him banned from public performance in his home city of Dundee. None of this bruised his delusions of being a genius.

In 1878, a year after he had chosen to become a poet, McGonagall decided to seek the patronage of Queen Victoria, so on a 'beautiful sunshiny day', he walked the sixty miles from Dundee to the Balmoral Estate. Inevitably he was turned back at the gate and had to walk the same distance home. Despite this minor setback, McGonagall chose to display the royal coat of arms at the top of his printed poems with no regard to having earlier received his marching-orders and leaving him, "Not in the least discouraged".

McGonagall was consistently impecunious and survived by selling or reciting his poems. He had many friends who supported him with donations. In 1880, he sailed to London to seek his fortune and in 1887 to New York, his return fare being paid by a benefactor. In his biography he describes his various misfortunes and on each occasion, returned unsuccessful.

In 1894, he received a letter purporting to be from the King of Burma in which he was informed that the King had knighted him as Topaz McGonagall, Grand Knight of the Holy Order of the White Elephant, Burma. It was evident that this was a fairly blatant prank but McGonagall would thereafter refer to himself as 'Sir William Topaz McGonagall, Knight of the White Elephant, Burma' for the rest of his life.

McGonagall wrote over two hundred poems, the most famous being '*The Tay Bridge Disaster*' which has been lampooned by critics as one of the worst poems in the English language. His risible choice of words, his puerile rhymes, inconsistent scansion, improvident subject matters and rambling narrative are usually coloured by the inclusion of inappropriate or naive details. Some scholars argue that his inappropriate rhythms and weak vocabulary combine to make his work amongst the most unintentionally amusing dramatic poetry in the English language but it is nevertheless evident that his reputation as the worst poet in British history is well deserved. That said, while his audiences ridiculed him, while his performances were banned due to the disruptions they caused, while his travels furth of Dundee proved spectacularly unsuccessful and despite being buried in a pauper's grave, his books remain in print to this day and he's remembered and is quoted long after more gifted contemporaries have been forgotten. A memorial plaque was erected to his memory in Greyfriar's Churchyard in Edinburgh in 1999. It reads;

'William McGonagall
Poet and Tragedian
Died 2nd September 1902
Buried near this spot'
'*I am your Gracious Majesty*
ever faithful to Thee.
William McGonagall,
The Poor Poet
That lives in Dundee'.

JOHN CHARLES WALSHAM REITH

1st Baron (John) Reith. Director General, BBC (1889 - 1971)

John Reith was born in Stonehaven on 20th July 1889 and was the fifth son and the youngest, by ten years, of the seven children of the Reverend Dr. George Reith and his wife Adah. Reith was educated first at Glasgow Academy then at Gresham's School in Norfolk before taking up a two year apprenticeship at the Royal Technical College which later became the University of Strathclyde in Glasgow.

This was followed by an apprenticeship as an engineer at the North British Locomotive Company which, following a merger, became the largest locomotive engineering works in Europe, building steam locomotives for countries all over the world. While there, he was commissioned into the 5th Scottish Rifles. In February 1911, he was commissioned as an officer in the Scottish Rifles' 5th Territorial Battalion and was shortly thereafter transferred to the Royal Engineers as a lieutenant. In October 1915, while fighting in France, he was severely wounded by a sniper's bullet through his left cheek which nearly cost him his life and left him with a significant scar. He received psychiatric treatment for his wounds but reputedly suffered suicidal depression for the rest of his life.

Reith resigned his commission in 1921 and returned to Glasgow where he became general manager of an engineering firm, William Beardmore & Co. A year later he returned to London where he started working as secretary to a group of London Tory MPs in the run up to the 1922 election. That general election's results were the first ever to be transmitted throughout the UK via radio. While in London, he saw an advert in The Morning Post for the General Manager of the planned British Broadcasting Company. Following a check in *Who's Who?* he noticed that the man interviewing him his was Aberdonian Sir William Noble so he re-wrote his CV to emphasise his own Aberdonian lineage. He wrote in his 1956 biography; '*Into The Wind", They didn't ask me many questions and some they did I didn't know the meaning of. The fact is I hadn't the remotest idea as to what broadcasting was. I hadn't troubled to find out. If had tried I should probably have found difficulty in discovering anyone who knew.'*

Despite a lack of any relevant experience, Reith was appointed. As the founding director general of the BBC from 1922 to 1938, he outlined four principles of his vision for a broadcasting system: it operated as a public service rather than for commercial motives; it offered national coverage; it depended on centralised control and it offered high standards of programming. He also insisted on BBC operational independence from political pressures. This was put to the test during the 1926 General Strike as he struggled to ensure editorial independence for the BBC. However, the following year he became Director-General of the reformulated British Broadcasting Corporation and was knighted in 1927 so it can be assumed that his editorial independence didn't upset the Establishment overmuch.

The British Broadcasting Company was a success. The number of listeners and licence-fee payers rocketed, the wireless manufacturers were making money and the BBC became established as part of the British way of life.

Reith was an enthusiastic admirer of Hitler's Germany, stating in his diaries following the 'Night of the Long Knives' event when the Nazis ruthlessly exterminated their internal dissidents, 'I really admire the way Hitler has cleaned up what looked like an incipient revolt. I really admire the drastic actions taken, which were obviously badly needed.' After Czechoslovakia was invaded by the Nazis in 1939, he wrote: 'Hitler continues his magnificent efficiency.'

These views notwithstanding, Prime Minister Neville Chamberlain, first invited him to resign from the BBC to become chairman of Imperial Airways before appointing him to several ministerial positions in the wartime government, thereafter being appointed to the House of Lords as Baron Reith. In 1967, he accepted the post of Lord High Commissioner to the General Assembly of the Church of Scotland, an appointment he treasured.

Reith died in Edinburgh after a fall aged 81. In accordance with his wishes, his ashes were buried at the ancient, ruined chapel of Rothiemurchus near Aviemore.

THE FATHER OF MODERN GEOLOGY

James Hutton. Geologist and Chemist (1726 - 1797)

James Hutton was born in 1726, in Edinburgh. His father, a merchant, died when he was young, leaving Hutton and his four siblings to be raised by their mother. From an early age, Hutton displayed a keen interest in science and nature. He studied at the University of Edinburgh, initially focusing on law, but soon switched to medicine, as he found the legal profession uninspiring.

His studies took him to Paris and Leiden, where he earned a degree in medicine. However, Hutton was more interested in chemistry and natural sciences than in practicing medicine. Upon returning to Scotland, he turned his attention to agriculture, managing a farm in Berwickshire. This hands-on experience with soil, erosion, and rock formations sparked his deep interest in geology.

At the time, most people believed in catastrophism, the idea that Earth's geological features were shaped by sudden, short-lived catastrophic events such as floods or divine interventions. The most widely accepted explanation for the Earth's formation was based on a literal interpretation of the Bible, which suggested that the planet was only 6,000 years old.

Hutton, however, observed that geological processes like erosion, sedimentation, and volcanic activity were slow and continuous. He concluded that these processes must have been occurring for vast periods, meaning the Earth was far older than previously thought. This idea became known as uniformitarianism, often summarised by the phrase, 'the present is the key to the past.'

Hutton proposed that mountains erode over time, sediments accumulate in oceans, and new rock layers form through heat and pressure. He argued that these processes had been happening for millions - even billions - of years, constantly reshaping the Earth.

Unlike many scientists of his time who relied on speculation, Hutton based his theories on careful observations of rock formations. One of his most famous discoveries was at Siccar Point, a coastal site near Cockburnspath in the Scottish Borders. Here, Hutton found unconformities - places where different layers of rock met at unusual angles. He realised that these rock formations told a story of immense geological time, that older layers of rock had been formed, tilted and eroded over time and that newer layers had then been deposited on top, showing that entire cycles of rock formation had taken place. This provided physical evidence that the Earth had undergone repeated geological transformations over millions of years. Another key discovery was made at Holyrood Park in Edinburgh, where Hutton observed intrusions of molten rock into existing formations. This led him to suggest that heat played a crucial role in rock formation, an idea that contributed to later studies of volcanic and igneous activity.

Hutton compiled his findings in his groundbreaking work, *'Theory of the Earth'* in 1795 in which he argued that the Earth's geological processes are cyclical and continuous, that rock cycle involves erosion, sedimentation, compaction and uplift, that heat from the Earth's interior plays a major role in rock formation and change and that the Earth is far older than previously believed - perhaps millions or billions of years old.

His work laid the groundwork for Charles Lyell's later refinements of uniformitarianism and influenced Charles Darwin's theory of evolution by suggesting that the Earth had been stable long enough for gradual biological changes to occur.

Hutton's ideas were not immediately accepted. Many scientists at the time were still influenced by religious beliefs about the Earth's creation. His complex writing style also made his work difficult to understand. It was not until the geologist Charles Lyell repopularised uniformitarianism in the 1830s that Hutton's theories gained widespread recognition.

Despite the initial skepticism, Hutton's contributions are now regarded as fundamental to geology. His concepts of deep time, slow geological processes and the rock cycle are cornerstones of modern Earth sciences. His ideas provided the foundation for geology as a scientific discipline. His work influenced later geologists like Charles Lyell, Charles Darwin and modern geologists, who use his principles to study plate tectonics, climate change, and natural disasters. He died in Edinburgh in 1797 and was buried in the vault of Andrew Balfour, opposite the vault of his friend Joseph Black in the now sealed south-west section of Greyfriars Kirkyard in Edinburgh.

SELECTED QUOTES

Ivor Cutler

There's nothing like a Scotch education. One is left with an irreparable debt. My head is full of irregular verbs still!"

"Right, that's it! I told you, I warned you! I'm leaving you!" (Ivor found backstage talking to his harmonium) "

Hamish Henderson

"Sae come all ye at hame wi' freedom.

Never heed whit the hoodies croak for doom.

In yer hoose a' the bairns o' Adam can find breid, barley bree and painted room."

"There's no principle in the world that says if you sit back and spectate, things will come right."

"They'll mind what he said here in Glasgie, oor city - and the haill warld beside". (About John Maclean)

"We're the D-Day Dodgers out in Italy
Always on the vino, always on the spree.
Eighth Army scroungers and their tanks
We live in Rome – among the Yanks.
We are the D-Day Dodgers, over here in Italy."

Tom Nairn

"There is no Stalinist like a Scottish Stalinist!"

"As far as I'm concerned, Scotland will be reborn when the last minister is strangled with the last copy of the Sunday Post!"

Margaret Skinnider

"We had obeyed all rules of war and surrendered as formally as any army ever capitulated." (Skinnider, incredulous that the leaders of the Easter Rising were executed.)

"All my reports were of death; nothing but death."

John Napier

"Seeing there is nothing that is so troublesome to mathematical practice, nor that doth more molest and hinder calculations, than the multiplications, divisions, square and cubical extractions of great numbers…I began to consider in my mind by what certain and ready art might I remove those hindrances."

Baron John Reith

"Somebody introduced Christianity into England and somebody introduced smallpox, bubonic plague and the Black Death. Somebody is minded now to introduce sponsored broadcasting."

"That bloody shit, Churchill."

"I'm very angry and I've spoilt a new tunic." (While lying wounded on a stretcher after being shot in World War One.)

William Topaz McGonigal

"Beautiful Railway Bridge of the Silv'ry Tay!
Alas! I am very sorry to say
That ninety lives have been taken away
On the last Sabbath day of 1879,
Which will be remember'd for a very long time."

"Ye lover of the picturesque, if ye wish to drown your grief,
take my advice and visit the ancient town of Crieff."

"Well, I must say that the first man who threw peas at me was a publican."

THE CREATION OF ORDNANCE SURVEY MAPS

Major General William Roy. Military Engineer and Cartographer (1726 - 1790)

William Roy was born in Milton Head in Carluke, South Lanarkshire in 1726. From an early age, he displayed a strong aptitude for mathematics and technical drawing. His father was a factor in the service of the Hamiltons of Hallcraig, as well as an elder of the Kirk. His grandfather had held a similar position as factor, and his uncle acted in that capacity for the Lockhart's of Lee. Thus Roy grew up in an environment where making land surveys and using maps was part of the daily business. He was educated in Carluke parish school and then Lanark Grammar School. There is no record of a further or higher education.

His skills led him to a career in surveying and by the age of twenty, he was working for the Board of Ordnance, the British military's engineering and mapping department.

Roy's career was shaped by the aftermath of the Jacobite Rebellion of 1745. After the failed uprising, the British government sought to tighten control over Scotland, particularly the Highlands, where the rebellion had gained the most support. One key issue was the lack of accurate maps, which had hindered the British army's ability to move troops and respond to threats.

Some time after 1738 (when Roy was 12) he moved to Edinburgh and gained experience of surveying and making plans, probably as a civilian draughtsman at the office of the Board of Ordnance at Edinburgh Castle. It is possible that he may have been employed there as a boy because it was normal procedure for the board to employ cadets aged ten or eleven who were trained to become civilian surveyors and draughtsmen. Roy was certainly associated with the board by 1746 (aged twenty), for he was the author of an official map of Culloden made soon after the battle. Following this, the government commissioned a detailed military survey of Scotland.

Roy was chosen to lead the project, marking the beginning of his lifelong contribution to cartography and military geography.

From 1747 to 1755, Roy led a team of surveyors in creating the first detailed map of Scotland. This project, known as the Military Survey of Scotland, was a massive undertaking that involved measuring distances, drawing maps and recording the landscape with unprecedented accuracy. The survey provided a comprehensive depiction of roads, rivers, mountains, and settlements, making it easier for the British military to navigate the country. He also adapted triangulation, a method of measuring distances and locations using a network of triangles, which would later become standard in modern surveying. However, while the maps were not published for public use, they provided the groundwork for later surveys, including those of the Ordnance Survey. They also had significant scientific and economic value, helping to improve infrastructure and land management in Scotland.

During the Scottish Survey, Roy took careful note of the locations of ancient Roman remains, primarily military camps wherever he encountered them and these were all marked precisely on the map sheets. This was the beginning of a lifelong interest in ancient Scottish history which he pursued whenever he was travelling the country in his capacity as Surveyor General.

In 1784, Roy was chosen to lead the Principal Triangulation of Great Britain, the first large-scale, scientifically accurate mapping of the country. His team first measured a precise baseline on Hounslow Heath, near London. This measurement was crucial for ensuring accuracy in the entire triangulation process. He worked with instrument makers like Jesse Ramsden to develop high-precision theodolites, which could measure angles with remarkable accuracy.

The Ordnance Survey was set up as part of the British military's efforts to improve national defence. At the time, Britain feared a French invasion and accurate maps were essential for military planning. Using Roy's methods, the Ordnance Survey undertook the first official mapping of Britain, starting with the south coast. His use of triangulation became the standard method for national mapping projects and his emphasis on accuracy and detail set the precedent for all future Ordnance Survey maps. Importantly his collaboration with instrument makers improved the quality of surveying tools, benefiting future generations of cartographers. The

Ordnance Survey eventually became one of the most respected mapping agencies in the world and its work continues today, producing highly accurate maps for a variety of purposes. Roy died in 1790, just a year before the British government officially established the Ordnance Survey in 1791.

THE MAN WHO DISCOVERED THE VICTORIA FALLS

David Livingstone. Missionary, Medic and Geographer. (1813 - 1873)

David Livingstone was born in 1813, in Blantyre, into a working-class family. His parents, Neil and Agnes Livingstone, were devout Christians who emphasised the importance of education and religion.

From a young age, Livingstone worked in a cotton mill while attending school in the evenings. His thirst for knowledge led him to study medicine and theology at Anderson's College (now the University of Strathclyde) and the University of Glasgow. He was deeply inspired by missionary work, particularly the efforts of Robert Moffat, a Scottish missionary in southern Africa.

After completing his medical studies, Livingstone was ordained as a missionary doctor and set sail for South Africa in 1841, marking the beginning of his lifelong connection to the continent.

Livingstone arrived in Kuruman, a mission station in modern-day Botswana, where he worked with his father-in-law and fellow Scottish missionary, Robert Moffat. However, he soon realised that existing missionary efforts were limited to settled African communities and did not reach deeper into the interior.

Determined to spread Christianity to unreached tribes, Livingstone embarked on expeditions into the unexplored heart of Africa. In the process, he became more than a missionary. He became an explorer and geographer.

Between 1849 and 1856, he led several expeditions, mapping previously unknown regions. Some of his most significant achievements during this period included crossing the Kalahari Desert in 1851 where he reached Lake Ngami, one of the first major bodies of water he discovered. He mapped the Zambezi River, proving that it flowed into the Indian Ocean which challenged existing beliefs. Famously, he discovered the

Victoria Falls in 1855, which he named after Queen Victoria. The local people called it '*Mosi-oa-Tunya*' meaning *'The Smoke That Thunders'*.

His 6,000-mile journey across Africa from Luanda (Angola) to Quelimane (Mozambique) made him a global celebrity when he returned to Britain in 1856.

While exploring Africa, Livingstone was horrified by the brutality of the Arab and Portuguese slave traders. He documented their atrocities and spoke out against the East African slave trade which saw thousands of Africans captured and sold. His reports influenced British policy, leading to increased efforts to suppress slavery in Africa. Livingstone believed that opening Africa to 'commerce, Christianity, and civilisation' would help end the slave trade and improve the lives of local people.

To support this vision, the British government funded his Zambezi Expedition (1858–1864) to explore the region's potential for trade. However, the expedition failed due to disease, logistical issues, and conflicts with local tribes. In 1866, Livingstone embarked on another mission to locate the source of the Nile River, a long-standing geographical mystery. This journey, however, was the most challenging of his life.

He suffered from malaria, dysentery, and extreme fatigue while struggling through dense jungles and hostile terrain. His letters back to Britain became infrequent and rumours spread that he was either lost or dead.

In 1871, the American journalist Henry Morton Stanley, sent by the New York Herald, found Livingstone in Ujiji (modern-day Tanzania). Upon seeing him, Stanley reportedly greeted him with the famous words, "Dr. Livingstone, I presume?"

Though Stanley urged him to return home, Livingstone refused, insisting on completing his mission. He spent his final years exploring and documenting the slave trade's horrors, but his health deteriorated rapidly. On May 1, 1873, Livingstone died in the village of Chitambo (now in Zambia) from malaria and internal bleeding. His loyal African companions, Susi and Chuma, embalmed his body and carried it over 1,500 miles to the coast where it was shipped back to Britain. His reports exposed the cruelty of the East African slave trade, pressuring Britain to take action. His influence contributed to eventual British intervention against the trade.

He was buried in Westminster Abbey, a rare honour that reflected his global significance.

THE PIONEER OF CHLOROFORM VAPOUR

James Young Simpson. Obstetrician and Gynaecologist (1811 - 1870)

James Young Simpson was born in 1811, in Bathgate, West Lothian. He was the youngest of seven children in a working-class family. His father, David Simpson, was a baker, and his early life was modest. Despite financial difficulties, Simpson displayed remarkable intelligence and academic promise.

At just fourteen years old, he enrolled at the University of Edinburgh, where he initially studied the arts before shifting his focus to medicine. By the age of eighteen, he was a medical student, and in 1832, at the age of twenty-one, he earned his medical degree. His early career was influenced by the renowned Scottish surgeon Robert Liston and he quickly developed an interest in obstetrics, a field that was still developing in the early 19th century.

Simpson became a professor of midwifery (now known as obstetrics and gynaecology) at the University of Edinburgh in 1840, succeeding James Hamilton. His lectures and teachings were influential, and he rapidly gained a reputation as an expert in childbirth and reproductive health. At the time, childbirth was a painful and dangerous process, often leading to high maternal and infant mortality rates. Pain relief during surgery and labour was minimal, relying on methods such as alcohol, opium, or even physical restraint. The introduction of anaesthesia was a groundbreaking shift in medical practice.

Ether had already been introduced as an anaesthetic by American dentist, William T. G. Morton in 1846. However, Simpson sought an alternative that was more effective and easier to administer. He and his colleagues conducted experiments with different chemical compounds.

On November 4, 1847, Simpson, along with his friends Dr. George Keith and Dr. Matthew Duncan, inhaled chloroform vapour in a controlled setting at his home. They quickly lost consciousness, proving its efficacy. Simpson recognised that chloroform was a more potent and reliable anaesthetic than ether. His findings were met with initial skepticism, particularly from religious groups which believed that pain in childbirth was divinely ordained. However, Simpson was a persuasive advocate for the use of anaesthesia, arguing that alleviating pain was both humane and ethical. His position gained widespread acceptance after Queen Victoria used chloroform during the birth of her eighth child in 1853. Her endorsement helped popularise chloroform and cemented Simpson's legacy in medical history.

Beyond anaesthesia, Simpson made numerous contributions to obstetrics and surgical procedures. He introduced the use of forceps to assist with difficult childbirth cases and developed improved techniques to manage labour complications. He also identified and named several medical conditions, including *placenta praevia,* a dangerous condition in which the placenta obstructs the birth canal. Simpson was also an advocate for antiseptic practices before Joseph Lister formally introduced germ theory. He promoted cleanliness in hospitals and labour wards, recognising the link between poor hygiene and maternal deaths due to infections like puerperal fever. His recommendations for hospital design included improved ventilation and sanitation which later influenced hospital architecture across Britain and beyond.

In addition to his medical advancements, Simpson was deeply committed to public health and social reform. He campaigned for better medical education, improved working conditions for doctors and hospital reforms to reduce infections and overcrowding. He was also a strong opponent of unregulated medical practices, advocating for stricter licensing of medical professionals.

His humanitarian efforts extended to working-class communities where he provided medical care to those who could not afford it. Simpson believed that medical treatment should be accessible to all, regardless of social class.Simpson's contributions earned him numerous accolades. In 1866, he was knighted by Queen Victoria, becoming Sir James Young Simpson. He was the first person to receive a baronetcy for services to medicine. He was also awarded honorary degrees from multiple universities and his influence reached beyond Britain to Europe and North America.

Simpson's legacy in medicine is profound. His discovery of chloroform anaesthesia transformed surgery and obstetrics, making medical procedures far less painful. His advocacy for antiseptic practices and improved hospital conditions laid the groundwork for modern healthcare standards.Sir James Young Simpson passed away in 1870 at the age of fifty-eight. His death was widely mourned, and he was given a public funeral in Edinburgh, attended by thousands. He is buried in Warriston Cemetery, Edinburgh.

THE CONQUEROR OF EVEREST AND THE EIGER

Duncan 'Dougal' Curdy MacSporran Haston. Mountaineer (1940 - 1977)

Dougal Haston was born in1940, in Currie, a small village near Edinburgh. From an early age, he exhibited a strong sense of adventure and a love for the outdoors. His passion for climbing began in the Scottish Highlands, where he honed his skills on the rugged cliffs of Ben Nevis and Glencoe. Like many great climbers, Haston was drawn to the challenge of conquering rock faces and testing his limits against the elements. Early in his career, he climbed numerous new Scottish routes such as *'The Bat'* on the *Carn Dearg Buttress* of Ben Nevis.

In 1965, shortly before his ascent of the Eiger, Haston was sentenced to 60 days in prison having run down and killed eighteen-year-old student, James Orr whilst driving drunk. He later attended the University of Edinburgh, but his heart was always in the mountains. He quickly became involved with the Scottish climbing community and gained a reputation as an exceptionally talented and determined climber. His early climbs in Scotland laid the foundation for what would become a legendary career.

By the early 1960s, Haston was making a name for himself in the European climbing scene. He moved to the Alps, where he joined a community of elite climbers tackling the continent's most formidable peaks. One of his most notable early achievements was his ascent of the North Face of the Eiger in 1966, a climb that solidified his reputation as one of the best mountaineers of his generation.

The Eiger's North Face, known as the *'Mordwand'* or *'Death Wall',* had claimed the lives of many climbers before Haston and his partner, John Harlin, attempted their route. Tragically, Harlin fell to his death during the climb, but Haston, along with German climber Siegfried Löw, completed the ascent. This climb, later dubbed the *'Eiger Direct,'* became one of the most famous in mountaineering history and was a testament to Haston's resilience and skill.

Haston's ambitions extended far beyond the Alps. By the 1970s, he set his sights on the Himalayas, where he would undertake some of the most daring ascents of his career. In 1970, he joined Chris Bonington's British expedition to Annapurna, one of the world's deadliest peaks. The team successfully summited via a new and highly challenging route, marking a significant achievement in Himalayan climbing.

His most famous ascent came in 1975, when he and Doug Scott became the first climbers to reach the summit of Mount Everest via the formidable Southwest Face. This route, pioneered by the British team led by Chris Bonington, was considered one of the most difficult and dangerous approaches to the world's highest peak. Haston and Scott made history when they stood on the summit on September 24, 1975, cementing their place among the greatest mountaineers of all time.

In addition to his mountaineering feats, Haston was a prolific writer and thinker. He wrote several books on climbing, including '*In High Places*' and '*The Eiger*'. These works provided insight into the mind of a mountaineer and chronicled the psychological and physical struggles of extreme climbing. His writing style was introspective and philosophical, offering a glimpse into the motivations that drove him to take on such immense challenges.

Haston also played a significant role in the development of mountain safety and training. In his later years, he became the director of the International School of Mountaineering in Leysin, Switzerland. Here, he mentored young climbers and passed on his vast knowledge and experience, ensuring that future generations could learn from his expertise.

Despite surviving some of the most dangerous climbs in history, Dougal Haston's life was cut short in a tragic accident. On January 17, 1977, he was caught in an avalanche while skiing near his home in Leysin. He was just 36 years old.

His death was a significant loss to the climbing world, but his legacy endures. Haston's bold ascents, groundbreaking achievements, and contributions to mountaineering literature continue to inspire climbers today. His name remains synonymous with courage, determination, and the relentless pursuit of adventure.

Dougal Haston was more than just a mountaineer; he was a pioneer who helped shape the future of climbing. His fearless approach to high-altitude challenges, combined with his deep understanding of the mountains, made him one of the greatest climbers of his era.

THE ARISTOCRATIC CHAMPION OF SCOTS GAELIC

The Honourable Ruaraidh Erskine of Marr. Aristocrat and Author (1869 - 1960)

Ruaraidh Erskine was born in 1869 into the distinguished Erskine family which had historical ties to the Scottish aristocracy. He inherited the title 'of Mar,' linking him to the ancient Earldom of Mar, one of Scotland's oldest noble lineages before amending the spelling to Marr. Despite his aristocratic background, Erskine was drawn to progressive and nationalist causes from an early age.

Educated in England, Erskine became fluent in multiple languages including Gaelic. His exposure to European nationalist movements, particularly in Ireland and the broader Celtic world, influenced his political outlook. Inspired by the Irish Gaelic revival and the growing call for Irish independence, he sought to apply similar ideas to Scotland, advocating for the cultural and political revival of the Scottish nation.

Erskine emerged as a key figure in the early Scottish nationalist movement at a time when the idea of Scottish independence was considered radical. In the late 19th and early 20th centuries, Scotland's political landscape was dominated by Unionist and Labour perspectives with little mainstream support for secession from the United Kingdom. However, Erskine believed that Scotland should be a self-governing nation with its own cultural and political identity.

In 1904, he founded *Guth na Bliadhna* (The Voice of the Year), a Gaelic-language journal that became an influential platform for nationalist ideas. Through this publication, he argued for Scottish self-rule, promoted the Gaelic language, and sought to inspire a cultural revival similar to the one happening in Ireland under leaders like Douglas Hyde and Eoin MacNeill.

Erskine was also involved in political activism, helping to form various nationalist organisations, playing a role in the National Party of Scotland and other early nationalist groups that would later influence the creation of the Scottish National Party (SNP). However, at this stage, Scottish nationalism remained a niche cause, lacking the widespread support that Irish nationalism had gained.

Beyond politics, Erskine was deeply invested in the preservation and promotion of Scottish Gaelic culture. He believed that the Gaelic language was a fundamental part of Scotland's national identity and that its decline was tied to the loss of Scottish independence. His writings often reflected a romanticised vision of Scotland's Celtic past, drawing upon mythology, folklore, and historical narratives.

He was an advocate for the teaching of Gaelic in schools, the promotion of traditional Scottish literature, and the preservation of Highland customs. He also supported the idea of a pan-Celtic movement, seeking solidarity between Scotland, Ireland, Wales, Brittany, and other Celtic nations. This idea of a broader Celtic identity was a recurring theme in his work.

Although an aristocrat, Erskine had complex political views that combined nationalism with socialist ideals. He believed that Scottish independence should be accompanied by economic and social reforms to benefit ordinary Scots, particularly in rural areas where poverty was widespread.

The account of his life and times, '*No Language! No Nation!*' by Gerard Cairns points out how he was influenced by European thinkers and had sympathies with the more radical elements of Irish nationalism. His support for Irish independence and his admiration for figures like Patrick Pearse and James Connolly reflected his belief that Scotland's struggle should not only be about culture but also about economic justice.

As the 20th century progressed, Scottish Nationalism remained a marginal movement, and Erskine's vision of an independent Scotland did not materialise in his lifetime. The interwar years saw the rise of socialist and Labour politics in Scotland, which overshadowed nationalist efforts. Nevertheless, his early advocacy laid the groundwork for later nationalist organisations, including the formation of the SNP in 1934. In his later years, Erskine continued to write and promote Scottish culture, but his influence waned as newer political movements emerged. He died in 1960, largely removed from mainstream political discourse. However, his contributions to the nationalist cause were later recognised as foundational to the modern Scottish independence movement. His life was marked by a deep commitment to Scottish self-determination, a fascination with the Celtic identity and a blend of aristocratic heritage with radical political ideas.

SCOTLAND'S LEGENDARY OUTLAW

Rob Roy MacGregor. Cattle Dealer (1671 - 1734)

Robert Roy MacGregor was born in 1671 at Glengyle, near Loch Katrine in the Scottish Highlands. He was a member of Clan MacGregor, a clan that had suffered persecution under Scottish law. The MacGregors had been stripped of their name and lands following conflicts with more powerful clans and the Scottish government. As a result, Rob Roy grew up in an environment where defiance against authority was both a necessity and a way of life.

The nickname, 'Rob Roy' comes from the Scots Gaelic *Raibeart Ruadh*, meaning 'Red Robert', a reference to his red hair. From an early age, he was trained as a warrior, skilled in sword fighting and cattle raiding, a common practice among Highland clans.

Like many Highlanders of his time, Rob Roy supported the Jacobite cause which aimed to restore the exiled Stuart monarchy to the throne of Britain. The MacGregors had historically backed the Jacobites and Rob Roy fought in the 1689 uprising alongside John Graham of Claverhouse, known as 'Bonnie Dundee'. Although that rebellion failed, it cemented Rob Roy's commitment to the cause. In 1693, at Corrie Arklet farm near Inversnaid, he married Mary MacGregor of Comar who was born at Leny Farm, Strathyre. The couple had four sons.

In the 1715 Jacobite Rising, Rob Roy played a more indirect role. While he did not fight in the major battles, he led raids against government forces and disrupted supply lines. His ability to outmanoeuvre British troops earned him a reputation as a skilled strategist. However, when the rebellion was crushed, he found himself a wanted man.

Before becoming an outlaw, Rob Roy was a respected cattle dealer. Highland cattle trading was an important business in Scotland and he acted as a middleman, purchasing cattle from Highland farmers and selling them to Lowland markets.

However, around 1712, his fortunes changed. Rob Roy borrowed a significant sum of money to invest in cattle but was betrayed by his business partner who disappeared with the funds. Unable to repay his debts, Rob Roy was declared an outlaw. The Duke of Montrose, a powerful landowner and political figure, seized his lands and property. This led to a long-standing feud between the two men with Rob Roy retaliating by raiding Montrose's estates, stealing cattle, and harassing his men.

Rob Roy's defiance against Montrose and the British government turned him into a folk hero. Many saw him as a champion of Highland justice, taking from the rich and redistributing to the poor. His reputation spread and his ability to evade capture only added to his legend.

Despite his outlaw status, Rob Roy continued his activities for years, often protected by sympathisers in the Highlands. However, in 1722, he was finally captured and imprisoned in Newgate Prison in London. A fictionalised account of his life, *The Highland Rogue*, was published making Rob Roy a legend in his own lifetime and George 1 was moved to issue a pardon for his crimes just as he was about to be transported to the colonies.

After his release, Rob Roy returned to the Highlands, where he lived peacefully for the remainder of his life. He died in 1734 at the age of 63 and was buried in Balquidder Churchyard where his grave remains a site of pilgrimage for those interested in Scottish history. It bears the legend, '*MacGregor Despite Them!*'

Much of what is known about Rob Roy today comes from legends, folklore, and romanticised accounts. The most famous of these is *'Rob Roy'* written in 1817, a novel by Sir Walter Scott. Scott's portrayal of Rob Roy as a noble outlaw helped solidify his image in popular culture. Scott's novel inspired further retellings of Rob Roy's life, including plays, songs, and later, films. The 1995 movie *'Rob Roy',* starring Liam Neeson, brought his story to a global audience although it took significant liberties with historical accuracy.

Even today, his name is associated with Scotland's national identity. The Rob Roy Way, a long-distance walking route through the Scottish Highlands, traces parts of his journey. His legacy also lives on in Scottish tourism, literature, and folklore, ensuring that the legend of Rob Roy will endure for generations to come.

WHO DARES WINS!

Lieutenant-Colonel Sir Archibald (David) Stirling, DSO, OBE. Army Officer and Seditionist. (1915 - 1990)

National Army Museum records that Stirling was born and raised in Keir House, Perthshire, into an aristocratic Scottish family with a proud military heritage. He was the son of Brigadier-General Archibald Stirling of Keir, and Margaret Fraser, daughter of Simon Fraser, the Lord Lovat.

Stirling was educated in England at a Yorkshire Catholic boarding school and joined Ampleforth Officer Training Corps. He briefly attended Trinity College in Cambridge before being expelled for twenty-eight transgressions. The Master of Trinity asked him to select the three which would give least upset to his mother. He then went to Paris unsuccessfully to become an artist. Standing at a strapping 6ft 6 inches, his nature then steered him into becoming a mountaineer and a reservist in the Scots Guards before declaiming that he was determined to become the first man to scale Mount Everest. However, when World War Two broke out in 1939, Stirling was in America working as a cowboy during an interlude to his mountaineering training. He promptly returned to Britain and re-joined the Scots Guards. A year later he volunteered for the newly-formed elite No 8 Commando unit serving in the Mediterranean but his unit was disbanded on 1 August 1941, leaving a frustrated Stirling convinced that there was an unrealised opportunity for a small, highly motivated and mobile force to cause considerable damage to the enemy.

Following an accident during parachute training in which he broke an ankle, he went on crutches to the Middle East headquarters in Cairo determined to see the Commander-in-Chief, General Claude Auchinleck. He ended up in the office of the British Deputy Commander in the Middle East, General Ritchie, who listened to Stirling's ideas, then conveyed them to Auchinleck. The result was the formation by Stirling of a unit with the deliberately confusingly named, 'L Detachment,

Special Air Service Brigade' to help bolster a deception under way that the British had a parachute brigade based in North Africa. Their first mission involved parachuting behind enemy lines in support of a more general attack in November 1941 and was a complete failure, with only twenty-two out of sixty-two troops reaching the rendezvous. Stirling, now promoted to Major, decided on a change of tactics and in subsequent operations, SAS troops were carried to an insertion point some distance from their target by the Long Range Desert Group, a motorised reconnaissance unit. They then attacked under cover of night on foot before being picked up once more by the LRDG, which the SAS nicknamed the Libyan Desert Taxi Service. Using this approach, Stirling organised attacks on the German airfields at Aqedabia, Sirte and Agheila, during which the SAS destroyed sixty-one enemy aircraft without a single casualty. At this point, the SAS had become so feared that German Field Marshal Rommel nicknamed David Stirling the 'Phantom Major'. Stirling recruited Irish and British and Irish Lions rugby internationalist Robert Blair Mayne, always known as Paddy and it was he who joined with Stirling in pioneering their tactics for raiding enemy airfields which basically involved driving up and down the lines of enemy aircraft and destroying them with machine-gun fire, hand grenades and special 'sticky' bombs. Field Marshal Bernard Montgomery was quoted as saying: "The boy Stirling is quite mad; quite, quite mad. However, in a war there is often a place for mad people." The high command approved of what he was doing – they formally approved the 1st SAS Regiment in September 1942 and Stirling was a promoted to Lieutenent-Colonel in charge. In the space of fifteen months, the German *Luftwaffe* and the Italian *Regia Aeronautica* suffered the loss of more than two hundred and fifty aircraft and dozens of supply dumps. In January 1943, Stirling was captured and though he managed to escape he was recaptured four times and was eventually sent to the maximum security prison at Colditz where he spent the rest of the war. Stirling retired with the rank of colonel and, after the war, took on an enterprise called the Capricorn Society which aimed to bring greater unity to Africa. Following that, Stirling organised deals to provide British weapons and military personnel to other countries such as Saudi Arabia for various privatised foreign policy operations. In 1975, he became increasingly worried about a political movement to the left in the UK and controversially decided to organise a private army to overthrow the Labour Government of Harold Wilson, created an organisation called Great Britain 75, recruited members from the aristocratic clubs in Mayfair and proposed that in the event of civil unrest resulting in the breakdown of normal Government operations, they would take over the running of the UK. He also created a secret organisation designed to undermine Trades Unions from within. None of these schemes made any headway. Despite his chequered post-war record he was knighted in 1990, the year he died at the age of seventy-four.

SELECTED QUOTES

David Livingston

"If you have men who will only come if they know there is a good road, I don't want them. I want men who will come if there is no road at all."

"Death alone will put a stop to my effort."

"And if my disclosures regarding the terrible Ujijian slavery should lead to the suppression of the East Coast slave trade, I shall regard that as a greater matter by far than the discovery of all the Nile sources together."

Sir James Young Simpson

"This is far better and stronger than ether!" (Said, having awoken from the floor after having first testing chloroform on himself.)

"I feel that the greater the good I can accomplish for my profession and for humanity, the greater will always be the temporary blame attempted to be heaped on me by the bigoted portion of the profession".

Dougal Haston

"It had been a night right for bitter dreams, but it is better to have bad dreams than good on a bivouac: waking up to harsh reality is less disappointing."

"Mountains are also a place to find the limits of your own mental and physical endurance."

Lord Erskine of Marr

"How long the Englishman is to dictate to the Scotsman is for the Scotsman to decide. How long the Englishman is to be permitted to trample upon the natural rights of Scotland remains not so much with Mr

Gladstone and his Scottish constituents as with the bulk of the people. In *their* hands rests the destiny of the country."

Rob Roy (attrib)

"Women are the heart of honour and we cherish and protect it in them. You must never mistreat a woman, or malign a man, nor stand by and see another do so."

"All men with honour are kings. But not all kings have honour."

David Stirling

"I was a bit unlucky because my parachute when it opened was attached to the tail plane. I descended a good deal faster than my companion."

"Who dares, wins!"

THE SCOTTISH SAMURAI

Thomas Blake Glover. Businessman and Industrialist (1838 - 1911)

Thomas Blake Glover was born on June 6, 1838, in Fraserburgh, in Aberdeenshire. His father, Thomas Berry Glover, worked as a coastguard officer. Educated locally, Glover showed an early aptitude for business and in 1859, he joined the British trading company Jardine, Matheson & Co. This opportunity led him to Japan during a time when the country was beginning to open up to foreign trade after more than two centuries of isolation under the Tokugawa shogunate. Arriving in Nagasaki in 1859, Glover established his own business, Glover Trading Company. His timing was opportune, as Japan's political landscape was shifting, with internal conflicts and pressure to modernise rapidly. Glover quickly recognised the potential for trade between Japan and the West, focusing on importing modern technology and exporting Japanese products such as tea and silk.

One of Glover's most significant contributions was his involvement in Japan's military modernisation. During the late Edo period, Japan faced growing threats from Western powers, which spurred the demand for modern weaponry. Glover supplied arms and warships to various Japanese domains, including the Chasha and Satsuma clans, both of which played pivotal roles in overthrowing the Tokugawa shogunate and establishing the Meiji government in 1868. By supporting these progressive factions, Glover indirectly contributed to Japan's transition from a feudal society to a modern nation-state.

Beyond military supplies, Glover introduced advanced technology that transformed Japan's industrial landscape. He was instrumental in developing the country's shipbuilding industry, establishing Japan's first modern dockyard in Nagasaki, which laid the foundation for Mitsubishi Heavy Industries. Additionally, Glover played a key role in the mining sector, particularly in coal mining, helping to meet Japan's growing energy needs as industrialisation accelerated.

Glover also facilitated the introduction of Western engineering and education in Japan. He supported Japanese students who traveled to Europe to study modern sciences, fostering a new generation of leaders who would drive Japan's modernisation. This cultural exchange strengthened Japan's technological capabilities and enhanced its position in the global economy.

Glover was a key figure in the industrialisation of Japan, helping to found the shipbuilding company which was later to become the Mitsubishi Corporation of Japan. Glover also helped establish the Japan Brewery Company, which later became the major Kirin Brewing Company. An urban myth has it that the moustache of the mythical creature featured on Kirin beer labels is in fact a tribute to Glover (who sported a similar moustache). In recognition of these achievements, he was awarded the Order of the Rising Sun.

Despite his successes, Glover's entrepreneurial journey was not without challenges. His ventures in shipbuilding and coal mining faced financial difficulties and by the late 1870s, Glover experienced significant financial losses. However, his partnership with the Mitsubishi conglomerate, founded by Iwasaki Yatara, helped stabilise his business interests. Mitsubishi's growth into one of Japan's largest industrial groups owed much to the foundations laid by Glover's early initiatives. His association with the rebellious samurai clans of Satsuma and Chòshù and his interest in samurai generally seems to have contributed to his being referred to as the "Scottish Samurai" in Scotland.

In addition to his business achievements, Glover's personal life and cultural impact further illustrate his unique position in Japanese society. He married Tsuru, a Japanese woman, and their mixed-heritage children symbolised the growing connections between Japan and the West. Glover's home in Nagasaki, known as Glover Garden, became a symbol of cultural exchange, blending Western architectural styles with Japanese aesthetics. Today, Glover Garden is a popular tourist attraction and a designated UNESCO World Heritage Site, preserving the legacy of this pioneering entrepreneur.

Thomas Blake Glover's legacy extends beyond his business ventures. As a cultural bridge between East and West, he helped foster mutual understanding and respect, paving the way for future diplomatic and economic partnerships. His contributions to Japan's modernisation during a critical period of its history underscore the importance of cross-cultural collaboration in driving progress. Both Scotland and Japan honour his memory, reflecting the enduring impact of his work in building a more interconnected world.Today, Glover is remembered as a symbol of entrepreneurship, innovation, and international cooperation.

A CONTROVERSIAL FORCE IN BRITISH POLITICS

George Galloway. Politician. (1954 -)

George Galloway was born in 1954, in Dundee. Raised in a working-class, socialist household, he was politically active from a young age. His father was a strong Labour supporter and Galloway joined the Labour Party at just thirteen years old. He quickly became involved in activism, particularly in opposition to the Vietnam War and apartheid in South Africa.

In the late 1970s, Galloway rose through the ranks of the Labour Party, gaining a reputation as a fiery speaker and a committed leftist. He became the youngest ever chairman of the Scottish Labour Party in 1981, marking the beginning of his national prominence. He was elected as the Labour MP for Glasgow Hillhead in 1987, later representing Glasgow Kelvin until 2005. From the start, he positioned himself as a left-wing voice within the party, opposing many of the centrist policies introduced under Prime Minister Tony Blair.

One of the defining aspects of Galloway's career has been his staunch opposition to Western intervention in the Middle East. He was a vocal critic of the Gulf War in 1991 and later became one of the most prominent figures opposing the Iraq War in 2003. His opposition to the war and his inflammatory rhetoric against Blair and US President George W. Bush put him at odds with the Labour leadership. In 2003, Galloway was expelled from the Labour Party for bringing the party into disrepute after he called on British soldiers to disobey orders in Iraq. However, his expulsion did not end his political career; instead, it allowed him to establish himself as a more radical, independent force.

Following his expulsion, Galloway co-founded the Respect Party, a left-wing, anti-war movement that attracted disillusioned Labour voters, Muslim communities, and socialist activists. His biggest political triumph came in the 2005 general election when he stood as a Respect candidate in Bethnal Green and Bow, an East London constituency with a large Muslim population. In a stunning upset, he defeated Labour incumbent Oona King, running on an anti-war, pro-Palestine platform.

During his victory speech, Galloway famously declared that the Iraq War had played a decisive role in his win, telling Prime Minister Blair, "All the people you have killed, all the lies you have told, have come back to haunt you".

Never one to shy away from publicity, Galloway gained international attention in 2005 when he testified before the US Senate over allegations that he had received illicit funds from the Iraqi government under Saddam Hussein. In a dramatic performance, he turned the tables on his accusers, denouncing US foreign policy and questioning the credibility of the investigation. His combative testimony made him a hero to anti-war activists while also further solidifying his reputation as a divisive figure. Galloway has also been a frequent presence in the media, hosting shows on Iranian state broadcaster Press TV and later on Russian-owned RT. His willingness to work with controversial media outlets has drawn criticism with opponents accusing him of aligning with authoritarian regimes. In January 2006, Galloway appeared on the TV programme *Celebrity Big Brother* and mimed licking imaginary milk from actress Rula Lenska's cupped hands whilst pretending to be a cat.

Galloway's political career has been marked by dramatic comebacks. In 2012, he pulled off another shock victory when he won the Bradford West by-election as a Respect candidate. However, in the 2015 general election, he was heavily defeated by Labour's Naz Shah, losing by a wide margin. After Respect dissolved in 2016, Galloway attempted several political comebacks. He ran unsuccessfully in various elections, including the 2016 London mayoral race and the 2019 West Bromwich East by-election. He remained a vocal critic of mainstream British politics, particularly of Labour under Keir Starmer. In 2021, Galloway launched the Workers' Party of Britain, a left-wing nationalist movement that opposes NATO, supports Brexit, and appeals to traditional working-class voters. He contested the Batley and Spen by-election that year, finishing third but drawing significant attention with his aggressive campaign against Labour. George Galloway's career spans decades of activism, controversy and dramatic electoral comebacks, making him one of the most distinctive politicians in the UK.

George Galloway is one of the most outspoken and polarising figures in British politics. A former Labour MP who later led his own political movements, he has been a relentless critic of Western foreign policy, a vocal supporter of various left-wing and anti-imperialist causes, and a master of political theatre. His career spans decades of activism, controversy, and dramatic electoral comebacks, making him one of the most distinctive politicians in the UK.

A CLAIM OF RIGHT FOR SCOTLAND

Canon Peter Derek Graystone (Kenyan) Wright. Cleric and Activist (1932 - 2017)

Kenyan Wright was born in Paisley in 1932, the son of a textile technician and attended Paisley Grammar School before going on to the University of Glasgow where he graduated with an MA (Hons.) degree in mathematics and philosophy. He then studied for a further degree at Fitzwilliam College in Cambridge where he was awarded a lower-second class degree in 1955.

Wright's early life and career offered foundational experiences that later shaped his role in Scotland. Originally studying theology, Wright was not confined to the ivory tower; his fervent belief in connecting faith with social action led him to involve himself in issues of public concern. Early in his career, he was driven by the principles of social justice, and this drove him into areas where religion intersected with everyday life, including the political sphere. His nickname '*Kenyan*'"came as a result of his early clerical work in Kenya and South Africa. During his time in these regions, Wright became acutely aware of the struggles against colonial rule and racial injustice. This *sobriquet* followed him throughout his life, emblematic of his commitment to fighting inequality and sowing the seeds of democratic governance.

Wright's prominence in Scotland began to crystallise in the late 20th century. Scotland, during this period, was experiencing growing dissatisfactions with its governmental structure, adding fuel to the desires for a devolution – a movement aiming for greater self-governance. In this environment, Wright's leadership became pivotal. His expertise and gravitas were further solidified when he became the chairman of the Scottish Constitutional Convention from its inception in 1989 until 1999.

The Scottish Constitutional Convention was a critical player in reviving and redefining Scotland's political landscape. Under Kenya Wright's chairmanship, the convention sought to delineate what a devolved Scottish Parliament would look like. The convention was noteworthy for its inclusivity, bringing in voices from politicians, civic figures, trade unionists, and representatives from various societal strata to create a blueprint that could genuinely reflect Scotland's aspirations.

One of Wright's enduring legacies from his time with the Convention was the 'Claim of Right for Scotland' document. This visionary declaration insisted on the sovereign right of the Scottish people to determine the form of government best suited to their needs—an echo of the democratic ideals resonant throughout Wright's life. It laid a philosophical and political foundation crucial for the subsequent enactment of the Scotland Act 1998, which established the devolved Scottish Parliament.

Wright wasn't merely satisfied with democratic processes being theorised; he was a staunch advocate for democratic engagement being accessible and functional for all. He communicated the ideals of the constitutional convention with eloquence and humility, always emphasising broad public participation and transparency. He believed that political progress was not only about politicians in parliament but about people on the ground engaging with these processes.

During this period, Wright's rhetorical skills, rooted in his background as a Canon, didn't just codify the language of devolution - they enlivened it. Many credits his ability to bridge divides, perhaps polished through years of ecclesiastical discourse and social engagement outside politics, with enabling differing groups to work towards a common goal.

In recognition of his contributions, Kenyan Wright received several accolades and honours throughout his career. In 1999, he was appointed as a Commander of the Order of the British Empire, a testament to his significant contribution to public life and the unity of political processes. Despite his many achievements, Wright remained humble and accessible. He continued, post-retirement, to pursue consultation roles and engage with initiatives fostering democratic dialogue. His patience and zeal for empowering communities within the political framework set a benchmark that remains influential in political discussions today in Scotland and beyond.

Wright retired from working as a priest in 2008 and went to live in the English Midlands. He died at his home in Stratford-upon-Avon on 11 January 2017 at the age of eighty-four.

AN ACADEMIC THORN IN THE FLESH!

Professor John Robertson PhD. OBA. Academic and Activist (1951 -)

John Robertson was born in Duns in Berwickshire to Margaret Sneddon, a textile worker and Hugh Robertson a plasterer.

When John was but a child, the family moved to Falkirk to stay with relatives due to the absence of work in Berwickshire. Young John attended the village primary school in Carronshore before going on to the local secondary school in Grangemouth where he left with Higher Art and History along with a school assessment that, 'This boy is bright - but not university material'.

Influenced by the general and societal ambience of young people in the sixties, Robertson was inclined towards the unconventional and more bohemian lifestyle of the times and was accepted by the Glasgow School of Art where, following his adopted more casual attitude of that period, he left after four months. He found employment as a trainee architect but his predisposition of a listless indifference towards his profession saw him dismissed four years into a seven year qualification. Finding engagement in the ICI Dye-works in Grangemouth and experiencing a requirement that all staff required to eliminate any harmful chemicals by finishing all shifts with a sauna, Robertson began reading voraciously as he sweated; his writer of choice being French philosopher, Jean Paul Sartre who opened his eyes to more societal concerns. Inspired, following an access course, he enrolled at the University of Stirling where he studied sociology and social policy, thereafter attending Callendar Park College where he graduated as a teacher. Following a period of teaching, he was appointed as a lecturer in Craigie College in Ayr teaching education and computing. When Craigie and Paisley Colleges merged with the West of Scotland University, Robertson found himself lecturing on media theory and used his research, aged sixty-one to obtain a Doctorate on Noam Chomsky's '*Propaganda'Model'*. Promoted to full professorship aged sixty-three, his teaching encompassed learning theories, technology-based education, and the critical analysis of socio-economic change. He led a module titled Global Cultural Industries, aiming to introduce students to the complexities of globalisation and its impact on social, cultural and economic transformations and also supervised PhD and honours dissertation students on diverse topics, ranging from media representations of disability to the effects of televised wrestling, his scholarly work being published in various peer-reviewed journals. His findings not only informed university-wide developments but also garnered attention in news media. In 2014, Robertson published a research report revealing clear media bias against the 'Yes' campaign in the lead-up to the 2014 Scottish Independence Referendum. This report gained significant attention and went viral shortly after its release. The findings were discussed on many varied platforms highlighting the challenges and criticisms Robertson faced from media outlets like BBC Scotland which complained bitterly that its hard won reputation (sic) for fairness had been tarnished and demanded his dismissal. They took their case to the University Vice Chancellor but after reviewing the evidence, Robertson was cleared and continued unsullied in his role, his assertions subsequently gaining considerable credibility. He was invited to give evidence on media bias to the Scottish Parliament and publicly eviscerated the three BBC representatives present. He retired through ill-health in 2016 and lives in Ayr with his wife, Bernadette.

Following his research on media bias, Robertson launched a blog called '*Thought Control Scotland*' in December 2014, which was later renamed *'Talking-up Scotland'*. The blog was conceived as a platform to counteract negative portrayals of Scotland in mainstream media, to rebut establishment untruths and to promote positive narratives about the country. For longer than the past decade, Robertson has published more than ten thousand posts on his blog, covering a wide array of topics pertinent to Scotland's socio-political landscape.

John Robertson is a distinguished academic and his commitment to challenging media narratives and advocating for Scottish self-respect remains unwavering. In June 2022, he was honoured with the Oliver Brown Award for advancing the cause of Scotland's self-respect, an accolade previously awarded to notable figures such as Alasdair Gray, Alex Salmond and Sean Connery. This recognition underscored his significant contributions to fostering a positive Scottish identity. Professor

John Robertson has played a pivotal role in shaping discussions around media representation and national identity in Scotland. His efforts have provided a counter-narrative to mainstream media portrayals, has encouraged critical engagement and has fostered a sense of pride among Scots.

MADAME ÉCOSSE

Winifred Margaret Ewing. Politician (1929 - 2023)

Winnie Ewing was born in Glasgow in 1929 to Christina Bell Anderson and George Woodburn, a small business owner. She was educated at Battlefield School and Queen's Park Secondary School. In 1946 she matriculated at Glasgow University where she graduated with an MA and an LLB in law. Although relatively inactive in politics at that time, she joined the Student Nationalists. Following her graduation, she qualified and practised as a solicitor - a rare achievement for women at the time - and was Secretary of the Glasgow Bar Association from 1962 to 1967

Although not initially involved in politics, Ewing became active in the SNP in the 1960s, attracted by the party's goal of Scottish independence and its potential to change Scotland's future.

Her political breakthrough came in 1967 when she won the Hamilton by-election. Standing as the SNP candidate, Ewing shocked the political establishment by defeating the Labour Party in what had been considered a safe seat. Her victory speech, in which she declared, "Stop the world, Scotland wants to get on!" became instantly iconic and signalled a new era in Scottish politics. The result electrified the independence movement and established the SNP as a serious political force. It was a turning point that challenged the dominance of the traditional Westminster parties in Scotland.

Although she lost her seat in the 1970 general election, Ewing remained a prominent figure in the SNP and continued to champion Scottish causes. In 1974, she returned to Westminster as the MP for Moray and Nairn, serving until 1979. During this time, she focused on issues such as fishing rights, oil revenues, and regional development—areas particularly important to her Highland constituency and to Scotland's economic self-sufficiency.

Her commitment to internationalism and Scotland's place in the wider world was demonstrated when she was elected as a Member of the European Parliament (MEP) in 1979. Ewing served in the European

Parliament for two decades, until 1999, representing the Highlands and Islands. She gained respect from her European colleagues and became a well-known advocate for regional voices within the EU. She argued passionately that Scotland had a distinct culture, economy, and political identity deserving of direct representation on the European stage. It was during her time as an MEP that she acquired the nickname *Madame Écosse* (French for 'Mrs Scotland') because of her advocacy of Scottish interests in Strasbourg and Brussels.

One of her major contributions as an MEP was building connections between Scotland and other European regions seeking greater autonomy. She believed strongly in the European principle of subsidiarity—that decisions should be made as close to the people as possible - and saw the EU as a potential ally in Scotland's pursuit of self-government. Her European experience also helped normalise the idea of Scottish representation beyond the UK, subtly reinforcing the SNP's argument for independence.

Ewing returned to domestic politics in 1999 when she was elected to the newly established Scottish Parliament as a list MSP for the Highlands and Islands. As the oldest member, she had the honour of presiding over the opening session. Her declaration, "The Scottish Parliament, adjourned on the 25th day of March in the year 1707, is hereby reconvened," was a powerful moment of historical continuity and emotional significance for many Scots. It marked a symbolic link between past and present and reinforced the legitimacy of the devolved Scottish Parliament.

Though she retired from frontline politics shortly afterward, Ewing remained a revered elder stateswoman within the SNP and continued to be a vocal supporter of independence. Her legacy was further cemented by the fact that her children, particularly Fergus Ewing and Annabelle Ewing, also pursued careers in politics, continuing the family tradition of service and advocacy.

Winnie Ewing passed away on June 21, 2023, at the age of 93. Her death was met with widespread tributes across the political spectrum, acknowledging her role as a transformative figure in Scottish political life. She was a woman of firsts - first SNP woman elected to Westminster, one of the first SNP MEPs and a foundational figure in the return of Scotland's own Parliament. Her career embodied resilience, passion, and unwavering belief in the right of Scotland to shape its own destiny.

THE DIVIDED SELF

Ronald David (R.D.) Laing MB, Ch.B., DPM. Psychiatrist. (1927 - 1989)

In 1927, Ronald Laing (usually referred to in later life as R.D.Laing) was born in Glasgow's Govanhill, the only child of civil engineer David Laing and his wife Amelia.

He was educated initially at Sir John Neilson Cuthbertson Public School just off Pollokshaws Road before being transferred to nearby Hutchesons' Grammar School where he was described as clever, competitive and precocious.

Laing studied philosophy at school and was also a musician, being made an Associate of the Royal College of Music before studying medicine at Glasgow University where he set up a 'Socratic Club', of which the philosopher Bertrand Russell agreed to be president. He failed his final exams but after spending six months working in a psychiatric unit, Laing passed the re-sits in 1951 to qualify as a medical doctor. He spent a couple of years as a Lieutenant psychiatrist in the British Army Psychiatric Unit in Southampton before returning to Glasgow in 1953 where he participated in an existentialism-oriented discussion group working at the Royal Mental Hospital in Glasgow and became the youngest consultant in the country. Laing's colleagues characterised him as unconventional for his opposition to Electro-Convulsive Therapy as well as new drugs that were being introduced to treat psychosis and schizophrenia.

In 1955, he moved to 1 Ruskin Place, Hillhead, Glasgow with the financial assistance of Anne's parents and took employment as Senior Registrar at the Southern General Hospital in Glasgow where the Department of Psychological Medicine of Glasgow University was situated. Only a year later he moved to Harlow New Town with wife Anne and three daughters Fiona, Susie and Karen and in 1956, started work at the Tavistock Clinic in Hampstead, London as a Senior Registrar, commuting from Harlow by bus. He began training as a psychoanalyst and undertook four years of psychoanalysis with Dr. Charles Rycroft as his analyst.

Two years later, whilst still in psychoanalysis, he completed the first draft of *'The Divided Self'* and, in 1960, was enrolled as a qualified psychoanalyst from the Institute of Psychoanalysis, London. In the same year, *'The Divided Self ; A Study of Sanity and Madness' was* published in hardback by Tavistock Publications, and was dedicated to Laing's mother and father whereupon he opened a private practice as a psychoanalyst at 21 Wimpole Street in London. His book became a phenomenon, selling 700,000 copies in the UK alone. Laing never denied the existence of mental illness, but viewed it in a radically different light from his contemporaries. During the seventies and eighties, Laing wrote several popular but controversial books, had several plays and films made about him and his work, and had affairs in which he fathered six sons and four daughters by four women. He travelled to India and America. Laing began to develop a team offering 'rebirthing workshops' in which one designated person was invited to re-experience the struggle of trying to break out of his mother's birth canal which was represented by the remaining members of the group who surrounded him or her. Many former colleagues regarded him as a brilliant mind gone wrong but there were some who thought Laing was somewhat psychotic.

He was possibly the world's most celebrated psychiatrist of the 1960s counterculture but his reputation slumped in his later years and there is still disagreement about whether he was a dangerous renegade or a visionary. At his peak he was revered as the high priest of anti-psychiatry, famous for his bestselling books and celebrity friends. The therapeutic community Laing set up for people with schizophrenia, which had no locks or strong medicaments, attracted visitors from around the world as well as celebrities, poets, and rock stars. His programme eventually disintegrated into chaos and did much to destroy Laing's reputation but many believe it inspired later, less mercurial, psychiatrists to treat patients outside the mental institution. Laing struggled with drink and drugs, experimenting with LSD in his later years after being influenced by the work of the psychedelic drug pioneer, Timothy Leary. As a psychiatrist, both brilliant and unconventional, RD Laing pioneered the humane treatment of the mentally ill. But as a father, clinically depressed and alcoholic, he bequeathed his ten children with four women over a period of thirty-six years a more divergent legacy. Laing died of a heart attack while playing tennis at the age of sixty-one.

A SCOTTISH SOCIALIST AND REPUBLICAN *INDEPENDENTISTA*

William (Oliver) Brown. Academic and Activist (1903 - 1976)

Oliver Brown was born in Paisley in 1903. He progressed through childhood education and studied Latin and French at Glasgow University before teaching French at secondary schools. He spent the majority of his teaching career at Pollokshields Secondary School in Melville Street. Built for Govan School Board, the school closed in 1962 with the removal of secondary pupils to Bellahouston Academy. His other teaching position was in Whitehill Secondary School in Glasgow's Dennistoun whose many luminaries include actors Rikki Fulton, Ford Kiernan, Dorothy Paul and Bill Paterson, journalist Jack House and singer Lulu. Teaching French and Latin, he also worked both as a courier for the British Council and was a broadcaster for the BBC. He was married to the painter and illustrator Margaret Oliver Brown with whom he had a daughter, Una Ozga.

His academic abilities were highly regarded and he contributed to both the English and French language editions of *La Grand Larousse Encyclopédique en dix volumes* which is a French Encyclopaedia.

Brown stood for the National Party, of which he was a founding member, at the 1930 East Renfrewshire by-election becoming the first National Party candidate to hold his deposit and, in 1934, when the National Party merged with the Scottish Party into the new Scottish National Party, he spoke at its first public meeting, along with Sir Compton Mackenzie.

Never one to be corralled within any one party, just prior to World War Two, Brown resigned and joined the Labour Party where he served in support of its Labour Council for Scottish Self-Government. He was a pacifist during the war and made many speeches attempting younger men to become conscientious objectors. Shortly thereafter, he launched the *Scots Socialist* journal, with others including Hugh MacDairmid, and acted as its editor until it ceased publication in 1949.

In 1943, he affiliated the Scottish Socialist Party with the SNP, but this lasted only a short while and it separated, remaining small and peripheral. That said, he routinely stood on his soapbox making speeches on the corner of Sauchiehall Street and Wellington Street in Glasgow, generally with only a small group of supporters.

In the 1950 general election, Brown stood in Greenock as an Irish Anti-Partitionist and Scottish Nationalist and was heavily backed by the Irish Anti-Partition League whose local branch had almost one thousand members. Brown was an unusual candidate for the party, given that he was neither Irish nor Roman Catholic and he refused to support the organisation's policy of establishing more Catholic schools in England. In consequence, he took last place in the poll, with just over seven hundred votes. Following the result, he claimed, "I appealed to the intelligent section of the electorate and the result shows that I have received their unanimous support".

In 1954, Brown claimed £3,000 in damages from the Scottish Daily Mail which claimed that he was linked to an unsuccessful effort to blow up one of the new red postboxes marked 'EIIR', in objection to the new Queen Elizabeth not being the second Elizabeth to rule in Scotland. He lost the case but no police action was forthcoming.

In 1967, he was one of the founders of the 1320 Club, a Scottish nationalist campaign group named after the date of the Declaration of Arbroath, a document proclaiming Scotland's independence from England. Membership of the organisation, other than between its leading figures, was kept secret and was by invitation only. This prompted sharp criticism from Hamish Henderson who rejected his invitation to join. The Club argued that Scotland should have the right to arm itself in defence against England, and this advocacy of armed action led the SNP to expel its members in 1968.

He wrote regularly for the *'Scots Independent'* newspaper which, following his death aged seventy-three in 1979, decided in 1983 to dedicate an award; the '*Oliver Brown Award'* to a journalist, author, critic, illustrator, radio or television performer who, in the opinion of the judges, did most in the preceding year to advance the cause of Scotland's self respect. The presentation of the award takes place every year at the Annual Scots Independent Lunch which is held in the Salutation Hotel, Perth.

THE WORLD'S FIRST SCIENTIST.

Mary Fairfax Somerville. Scientist and Polymath. (1780 - 1872)

Mary Somerville, was born in Jedburgh the daughter of Vice-Admiral Sir William Fairfax and Margaret Charters and raised in Burntisland, Fife where her mother was from. Her father's naval pay remained meagre, despite his elevated status and upon his return home when Mary was still young, he instructed that Mary must at least know how to write and keep accounts whereupon she was sent to a boarding school in Musselburgh where she learned the basics of writing, French and grammar. She also began to educate herself from the family library, encouraged only by her uncle, Thomas Somerville, who helped her with Latin. She read books on mathematics and algebra but her immediate family saw little point in her studies, thinking they would do more harm than good.

She married her cousin, Captain Samuel Greig of the Russian Navy aged twenty-four and they had two sons. Tragically her husband died after only three years of marriage. Widowed but now with a comfortable inheritance, she was no longer controlled by her parents or husband and was free to study as she wished. Five years later, she remarried another cousin, Dr. William Somerville, a British surgeon who was supportive of Mary's studies, thereby permitting her experimentation with magnetism. The following year her technical paper, *'The magnetic properties of the violet rays of the solar spectrum'* was the first paper written by a women to be published by the Royal Society. She translated and added to five exhaustive volumes of *'Mécanique Céleste'* and wrote an exposition of the mathematics behind the workings of the Solar System which was published in 1831, under the title of '*The Mechanism of the Heavens*' immediately making her famous.

Subsequently, she was elected honorary member of the Royal Irish Academy and the S*ociété de Physique et d'Histoire Naturelle de Genéve* in 1834. The British Crown granted her a civil pension of £200 a year in recognition of her eminence in science and literature.

Somerville's next book, *The Connection of the Physical Sciences* (1834), was even more ambitious in summarising astronomy, physics, geography and meteorology before writing nine subsequent editions over the rest of her life to update it. In the third edition, published in 1836, she wrote accurately that difficulties in calculating the position of Uranus may point to the existence of an undiscovered planet, leading to the discovery of Neptune. She was elected in 1835 to the Royal Astronomical Society, the first woman to receive such an honour.

Somerville had such an impact within her fields that in 1834, philosopher William Whewell coined the term 'Scientist' as a gender-neutral term for Somerville, making her the UK's and the world's first scientist.

In 1848, at the age of sixty eight, Mary Fairfax Somerville published yet another book, *'Physical Geography'* which proved to be her most successful yet and which was widely used in schools and universities for the next fifty years

From1833 onwards, the Somerville family spent much of their time in Italy, where Somerville continued to write and engage in current scientific debates. In 1868, four years before her death aged 91, she was the first person invited to sign John Stuart Mill's unsuccessful petition for female suffrage.

Following the demise of her second husband, her only remaining son, and her valued friend Sir John Herschel, she lived to complete two more works before her own death in Naples in 1872. Her last scientific book, *Molecular and Microscopic Science*, which was published in 1869 when Mary was eighty-nine, was a summary of the most recent discoveries in chemistry and physics. In that same year she completed her autobiography. A mathematician to the last, she spent the day before her death revising a paper on quaternions.

Two months after the publication of Somerville's critically acclaimed book '*Mechanism of the Heavens*', fellows of the Royal Society of London paid for a marble bust of Somerville by renowned sculptor, Francis Chantrey, to sit in their meeting room. Today, a copy of the Chantrey bust can be found in the Mary Somerville Room in Somerville College, Oxford University.

SELECTED QUOTES

George Galloway

“I have never solicited nor received money from Iraq for our campaign against war and sanctions. I have never seen a barrel of oil, never owned one, never bought one, never sold one.”

“Bush, and Blair and the prime minister of Japan and Berlusconi, these people are criminals, and they are responsible for mass murder in the world, for the war, and for the occupation, through their support for Israel, and through their support for a globalised capitalist economic system, which is the biggest killer the world has ever known.”

“If you are asking did I support the Soviet Union, yes I did. Yes, I did support the Soviet Union and I think the disappearance of the Soviet Union is the biggest catastrophe of my life.”

“Christianity doesn’t come into it. George Bush and Tony Blair are not Christians. Religious people believe in the prophets, peace be upon them. Bush believes in the profits and how to get a piece of them. So don’t ever confuse this with a war of civilisations.”

Oliver Brown

“I appealed to the intelligent section of the electorate and the result shows that I have received their unanimous support”. (Following his defeat in the 1950 General Election in Greenock, winning only 718 votes).

“The 1967 Hamilton by-election (won by the SNP) caused a shiver to run along the Scottish Labour benches looking for a spine to run up”.

Mary Somerville

“Who shall declare the time allotted to the human race, when the generations of the most insignificant insect also existed for unnumbered ages? Yet man is also to vanish in the ever-changing course of events. The earth is to be burnt up and the elements are to melt with fervent heat - to be again reduced to chaos - possibly to be renovated and adorned for other races of beings. These stupendous changes may be but cycles in those great laws of the universe, where all is variable but the laws themselves."

R D Laing

"Life is a sexually transmitted disease and the mortality rate is one hundred percent."

"Creative people who can't help but explore other mental territories are at greater risk, just as someone who climbs a mountain is more at risk than someone who just walks along a village lane."

Professor John Robertson

"So, on the objective evidence presented here, the mainstream TV coverage of the first year of the independence referendum campaigns has not been fair or balanced. Taken together, we have evidence of coverage which seems likely to have damaged the 'Yes' campaign."

"The BBC wrote to my principal and suggested that I'd brought the BBC into 'corporate disrepute'…no mention of 'moral disrepute'. Luckily, my principal was a supporter of academic freedom and backed me up."

"Commentators and voters are less likely to believe a politician with a reputation for lying, especially where there is a high incentive to deceive… except in Scotland it would seem!"

THE UNDIPLOMATIC DIPLOMAT

Craig John Murray. Diplomat, Author, Human Rights Campaigner and Journalist (1958 -)

Craig Murray was born in West Runton in Norfolk and was raised by his Scottish father, Robert and mother, Poppy in the nearby sea-side town of Sheringham. His education commenced at Sheringham Primary School thence to Sir William Paston's all-boys' grammar school located in the town of North Walsham.

He studied Modern History at the University of Dundee but decided not to attend any lectures, opting instead to use the facilities of the university to teach himself. He graduated in 1982 with a first class MA degree having spent seven rather than four years there as a consequence of two periods of electoral office of President of the Dundee University Students' Association.

In his second year as the Students' Association President, he sat the Civil Service Open Competition exams and, with an IQ hovering around 200, was placed at the top of his year. In consequence, he was offered a role in HM Diplomatic Service and served in a number of overseas postings with the Foreign and Commonwealth Office in Nigeria, Poland (in the 1990s, where he was first secretary heading the embassy's political and economic section) and Ghana. In London, he was appointed to the FCO's Southern European Department, as Cyprus desk officer, and later became head of the Maritime Section. In 1991 he worked in the Embargo Surveillance Centre monitoring the Iraqi government's attempts at smuggling weapons and circumventing sanctions. Aged only 43, he was appointed Ambassador to Uzbekistan, where he was formally in office from August 2002 to October 2004. However, in his role as ambassador and exhibiting the forthrightness for which he became notorious, he spoke at a Human Rights conference hosted by Tashkent, the capital and largest city of Uzbekistan, he said, "Uzbekistan is not a functioning democracy, nor does it appear to be moving in the direction of democracy. The major political parties are banned; Parliament is not subject to democratic election and checks and balances on the authority of the electorate are lacking. There is worse: we believe there to be between 7,000 and 10,000 people in detention whom we would consider as political and/or religious prisoners." Murray was advised by Whitehall not to antagonise the government in Tashkent any further and the Americans were said to have put pressure on the British government for Murray to tone down his comments. He was criticised several times by his London bosses, particularly over an internal letter he wrote them saying that MI6 were using intelligence provided by the CIA from the Uzbek authorities gained through torture and that Uzbekistan was being used as a base in the US programme of extraordinary rendition during the Afghan War and Iraq because it was tolerant of the use of torture. In 2014 he was recalled by the FCO and a week later was accused of 'gross misconduct'. After a lengthy internal inquiry, he was exonerated of all eighteen charges but was reprimanded for speaking about them publicly. In February 2005, Murray took a severance package and moved on. He was elected to the position of Rector of Dundee University and and was also executive chairman of Atholl Energy Ltd and chairman of Westminster Development Ltd, a gold mining company.

He stood unsuccessfully for election to the House of Commons three times, initially against his former boss, Jack Straw, then the MP for the constituency. In 2011 he left the Liberal Democrats and joined the SNP, supporting the Yes Campaign in 2014 before resigning from them in 2016 and later joining the Alba Party to support Alex Salmond. As an investigative reporter, he exposed four undisclosed meetings that took place from September 2009 between Britain's then defence minister Liam Fox MP and Fox's friend Adam Werritty and the UK Ambassador to Israel ostensibly to promote a deniable off-the-books foreign policy. He wrote extensively on the trial of Julian Assange and published detailed reports of each day's proceedings on his website. He was invited to Assange and Stella Moris's wedding at Bellmarch Prison but was barred from attending due to security concerns. He also attended Alex Salmond's trial in 2020 and wrote about the court proceedings alleging that the SNP leadership, the Scottish Government, the police and the Crown Office had conspired unsuccessfully to convict Salmond on charges of sexual harassment and attempted rape.The judge in the case found Murray to be in contempt of court as, in her view, his words could potentially lead to identifying some of the complainants and sentenced him to eight months' imprisonment. He served four. He has written several books, perhaps most prominently, *'Murder in Samarkand'*; a memoir about his time there as Ambassador. He won two awards for his campaigns on human rights and thrice refused an award from Queen Elizabeth for services to the nation.

THE PIONEER OF FINGERPRINT IDENTIFICATION

Henry Faulds. Doctor and Missionary (1843 - 1930)

Henry Faulds was born in Beith, North Ayrshire, into a family of modest means. Aged thirteen, he was forced to leave school and went to Glasgow to work as a clerk to help support his family, Aged twenty-one he decided to enrol at the Facility of Arts at the University of Glasgow where he studied mathematics, logic and the classics, later studying medicine and graduating with a physician's licence before deciding to work abroad as a medical missionary.

In 1873, Faulds traveled to Japan as a missionary and physician under the Church of Scotland. He settled in Tokyo, where he founded the *Tsukiji* Hospital and provided medical services to the local population. His work in Japan extended beyond medicine—he also engaged in anthropological studies and became interested in Japanese culture and archaeology.

It was in Japan that Faulds made his most significant discovery. While studying ancient pottery shards, he noticed distinct ridge patterns on human fingerprints left in the clay before firing. This observation led him to hypothesise that fingerprints could serve as a means of personal identification.

Faulds began systematically analysing fingerprints, conducting experiments that confirmed their uniqueness and permanence. He noted that even after injuries, fingerprint patterns remained unchanged once the skin healed. This realisation had profound implications, suggesting that fingerprints could be used both for personal identification and forensic investigations.

In 1880, Henry Faulds published his findings in '*Nature*', a leading scientific journal. In his article, he proposed that fingerprints could be used for crime detection and suggested a practical method for recording them using ink. He even described how fingerprints left at crime scenes could be matched to a suspect, effectively anticipating the modern use of forensic fingerprinting.

Faulds reached out to Charles Darwin, hoping the renowned scientist would promote his discovery. Darwin, however, was in poor health and forwarded Faulds' letter to his cousin, Francis Galton, a statistician and scientist. Galton later conducted extensive research on fingerprints and became more widely recognised for advancing Faulds' study.

Meanwhile, Faulds attempted to persuade Scotland Yard to adopt fingerprinting for criminal investigations, but his ideas were largely ignored at the time. Law enforcement authorities were still reliant on older methods such as anthropometry which involved measuring physical features to identify individuals.

A major controversy surrounding Faulds' legacy involves Sir William Herschel, a British civil servant stationed in India. Herschel had been using fingerprints for administrative purposes, such as preventing fraud in signing contracts, since the 1850s. However, he did not pursue a scientific study of fingerprints or recognise their forensic potential until after Faulds' work was published.

After Faulds' Nature article appeared, Herschel wrote to the journal, claiming he had been the first to use fingerprints for identification. This led to a long-standing dispute over who deserved credit for the discovery. While Herschel had indeed used fingerprints earlier, it was Faulds who recognised their uniqueness, permanence, and forensic application.

Despite his groundbreaking contributions, Henry Faulds did not receive the recognition he deserved during his lifetime. In 1886, he returned to Britain and continued working as a doctor in Staffordshire and later in London. He made further attempts to convince law enforcement agencies to adopt fingerprinting but was largely ignored.

It was not until the early 20th century that fingerprinting gained widespread acceptance. In 1901, Sir Edward Henry, the Commissioner of the Metropolitan Police, developed a systematic classification of fingerprints, which was adopted by Scotland Yard. This development marked the beginning of fingerprinting as an official method of criminal identification. Faulds, however, received little acknowledgment for his role in this scientific breakthrough. He spent his later years struggling financially and professionally, and he died in 1930 at the age of 86.

GROUSEBEATER...SCOTLAND'S MARK TWAIN

Gareth Wardell. Polymath and Polemicist (1946 -)

Born in Edinburgh in 1946 to a family of Irish Musicians on his mother's side and to a Sicilian father, he was schooled locally.

Leaving school he trained at the Royal Scottish Academy of Music and Drama (now the Royal Conservatoire of Scotland), thence to Jordanhill College of Education where he graduated as a teacher before moving into theatrical writing, teaching and lecturing.

He founded the Scottish Youth Theatre in 1976 and subsequently became its first Artistic Director before becoming active in television during the 1980s and '90s. His credits include the BAFTA-nominated, award-winning series '*Brond*' (1987) set in Glasgow and shown in the USA. It is a celebrated political thriller dealing with the Scottish Liberation Army and how the British State manipulates politics and economics against the interests of the Scottish people. Wardell followed this up with, *'Conquest of the South Pole'* two years later.

He remains active in public discourse, appearing in interviews and debates such as '*An Evening with Gareth Wardell'* hosted by pro-independence groups which reflect on both his creative journey and political engagement. In addition to his national focus, Wardell is also a most talented community development operator, transforming, with residents, an abandoned Edinburgh lane into 'Edinburgh's Most Beautiful Street.' As a 'relaxing hobby' he designs and plants large gardens.

Under the name *'Grouse Beater,'* Wardell writes incisive essays covering everything from Scottish history and politics to art, culture and personal memoir. On his WordPress site, he publishes long-form, thoughtful commentaries; articles which range from reflections on the '*Book of Deer*' and colonial museum practices to his responses on the lack of BBC impartiality. His students described him as 'The Common Man's Philosopher' and by Professor Alfred Baird as 'Scotland's foremost intellectual on Independence.' He frequently engages serious public figures through open letters.

His writings have been compiled into volumes entitled '*Essays: Grouse Beater*'. Reactions have been glowing, with reviewers calling them 'hugely entertaining' and praising their wit, conviction and originality in covering topics from grammar to the Scots language and film reviews. Readers from around the world have praised his eloquence and depth. Wardell is a passionate commentator in Scotland's constitutional debate. His writings frequently explore national identity and challenge establishment narratives. The Scottish National Party reacted strongly following a controversial article he penned about trade unions even though he wasn't a party member, a move that sparked debate and letters defending him flourished as his being unfairly targeted. Facing defamation from tabloid media and unions, he launched a public fundraiser to seek legal redress using proceeds to shed light on the grey areas of political smear campaigns.

In a poignant personal turn, Wardell revealed he had been diagnosed with incurable cancer. During this time, he was honoured by Alex Salmond with honorary ALBA membership for his service to Scotland, an act he described with wry humour as a potential 'cheque-free' symbol of reconciliation. Wardell writes with clarity, wit, and moral seriousness. He confronts political hypocrisy, cultural appropriation and media bias head-on, whether in open letters to the Director-General of the BBC or trenchant posts on Scotland's colonial legacy. His passion for art and history finds expression in essays like '*The Sorrow and the Shame*' . Undeterred by illness, his recent work reveals a reflective side as he recounts friendships, mortality and the power of thoughtful writing to change lives. By combining creative media, rigorous writing, and political engagement, Wardell has established a significant public voice. He bridges the arts and civic journalism with integrity using humour and honesty to explore Scottish identity, culture and conscience. His latest book, '*Thirty Tenets of Liberty*', is described as a guide book to social revolution which excoriates 'House Jocks, colonial watchdogs and a vindictive Westminster government' and unravels the democratic injustice where England's Westminster parliament outnumbers Scots in a ratio of 12:1.

Gareth Wardell is a gifted polymath of modern Scottish life. He blends art, politics, and introspection and in doing so, challenges readers to engage more deeply with their heritage. His outspoken reflections and cultivated style ensure he remains a significant, if often controversial voice in Scotland's cultural and political dialogue.

THE KILTED KILLER.

Colonel Sir Ronald Thomas Stewart (Tommy) Macpherson. CBE, MC**, TD, DL. CdG**. LdH. Businessman and War Hero. (1920 - 2014)

Tommy Macpherson was born in 1920 as the youngest of seven children. His father was a judge at the Indian High Court and was chancellor of Patna University. His mother, Helen Cameron, was the daughter of a clergyman. Although his family were from Newtonmore in the Highlands, he grew up in the city of Edinburgh.

Macpherson won a scholarship to Fettes where he was an outstanding athlete, winning the half mile, taking eight seconds off the school record for the mile and beating future four-minute-miler Roger Bannister in the process. He went to Trinity College in Oxford, and was awarded a first class degree in philosophy, politics and economics. He was a Scottish international student athlete and also represented Oxford in hockey, rugby and athletics.

With the advent of World War Two, Macpherson was commissioned in the Queen's Own Cameron Highlanders in 1939, before serving with the No. Eleven Scottish Commando Unit during the war. In 1941, during a daring four man raid to capture Erwin Rommel in North Africa, he was captured and held in several prisoners-of-war camps. He made repeated attempts to escape but was caught each time. However, interrogated by the Gestapo before ending up in a remote camp on the far eastern borders of Germany, he slipped away wearing a French uniform, made it to the Baltic coast and stowed away on a ship to neutral Sweden from where he returned to Scotland.

Upon eventually escaping and returning on a home run to Scotland, Churchill personally ordered that he return 'to set Europe ablaze!' In consequence, he was parachuted behind enemy lines in France and began a long campaign of destruction alongside the French Resistance. The Germans placed a 300,000 franc bounty on his head and referred to him as *'The Kilted Killer'*.

McPherson was highly active. On one occasion when a German staff car was approaching a level crossing, Macpherson booby-trapped the barrier arm so it crashed down on the vehicle, decapitating the local commandant and his driver. He single-handedly captured over twenty-three thousand German soldiers and one thousand vehicles one night simply by persuading a German General that he was in command of the Allied Forces in the area and that they'd no way out.

Throughout his guerrilla campaign he wore the kilt and carried a *sgian dhu* - the traditional Scottish dagger - tucked into his sock. Instead of merging with the local population to avoid detection, he took the view that he'd rather the French gained confidence from the knowledge that an Allied Scotsman was responsible for the constant and considerable carnage that was being waged on the Axis powers.

With three Military Crosses, three Croix de guerre, a Légion d'honneur, and a papal knighthood for his heroics during the Second World War, Sir Tommy Macpherson was the most decorated soldier of the British Army.

After the war, Macpherson married Jean Henrietta Wilson, who was patroness of the Royal Caledonian Ball. They had two sons and a daughter. He also took a First Class Degree at Oxford and enjoyed a successful business career, including periods variously as the Managing Director and Chairman of the Mallinson-Denny Group, as a director of Brooke Bond Group, Scottish Mutual Insurance and the the National Coal Board. He was also President of *Eurochambres* (the Association of European Chambers of Commerce) between 1992 and 1994. He was proud of being the chieftain of the Newtonmore Highland Games, president of the British Legion for Badenoch and vice-president of the Newtonmore shinty club.

He spent his laters years at his home in the Highlands, Balival House, near Newtonmore which was located at the heart of the ancestral lands of his Clan MacPherson.

He died aged 94 on 6 November 2014

OOR WULLIE, THE BROONS AND CONSERVATISM

David Couper (DC) Thomson DL. Newspaper Proprietor (1861 - 1954)

Thomson was raised in Fife's Newport-on-Tay by his mother, Margaret Couper, and his father, William Thomson who was a successful draper and later a shipowner. In 1884, aged twenty-three, he became the major shareholder of the *Dundee Courier & Daily Argus.* In *1914,* he founded *The Sunday Post* which rapidly blossomed to develop a significant circulation across Scotland, Ulster and parts of Northern England. Sales of *The Sunday Post* in Scotland became so saturated within the Scottish population that it was recorded in *The Guinness Book of Records* as the newspaper with the highest *per capita* readership penetration of anywhere in the world. In 1969, its total estimated readership of 2,931,000 represented more than eighty per cent of the entire population of Scotland aged sixteen and over.

Between 1920 and 1922, Thomson actively campaigned against an M.P. for Dundee; then Liberal politician Winston Churchill. At the 1922 General Election, both of the local newspapers owned by Thomson advised their readers to reject Churchill who subsequently, came only fourth in the poll and lost his seat in Parliament. Thomson barred Churchill's name from his newspapers until World War Two made occasional use of it unavoidable.

D.C. Thomson married Margaret McCulloch and had a daughter, Irene and son, Conrad. He was a particularly conservative individual and would not allow either members of Trades Unions or Roman Catholics to be employed in his titles. The company has in the past excited a good deal of interest because it has always shrouded its activities in secrecy and has never allowed scholars access to its archives.

Its regular columns include; *My Week* by Francis Gay which featured sentimental stories and a weekly short poem, *The Honest Truth* – a question and answer celebrity interview feature, *Raw Deal* which dealt with consumer problems, *The Doc Replies* which offered medical advice, Y*our Money,* a Personal finance feature, *On The Box, a* TV review column and *The HON Man* a report from an unidentifiable peripatetic man who travelled Britain, meeting people and exploring local tourist attractions (*HON* being short for '*Holiday on Nothing*').

There were also two enormously popular strip cartoons in the paper; *Oor Wullie*, drawn by cartoonist Dudley D Watkins who continued to draw *Oor Wullie* until his death in 1969 and *The Broons*, a second comic strip which made use of the Scots' language (as spoken in Broughty Ferry near Dundee where Watkins lived and which used local terms such as 'bairn' instead of the West of Scotland's more common use of 'wean') and which featured a family called Brown (Broon), that lived in a tenement flat at 10 Glebe Street in the fictional Scottish town of Auchentogle.

In addition to his newspapers portfolio, Thomson published magazines including the *People's Friend* and *Scot's Magazine* which came into existence in 1739 and which claims to be the oldest magazine in the world still in publication although there have been several gaps in its publication history. It has reported on events from the 1745 Battle of Culloden to to the creation of the new Scottish Parliament in 2000. However, in terms of UK exposure, his weekly comics including the Beezer, the Hotspur, the Beano, Commando, the Dandy, the Victor and the Rover among many others introduced extremely popular characters as Desperate Dan, Lord Snooty, Alf Tupper, Biffo the Bear, Bananaman, the Bash Street Kids, Rodger the Dodger and Denis the Menace to an enthusiastic audience.

The Sunday Post has seen a decline in circulation in common with other print titles; in 1999, circulation was around 700,000, dropping to just under 143,000 in December 2016, it experienced a year-on-year fall of 13.5% and in 2024 it achieved sales of only 34,000 - still outselling many other titles. The newspaper backed a 'No' vote in the Referendum on Scottish Independence in 2014 doubtless in keeping with the views and attitudes of its major proprietor, David Couper Thomson. Although Thomson was less involved with the company after 1933, he remained chairman of the company until his death, aged 93. David was Deputy Lieutenant of Dundee for fifty years, Governor of University College, Dundee for nearly sixty years and was also an active member of Dundee Chamber of Commerce and Dundee Eye Institute. He died in 1954 and is buried in the Western Cemetery, Dundee.

THE RED DUCHESS

Katharine Marjory Stewart-Murray, Duchess of Atholl. Aristocratic Rebel. (1874 - 1960)

Katharine Ramsay was born in Edinburgh 1874, into an aristocratic Scottish family; the daughter of Sir James Henry Ramsay and Charlotte Fanning Ramsay. During her school years she was known as Kitty Ramsay. Her father, Sir James Ramsay, was the 10th Baronet of Banff, a lineage that gave her a privileged upbringing. She was well-educated and developed an early interest in literature, politics, and social reform which would define her later career.

In 1899, she married John Stewart-Murray, the 8th Duke of Atholl, a Scottish peer" and military officer. As the Duchess of Atholl, she took on the traditional responsibilities of managing estates and supporting local charitable causes. However, she was far from a conventional aristocratic wife - she had strong political opinions and a deep interest in public affairs.

Her political career began in earnest in 1923 when she was elected as the Member of Parliament for Kinross and West Perthshire. Running as a Conservative, she became Scotland's first female MP and one of the few women in British politics at the time.

Despite being a Conservative, the Duchess of Atholl was often at odds with her party, particularly on issues of social justice, education and international affairs. She supported progressive policies, especially in education and was a strong advocate for improving schools in Scotland. She was also deeply concerned with the rights of women and children, supporting policies that promoted their welfare.

Between 1924 and 1929, she served as the Parliamentary Secretary to the Board of Education under Prime Minister Stanley Baldwin. In this role, she worked on education reform, promoting better access to schooling and higher standards for teachers. However, her most defining political positions came in the 1930s when the rise of fascism in Europe became a major global issue.

The 1930s saw the rise of authoritarian regimes in Europe, including Nazi Germany, Mussolini's Italy, and Francoist Spain. While many in the British establishment took a policy of appeasement, Katharine Stewart-Murray became one of the most vocal opponents of fascism within her party.

She was particularly outspoken against Franco's regime during the Spanish Civil War which took place between 1936 and 1939. She visited Spain and was horrified by the brutality of Franco's forces which were backed by Hitler and Mussolini. She wrote *'Searchlight on Spain'*, a book that condemned Franco's regime and exposed the atrocities committed against civilians and political opponents. Her outspoken stance put her in direct conflict with her own party leadership, who preferred a neutral stance toward the war. Her book led to her being nicknamed the 'Red Duchess' by some. She became active in the National Joint Committee for Spanish Relief, a cross-party group coordinating aid to Spain

Her strong anti-fascist position ultimately led to her resignation from the Conservative Party in 1938. She chose to stand as an Independent candidate in the ensuing by-election, campaigning on a platform of anti-fascism and international justice. However, she lost her seat to a Conservative opponent. Despite this political defeat, she remained active in humanitarian efforts and continued to speak out against fascism and oppression.

During World War Two, the Duchess of Atholl continued her humanitarian work. She was a vocal advocate for refugees fleeing Nazi persecution and worked with various organisations to support those displaced by war. She remained a passionate critic of totalitarian regimes, whether fascist or communist and continued to write and lecture on international affairs.

After the war, she did not return to Parliament but remained an influential figure in British political discourse. She continued advocating for democracy, human rights, and social reform, using her aristocratic influence to support charitable causes and political activism.

Her contributions to education, her opposition to fascism and her humanitarian efforts during times of conflict set her apart from many of her contemporaries. While she may not have had a long political career, her principled stands continue to be remembered as examples of moral leadership in times of crisis.

She lived out her later years in Scotland, where she remained engaged in writing and public affairs until her death on October 21, 1960.

THE SLAB BOY

John Patrick Byrne CBE. Artist and Playwright (1940 - 2023)

John Patrick Byrne was born into a family of Irish Catholic descent in Paisley, Renfrewshire where he grew up in Ferguslie Park. His mother, Alice McShane, was married to Patrick Byrne when he was born. He discovered in later life that he had been conceived from an incestuous affair between his mother and her father, Patrick McShane.

Ferguslie Park, a profoundly deprived area in Paisley, was notorious in the nineteen-forties through the nineties for high levels of crime, poverty and poor housing but offered the young Byrne an upbringing that inevitably shaped his artistic vision. His father worked as a labourer while his mother took on domestic duties. These humble beginnings instilled in Byrne a deep understanding of working-class culture and a fascination with the lives of ordinary people, themes that would feature prominently in his later work. His interest in art was evident from an early age and he studied at the Glasgow School of Art, graduating in 1963. It was during this time that he developed a distinctive style that blended surrealism, pop art, and a strong sense of narrative. Byrne was heavily influenced by painters such as Diego Rivera and Stanley Spencer, whose works are notable for their intricate detail and social themes. These influences, coupled with Byrne's own Scottish heritage, created a unique visual language that set him apart in the contemporary art world.

John Byrne's visual art is characterised by its vibrant colours, exaggerated forms, and an almost cartoonish quality that belies its deeper emotional and social undertones. His paintings often depict fantastical, semi-autobiographical scenes set in Scottish urban and rural landscapes and captures the grit and charm of working-class life, celebrating its humour and resilience while also addressing its struggles.

One of his most iconic contributions to the art world came in the form of album cover designs. In the 1970s, Byrne created striking artwork for artists such as The Beatles, Billy Connolly and Gerry

Rafferty, whose *'City to City'* and *'Night Owl'* albums featured his surreal, narrative-rich illustrations. These designs brought his work to a broader international audience and showcased his ability to blend fine art with popular culture.

Byrne's foray into playwriting came in the early 1970s when he turned his attention to theatre. His debut play, *'Writer's Cramp'*, was a critical success, demonstrating his ability to craft compelling stories that were both humorous and poignant. This was followed by *'The Slab Boys'*, the first in a trilogy of plays (followed by *'Cuttin' A Rug'* and *'Still Life'*) that would establish Byrne as one of Scotland's most significant dramatists. The plays draw on his own experiences working in a carpet factory in Paisley, offering a richly detailed portrait of working-class life in post-war Scotland. The trilogy resonated deeply with audiences and critics alike, earning Byrne comparisons to great playwrights like John Osborne and Harold Pinter. A recurring theme in Byrne's work was the tension between aspiration and limitation. Whether in his visual art or his plays, Byrne explored the struggles of individuals striving to escape the confines of their social and economic circumstances. His characters are often dreamers, rebels, or misfits, grappling with the challenges of identity, ambition, and belonging.

In addition to his work in painting and theatre, Byrne made significant contributions as a set designer, most notably for productions at the Royal Court Theatre and the National Theatre. His ability to create immersive visual environments has enhanced the theatrical experience for countless audiences. He received numerous accolades throughout his career, including an honorary doctorate from the University of Paisley and the title of Commander of the Order of the British Empire in 1996. Despite his international success, he remained deeply connected to Scotland and continued to live and work there, drawing inspiration from its people and landscapes.

In his personal life, Byrne was also been a figure of intrigue. His relationship with acclaimed actress Tilda Swinton with whom he shared two children brought him additional media attention. They separated in 2004. He began a relationship with the theatre lighting designer Jeanine Davies in 2006, marrying her in 2014.

His ability to move seamlessly between painting and playwriting demonstrates a rare versatility while his commitment to exploring working-class life has ensured the relevance and authenticity of his work. Whether through his visually stunning paintings or his emotionally resonant plays, Byrne captivated audiences and inspired new generations of artists. As a cultural icon, his legacy is firmly cemented, ensuring his place as one of Scotland's most cherished creative talents.

SHERLOCK HOLMES AND MORE...

Sir Arthur Ignatius Conan Doyle. Author and Physician (1859 - 1930)

Arthur Conan Doyle was born in 1859 at 11 Picardy Place, Edinburgh. His father, Charles Doyle was born in England, of Irish Catholic descent and his mother, Mary, was Irish Catholic. His parents married in 1855 but in 1864 the family was rent asunder due to his father, Charles's growing alcoholism. The children were temporarily housed across Edinburgh. Arthur lodged with the aunt of a friend, at Liberton Bank House on Gilmerton Road, while studying at Newington Academy. Hs mother, Mary, was an avid storyteller who greatly influenced young Arthur's imagination, her vivid tales laying the groundwork for his narrative prowess.

Doyle attended the Jesuit preparatory school, Stonyhurst College and later studied medicine at the University of Edinburgh. During his time at university, he encountered influential figures, including Dr. Joseph Bell, a professor of surgery whose keen powers of observation and logical reasoning inspired the creation of Sherlock Holmes. Doyle's education was marked by a balance of rigorous scientific training and a growing passion for writing, which would eventually become his primary career.

After graduating in 1881, Doyle worked as a ship's doctor on a whaling vessel and later set up a medical practice in Southsea, England. His practice initially saw few patients, allowing him ample time to write. In 1887, he published *'A Study in Scarlet'*, the first novel featuring Sherlock Holmes and his loyal friend Dr. John Watson. The novel introduced readers to the detective's brilliant analytical mind, his methodical approach to solving crimes, and his characteristic aloofness. Its success marked the beginning of Doyle's literary career. Over the years, he wrote fifty-six short stories and three more novels featuring Holmes, including *'The Sign of the Four'*, *'The Hound of the Baskervilles'*, and *'The Valley of Fear'*. These works gained immense popularity and established Holmes as one of the most enduring fictional characters in literary history. Holmes' adventures were serialised in The Strand Magazine, captivating readers worldwide and solidifying Doyle's reputation as a master storyteller.

While Sherlock Holmes brought Doyle fame and fortune, the author grew increasingly frustrated with the character's overshadowing presence in his literary portfolio. Doyle believed his historical novels were his greatest achievements. Feeling constrained by Holmes' popularity, Doyle controversially killed off the detective in the 1893 story *'The Final Problem'* only to resurrect him due to public demand in 1903 with *'The Adventure of the Empty House'*.

Doyle also penned historical novels, adventure stories, ghost tales, and essays on political and social issues. He was also a keen sportsman, playing goalkeeper for Portsmouth FC, and was a cricketer for Marylebone Cricket Club. He founded the Undershaw Rifle Club, was one of three judges for the world's first major bodybuilding competition and was an amateur boxer and keen golfer. He entered the English Amateur Billiards Championship in 1913 and following a move to Switzerland, took up skiing. Doyle served as a volunteer physician in the Langman Field Hospital at Bloemfontein in 1900 and was also a fervent advocate of justice, personally investigating two closed cases which led to each man being exonerated of the crimes of which they were accused.

In 1885 Doyle married Louisa Hawkins and, in 1907, the year after her death from tuberculosis, he married Jean Elizabeth Leckie. Doyle fathered five children; two from his first marriage and three from his second.

Doyle's books have been adapted countless times into films, television series and stage productions but his influence extends beyond entertainment. The methods of deduction and forensic science employed by Holmes have inspired advancements in real-world criminal investigations. His stories also contributed to the development of the modern detective genre, paving the way for authors like Agatha Christie and Raymond Chandler.

Despite his frustrations with being forever associated with Sherlock Holmes, Doyle's literary genius and imaginative storytelling continue to captivate audiences more than a century after his works were first published. Sir Arthur Conan Doyle was knighted in 1902 for his service to literature and his involvement in the Boer War, reflecting the broad scope of his contributions to society.

In July 1930, he died of a heart attack at the age of seventy-one and was buried in Windlesham before later being reinterred together with his wife in Minstead churchyard in the New Forest. A statue of Conan Doyle was erected outside his Edinburgh home; another honours Doyle in Crowborough, in England where he lived for twenty-three years.

'IT'S A SMALL WORLD, BUT I WOULDN'T WANT TO HAVE TO PAINT IT.'

Charles Thomas McKinnon (Chic) Murray. Actor and Comedian (1919 - 1985)

Charles Thomas McKinnon Murray was born in 1919 just after the First World War, in Greenock on the south bank of the River Clyde. After leaving school at the age of fourteen in 1934, he started work as an apprentice engineer in the local Kincaids Shipyard. In his spare time he was using his talents as an entertainer with amateur groups such as 'Chic and his Chicks'. He played various instruments (including the piano, organ, banjo, mandolin and guitar), sang, yodelled and told jokes.

Chic's mother worked at the Greenock Empire theatre and put one of the performers, Maidie Dickson, up in her home. Subsequently, Maidie who was a well-regarded and in-demand performer, gave Chic parts within her own act and over time, they formed a double-act. Billed as *'The Tall Droll with the Small Doll'* (Chic was 6'3" tall, Maidie was 4'11") and also as *'Maidie and Murray'*, their combination of jokes and songs made them popular in theatres throughout the country and eventually on television. They married and had two children, Annabelle and Douglas.

They were signed up by the powerful Bernard Delfont agency in 1955 and made the breakthrough beyond Scotland to UK-wide performing circuits, rising rapidly up the bill. The double act became very popular and achieved significant popularity at the Prince of Wales Theatre in London which culminated in an invitation to appear on the bill at the Royal Variety Performance in the London Palladium before the Queen, but the short-lived Suez Crisis when Egyptian president Gael Abdel Nasser nationalised the Canal resulted in the show being cancelled. Gradually, Murray began to perform on his own.

Chic Murray was an original. While television audiences were fed comedians like Colin Crompton, Ken Goodwin, Bernard Manning, Mick Miller, Tom O'Connor, Mike Reid, Roy Walker and Charlie Williams who told old jokes about their mother-in-law and were reliant on standard one-liners and formulaic anecdotes, Murray was innovative, subversive and surreal.

Many aspects of his act bordered on the absurd. 'After I told my wife that black underwear turned me on, she didn't wash my Y-fronts for a month'.... 'The police stopped me when I was out in my car. They told me it was a spot check. I admitted to two pimples and a boil'... 'I met this cowboy with a brown paper hat, paper waistcoat and paper trousers. He was wanted for rustling'... 'I rang the bell of this small bed-and breakfast place, whereupon a lady appeared at an outside window. "What do you want?", she asked. "I want to stay here", I replied. "Well, stay there then", she said and closed the window.' These, and many more, entertained audiences, particularly in Scotland.

Murray acted in films such as *'Casino Royale'* and *'Gregory's Girl'* in which he played a piano-playing headmaster. He also played former Liverpool Football Club manager Bill Shankly in the musical play, *'You'll Never Walk Alone'* and made cameo appearances as an itinerant poacher in a few episodes of Scottish Television's soap opera '*Take The High Road'*. He also played roles in popular comedy films *such as 'What's Up Nurse?', What's Up Superdoc?, 'Secrets of a Door-to-door Salesman' and 'I'm Not Feeling Myself Tonight'*.

He divorced former wife Maidie in the 1970s but remained on good terms. In later years, he developed an unhealthy relationship with alcohol and when he died of a perforated ulcer in Edinburgh in 1985 at the age of 65, tributes were many and heartfelt. Scottish comedian Billy Connolly considered him his favourite funny-man. 'He was the guv'nor. I saw him live several times. He was the funniest man on earth'. Eric Sykes adored his naturally droll character; Bruce Forsyth was in awe of his timing, 'immaculate and so different'; Jimmy Tarbuck said, 'Chic was the comedian all the other comedians wanted to watch' and Ronnie Corbett described him as 'a true original: a funny, sweet and engaging man who as a comic was ahead of his time'. Two plays were written, celebrating his work.

Let's give him an encore... 'I got up this morning. I like to get up in the morning; it gives me the rest of the day to myself. I crossed the landing and went down stairs. Mind you, if there had been no stairs, I wouldn't even have attempted it'... 'So there I was lying in the gutter. A man stopped and asked '"What's the matter? Did you fall over?" I said "No. I've a bar of toffee in my back pocket and I was just trying to break it."...

'I was looking for lodgings. So I went up to this boarding house. The landlady said, "Do you have a good memory for faces?" I said, "Yes. Why?" She said, "There's no mirror in the bathroom". At his funeral, his tartan bunnet was atop his coffin as it was lowered and everyone in the church stood up and applauded. Billy Connolly shouted, 'Please...please, not too much. The bugger'll come back and do twenty minutes!'

THE FIRST BLACK FOOTBALLER

Andrew Watson. Footballer and Football Administrator (1856 - 1951)

Watson was the son of a wealthy Scottish plantation owner, Peter Miller Watson, and a local Guyanese woman named Hannah Rose. After his father's death, Watson inherited a considerable fortune and moved to Britain for his education. He attended prestigious schools in England before enrolling at the University of Glasgow to study philosophy, mathematics, and engineering. During this period, he also began playing football, a sport that was rapidly growing in popularity in Britain.

Watson joined Queen's Park Football Club in the early 1880s, a time when the club was a dominant force in Scottish football. Queen's Park was known not just for its success on the pitch, but for its progressive football philosophy. It played a pioneering role in shaping the modern passing game, as opposed to the more physical English style of the time. For Watson, a cultured and intelligent player, Queen's Park was a natural fit.

Playing as a full-back, Watson quickly established himself as a talented and composed defender. He possessed excellent positional sense, great athleticism and an innate understanding of the game. His performances at club level caught the attention of the Scottish Football Association and in 1881 Watson made history when he was selected to play for the Scottish national team. This made him the first black player to represent a national football team, decades before other black footballers would break through in international or club football in Europe.

Watson earned three caps for Scotland between 1881 and 1882. During his international debut, Scotland thrashed England 6 - 1 in London; a remarkable result that underscored Watson's impact. He captained Scotland in one of his subsequent matches, making him not only the first black international footballer but also the first black player to captain a national team. His international career was short, but it was historic and impactful.

After signing for Queen's Park, then Britain's largest football team he became their secretary in November 1881. During his time with Queen's Park, Watson won multiple Scottish Cup titles, contributing to the club's dominance in the Scottish game. He also played for other clubs, including Parkgrove and Corinthians, but Queen's Park remained the centrepiece of his footballing legacy. The club's amateur values and commitment to the purity of the game aligned with Watson's own principles, particularly in an era when professionalism in football was still controversial.

One of the most remarkable aspects of Watson's career is that he achieved such prominence during a time of widespread racial prejudice. While historical records do not provide extensive commentary on how his race was perceived at the time, it is clear that Watson was highly respected by his peers. His wealth and education may have shielded him somewhat from the worst of the discrimination faced by black athletes in later years, but his success still challenged the then racial norms of Victorian society.

Andrew Watson's story was largely forgotten for many decades. For much of the 20th century, the contributions of black players to early football history were under-recognized or ignored. It wasn't until the late 20th and early 21st centuries that historians began to rediscover Watson's pioneering role. Today, he is rightly celebrated as a trailblazer - not just in Scottish football, but in the global game.

Queen's Park has played a significant role in honouring Watson's legacy. The club has embraced its connection with this pioneering figure and has worked to educate new generations of fans about his contributions. Statues, plaques, and exhibitions have helped to bring Watson's story back into the public consciousness and his legacy continues to inspire black players and fans across the footballing world.

Andrew Watson's time at Queen's Park Football Club was instrumental in his rise as the first black international footballer. A gifted player and a thoughtful, dignified figure, Watson broke racial barriers at a time when few people of African descent were seen on British sports fields. His contributions to football, both on and off the pitch, are a testament to the power of talent, integrity, and perseverance. His story, once nearly forgotten, is now celebrated as an essential part of football's rich and diverse history.

SELECTED QUOTES

Craig Murray

"If you achieve a voice that will be heard, you should use it to speak up for the voiceless and oppressed. If you possess any power or authority, you must strive to use it to help and empower the powerless."

"As a rule of thumb, if the government wants you to know it, it probably isn't true."

"The hands of the British state are all over this. The roots of it was a political conspiracy against Alex Salmond, to destroy both his reputation and career, and why? Because he was a threat to the British state, one of the biggest threats in three hundred years who had taken the country to the brink of independence."

Tommy MacPherson

"The clincher was when I told him that I was in contact with London by radio and could at any time call up the RAF to blow his people out of sight. The truth, the only thing I could whistle up was Dixie, but the Germans had no way of knowing that. We had just finished these negotiations and got the General's signature when up came American Lieutenant Samuel Magill of the 329th Infantry accompanied by Lieutenant Colonel Jules French, who saluted politely and said he would be very pleased indeed to take immediate responsibility for all 23,000 Germans'.

"The tiger and the lion may be more powerful but the wolf does not perform in the circus"

Katharine Marjory Stewart-Murray

"Handing over territory to Germany means handing over human beings. Knowing what we do of the brutalities of the Nazi regime, have we any right to expose other people to this danger?"

"I have enjoyed the battles of my life."

John Byrne

"I cannae no' paint. I cannae no' paint. I cannae no' do it. If I don't paint, I'm not well, I'm no' myself. I love doing it, but it's a necessity."

"Even at deaths and funerals, in the most tragic circumstances, the funniest things happen. Life is funny. I think I could only write a funny play. To write a serious one would be utter hell."

"It's been a real pleasure working with Glasgow Museums on this retrospective. I've been in and out of Kelvingrove my whole life. It's a delight to be reunited with works I've not seen in years, especially as they are hanging on the walls of a place I, and so many people, love."

Chic Murray

"My wife went to a beauty parlour and got a mudpack; for two days she looked nice, then the mud fell off."

"My sister wanted a cat for a pet... I wanted a dog, so my parents bought a cat and taught it to bark."

"My parents never understood me; they were Japanese."

Gareth Wardell

"A Scotsman's worst enemy is not an Englishman but another Scotsman keen to be an *ersatz* Englishman."

"Each time I convince someone to see the blazing light in independence restored, I regard that as a tiny revolution."

A SCOTS-ITALIAN VISIONARY

Richard Demarco CBE. Artist, Curator and Promoter. (1930 -)

Born in 1930, in Edinburgh to an Italian-Scottish family, the son of Carmino Demarco and his wife Elizabeth Valentina Fusco, Demarco's contributions to the world of art extend far beyond his work as a painter. He is best known as a visionary artist, curator, educator, and tireless promoter of the arts, particularly through his efforts to connect Scotland with the broader European cultural scene. His life's work has been dedicated to fostering dialogue between artists and audiences and positioning Edinburgh as a global hub for contemporary art and ideas. His childhood was shaped by the city's rich history and his dual cultural heritage. His father's Italian roots introduced him to the Mediterranean's artistic traditions, while his Scottish upbringing instilled in him a deep appreciation for his homeland's cultural and natural landscapes. These early influences would later inspire much of his artistic and curatorial work, which often sought to blend local and international perspectives.

Demarco studied at the Edinburgh College of Art, where he developed his skills as a painter. His early works were inspired by his surroundings, reflecting the interplay between Scotland's rugged landscapes and its architectural heritage. However, it soon became clear that Demarco's ambitions went far beyond his own artistic practice. He had a vision of art as a means of connection and cultural exchange and in 1963, he co-founded the Traverse Theatre, which quickly became a cornerstone of Edinburgh's cultural life. Although initially focused on experimental theatre, the Traverse soon became a multidisciplinary platform for emerging talent in art, music, and literature. Demarco's involvement in the theatre marked the beginning of his lifelong mission to challenge traditional boundaries between artistic disciplines and create spaces for innovation and collaboration.

In 1966, Demarco established the Richard Demarco Gallery, which became a vital force in Edinburgh's art scene. Unlike conventional galleries, Demarco's space was dedicated to showcasing contemporary and avant-garde art that challenged traditional norms. Through the gallery, Demarco introduced Scottish audiences to groundbreaking international artists, including Joseph Beuys, Marina Abramoviç, and Tadeusz Kantor. His collaborations with these artists helped to position Edinburgh as a significant player in the global art world.

Demarco's work is inseparable from the Edinburgh Festival which he used as a platform to bring diverse and often radical artistic voices to the city. From the late 1960s onwards, he organised exhibitions, performances, and events that pushed the boundaries of contemporary art and was instrumental in introducing audiences to conceptual and performance art, often at a time when such practices were met with skepticism or resistance. One of Demarco's most notable partnerships was with the German artist Joseph Beuys. Demarco first invited Beuys to Scotland in 1970 and their collaborations became legendary. Beuys' performances, such as the Celtic (Kinloch Rannoch) Scottish Symphony, were deeply influenced by Scotland's landscapes and cultural traditions and they embodied Demarco's belief in art as a means of cultural exchange.

Demarco's European connections extended beyond individual artists. He was a passionate advocate for Scotland's place within the broader European cultural and intellectual tradition and he used his gallery and festival projects to foster dialogue between Scottish and European artists. In doing so, he positioned Edinburgh as a gateway between Scotland and the rest of the world.

In addition to his work as a curator and promoter, Demarco has remained committed to his own artistic practice. His paintings and drawings often explore themes of identity, heritage, and the relationship between humanity and the natural world. Demarco's contributions to art and culture have been widely recognised. He has received numerous awards and honours, including a Commander of the British Empire medal in 1993 and the European Citizen's Prize in 2013. His archive, which documents decades of artistic activity, is considered one of the most important cultural resources in Scotland. Demarco's career has not been without its challenges. His uncompromising vision and willingness to champion unconventional art have sometimes put him at odds with traditional institutions and funding bodies. Financial difficulties have also been a recurring theme, particularly in relation to maintaining his gallery and archive. However, these struggles have only reinforced his reputation as a passionate and principled advocate for the arts. Today, Richard Demarco stands as an artist, curator, and cultural ambassador and as a symbol of creativity, resilience, and the enduring power of art.

TRIDENT PLOUGHSHARE AND THE DISTRIBUTISTS

Brian Quail. Academic and Anti-Nuclear Campaigner (1938 -)

Brian Quail was born in 1938 in Carmyle on the north bank of the Clyde in Glasgow and attended St Conval's, Holycross and Holyrood schools before enrolling at Glasgow University where he studied Classics from 1956 - 1960. Following the further acquisition of a teaching qualification in Jordanhill College of Education, Quail was appointed as a teacher of Classics during which time he also undertook an immersion course in Russian.

Brian Quail was only seven years old when the *Enola Gay,* a Boeing B-29 Superfortress named after Enola Gay Tibbets, the mother of the pilot, Colonel Paul Tibbets, dropped its Atomic Bomb over Hiroshima. Quail still remembers Glasgow tramcars at that time carrying the letters, *'VJ'* symbolising the *'Victory in Japan'* events that followed. In later years he listened to a young Robin Cook speak at a large gathering in George Square in Glasgow and was further inspired to protest the creation, maintenance and use of nuclear weapons. Quail was married to Mary McCormick for over twenty years and had six children by her before meeting Barbara after this marriage ended. Barbara (the mother of his youngest son *Seonaidh*) has now remarried but remains a friend having been a peace and Gaelic activist from Stornoway. Brian is also a member of the Scottish Republican and Socialist Movement and became a prominent member of '*The Distributists*', a movement arguing a socio-economic progress primarily associated with G.K. Chesterton and Hilaire Belloc, which advocated the widespread ownership of productive assets in society. He also joined the *'Trident Ploughshares'*, an activist anti-nuclear weapons group, founded in 1998 with the aim of beating swords into ploughshares as cited in the *Book of Isaiah* specifically by attempting to disarm the UK Trident Nuclear Weapons System in a non-violent manner. He is also a member of the '*Iona Community'* which seeks to close the gap between the church and working people. He took early retirement from teaching in his mid-fifties and dedicated subsequent decades to the employment of non-violent direct action against nuclear weapons.

Throughout his activism, Quail has been involved in numerous protests, often leading to legal confrontations. In March 2016, at the age of 78, he was acquitted of breach of the peace charges after halting a convoy believed to be transporting nuclear warheads. Quail achieved this by calmly using a pedestrian crossing in Balloch, then lying down on the road, effectively stopping the convoy. Representing himself in court, he argued that his actions were a lawful attempt to prevent the movement of illegal weapons. The presiding Justice of the Peace concluded that Quail's actions did not constitute a breach of the peace, leading to his acquittal. In September 2016, Quail participated in another protest against a nuclear convoy passing through Stirling. Quail manoeuvred himself under one of the lorries, delaying the convoy for approximately twenty minutes. He was subsequently arrested and charged with breach of the peace. Despite being fined £200 (still unpaid), Quail remained steadfast in his principles, declaring he would not pay the fine as it implied acceptance of the legitimacy of Trident, the UK's nuclear weapons system. He has been imprisoned on six occasions for refusal to pay a fine.

Quail's dedication to the cause has not waned with age. In 2021, at 83, he urged Pope Francis to visit the Faslane naval base, home to the UK's Trident nuclear submarines, during the COP26 climate conference in Glasgow, believing that a papal visit would underscore the immorality of nuclear weapons. In an open letter, he referenced the Pope's 2019 declaration that the possession of nuclear weapons is immoral, aligning with Quail's long-held beliefs. Beyond his direct actions, Quail has been an active member of various organisations dedicated to nuclear disarmament. He serves on the committee of the Scottish National Party Campaign for Nuclear Disarmament, working towards a nuclear-free, independent Scotland. In 2022, Quail was involved in organising a gathering at the Faslane and Coulport nuclear weapon complexes aiming to peacefully confront the UK's possession and deployment of nuclear weapons. Quail's activism has garnered support from various quarters, including former students. Notably, comic book writer Mark Millar, known for works like '*Kick-Ass*', was taught Latin and classics by Quail.

Millar has publicly supported his former teacher, expressing admiration for Quail's convictions and offering to cover his legal costs during protests. Despite facing legal challenges, health issues and advancing age, Brian Quail's resolve remains unshaken. His life exemplifies a profound commitment to peace and a nuclear-free world, inspiring many within and beyond Scotland to advocate for disarmament and global harmony.

THE WOMEN'S FREEDOM LEAGUE

Janet (Jenny) McCallum. Suffragist and Trades Unionist (1881 - 1946)

Jenny McCallum was the eldest of thirteen children born to John McCallum, a stonemason involved in constructing the Forth Bridge and Janet McCallum (née Hutchison). Growing up in a large working-class family, she began working in a linen weaving factory in Dunfermline, a common occupation for women in the area at the time. Despite the demanding nature of her work, McCallum became actively involved in trade unionism, advocating for better working conditions and fair wages for women.

In 1907, McCallum organised a significant demonstration in West Fife, bringing national leaders of the Women's Social and Political Union (WSPU), including Christabel Pankhurst, to the region. Her efforts aimed to galvanise support for women's suffrage among the local working-class population. However, disillusioned with the autocratic leadership of the Pankhursts, McCallum joined the Women's Freedom League (WFL) in 1908, a breakaway group advocating for democratic principles within the suffrage movement.

On 27 October 1908, McCallum participated in a coordinated WFL demonstration in London, protesting outside the Houses of Parliament. She was arrested alongside fourteen others after staging a demonstration in Old Palace Yard, where some activists climbed onto a statue. Reports of her trial described her as 'a little Scotch girl with a decided accent' and treated her as a figure of fun. Offered the choice between paying a £5 fine or serving a one-month sentence, McCallum chose imprisonment, spending five days in Holloway Prison before being released due to health concerns. Her incarceration highlighted the sacrifices made by working-class women in the fight for suffrage.

On 18 June 1910, she took part in a Grand Procession in London, one of the earliest mass marches organised by the suffrage movement. She was among a group of prisoners who had been sent to prison for the cause.

Other groups were graduates, teachers, athletes, musicians and actresses. Many of the groups carried banners.

As a wage-earner, McCallum's income was important to her family. When she returned to her home in Dunfermline, she was blacklisted by her employer, and it took her a year to secure another job in a mill. She resumed her trade union activities and became the full-time organiser of the Scottish Textile Workers Union while continuing her activism, working with the WFL in Glasgow and participating in various campaigns, focusing on improving labour conditions for women in the textile industry. In 1919, McCallum played a pivotal role in a women-led rent strike in Rosyth, challenging the Scottish National Housing Company over unfair rent increases. She successfully enlisted Sylvia Pankhurst to speak on behalf of the tenants, demonstrating her ability to mobilise support and effect change.

In 1915, McCallum married Harry Richardson, a machinist at the Rosyth Dockyards, and they had three children together. Facing limited employment opportunities in Scotland, the family emigrated to South Africa in the 1920s. McCallum continued her advocacy work abroad, though details of her activities in South Africa remain limited. She passed away on 24 March 1946 in Pretoria, leaving behind a legacy of resilience and dedication to social justice.

Janet McCallum's contributions to the suffrage movement and labor rights have often been overlooked in historical narratives dominated by middle and upper-class figures. However, recent efforts have sought to honour her legacy. In Inverkeithing, local initiatives have aimed to commemorate her work, including proposals to name a new high school after her as Inverkeithing High School is being replaced and a new high school is already under construction on a new site in Rosyth. As the new school will not be in Inverkeithing, a new name for the school is now being sought and Janet McCallum Academy is high on the short-leet.

McCallum's life exemplifies the critical role of working-class women in advancing social change. Her unwavering commitment to equality and justice serves as an enduring inspiration, reminding us that the struggle for rights and representation transcends class boundaries.

In 2021 McCallum was included in an educational resource called *Scotland's Suffrage Education Pack* which was produced by crowdfunding and given to one hundred Scottish schools to increase awareness of suffrage activism across the country.

THE SCOT WHO SOLD A COUNTRY

Gregor MacGregor. Soldier and Con-man (1786 - 1845)

Gregor MacGregor was born on Christmas Eve 1786 at his family's ancestral home of Glengyle, on the north shore of Loch Katrine. He was the son of Daniel MacGregor, an East India Company sea captain and his wife Ann. The clan had a turbulent history, having been outlawed for much of the 17th century due to conflicts with the government. Despite his family's past, Gregor received a good education and later joined the British Army in 1803 at the age of sixteen.

He served in the Peninsular War against Napoleon's forces in Spain and Portugal, rising to the rank of lieutenant. However, he resigned from the army in 1810, possibly due to frustration over his slow advancement. After leaving the British military, he sought adventure elsewhere.

With Europe largely at peace following Napoleon's defeat, MacGregor set his sights on the New World. South America was in the midst of its wars of independence from Spanish rule and MacGregor saw an opportunity to make a name for himself. He traveled to Venezuela and joined the forces of Simón Bolívar, the revolutionary leader fighting Spanish colonial rule.

MacGregor quickly established himself as a daring and sometimes reckless military leader. He led a number of campaigns, including an ambitious but ultimately disastrous attempt to take Florida from Spain in 1817. Despite setbacks, he managed to style himself as a heroic general, marrying into a wealthy Venezuelan family and gaining prestige. However, by 1820, his military exploits had waned and he sought a new way to make his fortune - through deception.

In 1821, MacGregor returned to Britain with an extraordinary story. He claimed that he had been granted a vast territory in Central America, known as Poyais, by the indigenous Mosquito King. According to MacGregor, Poyais was a paradise, filled with fertile land, rich natural resources and a welcoming native population eager for European settlers.

He declared himself '*Cazique* of Poyais' (a title meant to signify a ruling prince) and began promoting his imaginary nation as a golden opportunity for British investors and emigrants.

MacGregor printed elaborate promotional materials, including maps, pamphlets, and even a constitution for Poyais. He described a land of prosperity, where European settlers would find a ready-made society complete with government buildings, infrastructure and even a bank that issued its own currency. He also sold 'Poyaisian bonds' to investors, raising significant sums of money.

The conman was so convincing that he managed to recruit around two hundred and fifty settlers, who sailed from Britain to what they believed would be their new home. When they arrived in the supposed Poyais territory, which was actually an undeveloped part of Honduras, they found nothing but jungle. The promised settlements, roads, and resources did not exist. Many perished from disease and starvation.

News of the disaster eventually reached Britain and authorities began investigating MacGregor's claims. By the mid-1820s, his fraud was exposed and he fled to France, where he attempted to run the same confidence trick again. However, the French government arrested him in 1826. Despite facing trial for fraud, he managed to escape conviction due to lack of evidence.

After his release, MacGregor faded into obscurity. In the 1830s, he returned to Venezuela, where he was granted a pension for his earlier military service. He lived the rest of his life quietly and died in Caracas in 1845, remarkably unpunished for his elaborate hoax.

Gregor MacGregor's Poyais fraud remains one of the most ambitious cons in history. His ability to fabricate an entire country, complete with official-looking documents and financial instruments, was unprecedented. His victims included not only impoverished settlers but also wealthy investors who lost thousands.

While MacGregor's scheme was unique in scale, it highlighted the speculative frenzy of the early 19th century, where grand colonial projects often attracted blind enthusiasm. His story is now studied as a classic example of confidence trickery, demonstrating how persuasive storytelling can be more powerful than reality.

THE REFORMING AND HUMANE INDUSTRIALIST

David Dale. Businessman and Industrialist (1739 - 1806)

David Dale was born in 1739, in Stewarton, Ayrshire, but his early life did not foretell his eventual influence in the world of industry. His father, William and his mother Martha Dunlop were modest grocers. Dale began his working life as an apprentice to a hand-loom weaver. Through ambition, intelligence and diligence he later moved to Glasgow, a burgeoning centre of trade and commerce where Dale set up his own linen business in the 1760s. His determination and business acumen paid off, establishing him as a successful merchant ultimately with interests in cotton spinning, banking, and shipping.

Dale came to broader prominence as he seized upon the burgeoning potential of the cotton industry. The advent of Richard Arkwright's spinning technology, which greatly increased the efficiency of cotton production, presented entrepreneurs with unprecedented opportunities. In collaboration with Arkwright, Dale established Scotland's first rotary spinning mill in 1785, located at New Lanark, near the Falls of Clyde. Here, Dale's idealistic vision took shape, as he endeavoured to create a model industrial community that combined the pursuit of profit with the welfare of workers.

The business grew rapidly and Dale became a wealthy merchant in the city. In 1777, at the age of thirty-eight, he married twenty-four year-old Anne Carolina Campbell, whose late father had been the Chief Executive of the Royal Bank of Scotland. In 1783 Dale had his own mansion built in Glasgow's fashionable Charlotte Street. The couple were together for fourteen years until the death of Carolina. During that period, they had nine children, four of whom, including their only son, died in infancy.

New Lanark became the embodiment of Dale's progressive outlook. While the industrial revolution often meant harsh conditions for workers, including child labour, Dale offered comparatively humane alternatives.

He built housing, schools and recreational facilities for his workers, opting to care for his workforce in ways that were innovative for the time. Particularly noteworthy was his concern for child labourers, many of whom were orphans brought to New Lanark under the care system of the time. Dale provided schooling and decent living conditions, practices that were relatively unheard of in the industrialised world. At one stage, the school roll totalled more than five hundred pupils and Dale was employing sixteen trained teachers to teach more than eight classes. The pupils were grouped according to their ability and promoted to the next class after suitable tests. Teachers received a bonus for each pupil promoted.

His philanthropic values extended beyond the mill. Dale was a devout Christian and a member of the Old Scotch Independents which deeply influenced his approach to business and social responsibility. He was known for his generous support of various charitable causes, often emphasising education and the alleviation of poverty. His belief in moral and religious instruction as keys to social improvement was reflected in the operation and ethos of New Lanark.

Dale's efforts in education were pioneering; he introduced free school systems at New Lanark that emphasised not only literacy and numeracy but also moral education and self-improvement. These principles became integral to the community, improving the lives of the workforce's children and instilling a sense of agency and hope.

In the midst of his successes, David Dale became connected with Welshman Robert Owen, another pivotal figure who would carry forward and amplify Dale's vision. Owen married one of Dale's daughters and took over the management of New Lanark in 1799. While Dale laid the foundations of what became one of the most influential social experiments of the 19th century, Owen expanded on these practices to further push the boundaries of social reform and community welfare.

Dale retired from active business life around the turn of the century, remaining a respected figure in Scottish commerce and philanthropy until his death on March 17, 1806. His legacy grew as New Lanark under Owen became internationally renowned for its extensive reforms and humane conditions, serving as a model community and a symbol of what industrial society could aspire to in terms of social consciousness and economic innovation.

THE DEVELOPMENT OF WIND POWER

James Blyth. Teacher and Inventor (1838 - 1906)

James Blyth was born in Marykirk in Kincardinshire in 1839 to John Blyth, an innkeeper and small farmer, and his wife Catherine. He attended the Marykirk Parish School and later, Montrose Academy before winning a scholarship to the General Assembly Normal School, Edinburgh in 1856.

He completed his Master of Arts in 1871 and in the same year married Jesse Wilhelmina Taylor at the United Presbyterian Church in Edinburgh. They had two sons and five daughters, two of whom died in infancy.

In 1880 he was appointed as the Professor of Natural Philosophy at Anderson's College, Glasgow, which, in 1886, became the West of Scotland Technical College and is now the University of Strathclyde. Whilst teaching at the technical college he pursued an active research programme with a particular interest in the generation and storage of electricity from wind power. He was deeply interested in electrical energy and its potential applications, particularly in rural areas where conventional power sources were scarce.

During the late 19th century, electricity was still a developing field, and most power generation relied on coal-fired steam engines. The idea of using wind to generate electricity was virtually unheard of, making Blyth's experiments revolutionary. His work laid the foundation for what would later become the modern wind energy industry.

In 1887, James Blyth constructed the world's first wind turbine capable of generating electricity. It was installed in the garden of his holiday cottage in Marykirk and consisted of a cloth-sailed windmill that powered a dynamo which in turn charged accumulators which were an early form of battery. The stored energy was then used to power the lights in his home, making it the first residence ever lit by wind-generated electricity.

Blyth's wind turbine had a vertical axis and stood around thirty-three feet high. While simple by today's standards, it was groundbreaking at the time. It operated successfully for several years, demonstrating that wind energy could be a viable alternative to fossil fuels.

Recognising the potential of his invention, Blyth sought to expand its use beyond his own home. He offered to provide free wind-generated electricity to a local hospital in Montrose, but the offer was declined as the technology was seen as too unconventional and unreliable - a reaction that highlights the resistance to renewable energy that has persisted throughout history.

After his initial success, Blyth continued to refine his wind turbine designs. He built several more turbines, each improving on the last. His largest wind turbine, erected at Anderson's College in Glasgow, produced enough electricity to power lighting for the entire college.

In 1891, Blyth patented his wind turbine design, further solidifying his role as a wind power pioneer. His patent outlined key innovations, such as improvements to turbine blade design and efficiency. While his work did not immediately lead to widespread adoption, it influenced later developments in wind energy technology.

Despite his achievements, James Blyth did not receive widespread recognition during his lifetime. His work was overshadowed by the rapid expansion of coal-fired power plants and hydroelectric dams which were seen as more reliable sources of electricity at the time. However, in recent decades, as concerns about climate change and fossil fuel dependence have grown, Blyth's contributions to wind power have gained renewed appreciation.

Today, wind power is one of the fastest-growing renewable energy sources in the world. Modern wind turbines, capable of generating megawatts of power, owe much to the pioneering efforts of Blyth and his contemporaries. Countries like Denmark, Germany, and the United States have invested heavily in wind energy, proving that Blyth's vision of harnessing wind for electricity was ahead of its time.

Scotland now generates a significant portion of its electricity from wind farms, with ambitious targets for further expansion. The success of these efforts is a testament to Blyth's early work and his belief in wind energy's potential.

THE INDUSTRIALIST AND PHILANTHROPIST WHO TRANSFORMED AMERICA

Andrew Carnegie. Industrialist and Philanthropist. (1835 - 1919)

Andrew Carnegie was born in 1835, in Dunfermline. His family lived in modest conditions, with his father working as a handloom weaver. However, as industrialisation advanced, traditional weaving jobs declined leaving many families struggling including the Carnegies.

In 1848, seeking better opportunities, Carnegie's family emigrated to the United States, settling in Allegheny, Pennsylvania. At just thirteen years old, Carnegie began working in a cotton mill earning a mere $1.20 per week. Despite his limited formal education, he was a voracious reader, borrowing books from a local benefactor's personal library. This self-education would play a crucial role in shaping his future success. His first significant career step came when he secured a job as a telegraph messenger boy with the Pennsylvania Railroad Company. His dedication and ability to learn quickly impressed his superiors and he soon climbed the ranks, becoming the personal secretary to Thomas A. Scott, a top executive at the railroad.

During his time in the railroad industry, Carnegie learned valuable lessons about business, efficiency, and investment. He began investing in railroad-related businesses, including ironworks and bridges. His keen eye for emerging industries led him to recognise the growing demand for steel - a material crucial to building railways, bridges, and skyscrapers. In the 1870s, Carnegie fully committed to the steel industry, founding Carnegie Steel Company in Pittsburgh. He introduced innovative production techniques, including the Bessemer process, which significantly lowered the cost of steel production while increasing efficiency. His company became the largest and most profitable steel producer in the world. He became known for his aggressive business tactics. He implemented vertical integration, controlling every aspect of steel production - from raw materials to transportation and manufacturing. This strategy allowed him to outcompete rivals and amass extraordinary wealth.

By the late 19th century, Carnegie Steel was a dominant force in American industry. In 1901 he sold the company to banker J.P. Morgan for $480 million (equivalent to billions today). This deal led to the creation of U.S. Steel, the first billion-dollar corporation. With his fortune secured, Carnegie turned his focus to philanthropy.

Carnegie firmly believed in the principle of '*The Gospel of Wealth*', an essay he wrote in 1889. In it he argued that the rich had a moral obligation to use their wealth for the betterment of society. He opposed excessive inheritance, believing that passing down vast fortunes to heirs could encourage idleness. Instead, he advocated for using wealth to fund public goods that would empower individuals, such as education, libraries, and scientific research. His philanthropic efforts were vast and transformative including the construction of over 2,500 libraries worldwide, including nearly 1,700 in the United States and a great many in Scotland - all of which had to be made of stone. He developed the Institution for Science which supported research and innovation. He advocated for world peace, funding the Carnegie Endowment for International Peace and donating funds for the construction of the Peace Palace in The Hague, Netherlands and donated to hospitals, music halls and universities, ensuring that his fortune contributed to society's long-term benefit. By the time of his death, Carnegie had given away nearly 90% of his wealth, demonstrating his commitment to his philosophy of responsible wealth distribution.

Despite his philanthropy, Carnegie's legacy is not without criticism. His business practices were often ruthless and he was involved in some of the most controversial labour disputes in American history. The most infamous event was the Homestead Strike of 1892, a violent labour conflict at Carnegie Steel's Homestead plant in Pennsylvania. When workers protested wage cuts, the company, under the management of Henry Clay Frick, hired private security (Pinkerton agents) to break the strike. A bloody clash ensued, resulting in multiple deaths. Carnegie, who was in Scotland at the time, later expressed regret over the violence but many saw his company's actions as prioritising profit over worker welfare. Carnegie also opposed labor unions, believing that industry should not be constrained by collective bargaining. This stance put him at odds with many workers, leading to accusations of hypocrisy. Some critics questioned how a man who preached social responsibility could tolerate harsh working conditions in his own factories. Carnegie died on August 11, 1919, leaving behind a complex but undeniable legacy. He transformed the steel industry, helped shape modern philanthropy and contributed to the intellectual and cultural development of countless individuals. His contributions to education, libraries and scientific research continue to benefit society.

THE INVENTOR OF REFRIGERATION

William Cullen. Chemist and Inventor (1710 - 1790)

William Cullen was born in 1710, in Hamilton. He came from a relatively well-off family and had access to good education. His father, William was a lawyer retained by the Duke of Hamilton as a factor and his mother was Elizabeth Roberton of Whistlebury. He studied at the Old Grammar School of Hamilton (renamed in 1848 as Hamilton Academy) and subsequently at the University of Glasgow, where he developed an interest in medicine and chemistry. Later, he moved to the University of Edinburgh, where he continued his studies and began making a name for himself in the scientific community.

After completing his education, Cullen briefly worked as a physician but his true passion lay in research and teaching. He returned to academia and held various teaching positions, eventually becoming a professor at the University of Glasgow and later at the University of Edinburgh. Cullen was widely respected for his engaging lectures and his ability to make complex scientific concepts accessible to his students.

One of William Cullen's most important contributions to science came in 1756 when he demonstrated the first known instance of artificial refrigeration. At the time, cooling was primarily achieved through natural means such as storing ice harvested from frozen lakes or using underground cellars. Cullen's work showed that cooling could be achieved artificially, paving the way for modern refrigeration.

His experiment involved the use of a pump to create a vacuum in a container of diethyl ether, a volatile liquid. As the pressure inside the container dropped, the ether began to boil at a much lower temperature than normal. This boiling process absorbed heat from the surrounding environment, causing the container to cool significantly. Although Cullen's experiment did not have any immediate practical applications, it demonstrated the principle that underlies modern refrigeration; the use of evaporating liquids to absorb heat and lower temperatures.

While William Cullen did not build a practical refrigerator, his demonstration provided a crucial scientific foundation. His work inspired later scientists and inventors to explore ways to harness refrigeration for practical use. Over the next century, other inventors built upon Cullen's discovery, refining the process and developing machines capable of producing controlled cooling.

In the early 19th century, American inventor Jacob Perkins created one of the first working refrigeration systems using vapour compression, a concept closely related to Cullen's original experiment. Later, James Harrison, an Australian journalist and engineer, developed the first commercial refrigeration system, which was used (perhaps not surprisingly) to cool beer and meat. These advancements eventually led to the development of the household refrigerators and industrial cooling systems we use today.

Although refrigeration is what William Cullen is best remembered for, he made many other important contributions to science. As a physician, he was a key figure in medical education and was highly respected for his work in medical chemistry. He published several influential medical texts, including works on the nervous system and diseases of the digestive system.

Cullen was also an important figure in chemistry, particularly in the study of gases and the properties of heat. His work on latent heat - how substances absorb and release heat without changing temperature - was an important step toward understanding thermodynamics. His lectures on chemistry were widely attended, and his students included some of the leading scientists of the next generation, including Joseph Black, who made significant discoveries in heat and gases.

Today, refrigeration is essential to modern life. It allows us to preserve food for longer periods, transport perishable goods across great distances, and create controlled environments for medical and scientific purposes. While Cullen's experiment in 1756 was a small step, it set in motion a series of advancements that have shaped the way we live.

William Cullen passed away on February 5, 1790, but his legacy lives on in multiple fields of science. His work on refrigeration was foundational and while he did not invent the modern refrigerator, he provided the first scientific proof that artificial cooling was possible. His research influenced the development of cooling systems that revolutionised food storage, medicine, and industrial processes.

THE TELEPHONE VISIONARY

Alexander Graham Bell: Scientist and Inventor. (1847 - 1922)

Alexander Graham Bell was born in 1847 in Edinburgh to a family deeply involved in speech and communication. His father, Alexander Melville Bell, was a phonetician who developed Visible Speech, a system of symbols designed to help deaf individuals learn spoken language. His grandfather and uncle were also elocutionists, making speech and sound a central theme in Bell's upbringing.

Bell showed an early curiosity for science and problem-solving. As a child, he conducted experiments in sound and mechanics, demonstrating an inventive mind. He received his early education at the Royal High School in Edinburgh but was not an outstanding student. Despite this, he was passionate about learning, especially in areas related to speech and sound. In 1865, Bell moved to London to continue his studies. However, after the deaths of his two brothers from tuberculosis, his family immigrated to Canada in 1870, seeking a healthier climate. Shortly after, in 1871, Bell relocated to the United States, where he accepted a teaching position at the Boston School for the Deaf. His work with the deaf community greatly influenced his scientific interests and ultimately led to his greatest invention.

Bell's research in sound and speech inspired him to explore ways of transmitting voice electronically. During the 1870s, he experimented with various sound transmission methods and worked closely with his assistant, Thomas Watson. Bell's goal was to create a device that could send speech over electrical wires.

On March 10, 1876, Bell successfully transmitted his first intelligible sentence over the telephone; "Mr. Watson, come here, I want to see you". This breakthrough was a pivotal moment in communication history. Later that year, Bell showcased his invention at the Centennial Exposition in Philadelphia, where it captured the attention of Emperor Dom Pedro II of Brazil and British scientist Sir William Thomson (later Lord Kelvin), bringing Bell international recognition.

In 1877, Bell co-founded the Bell Telephone Company, which played a crucial role in expanding telephone technology. Over time, the telephone evolved from a novel invention into a global necessity, transforming personal and business communications.

Bell's telephone patent (U.S. Patent No. 174,465) became one of the most contested patents in history. Several inventors, including Elisha Gray, claimed to have developed similar devices around the same time. A notable controversy arose when Elisha Gray filed a caveat (a legal notice of intention to patent an invention) on February 14, 1876, just a few hours after Bell's patent application.

Despite numerous legal challenges, Bell's patent held up in court, securing his place as the recognised inventor of the telephone. The Bell Telephone Company grew rapidly, eventually becoming AT&T, one of the world's largest telecommunications corporations.

While the telephone was Bell's most famous invention, he continued to innovate in various fields. Some of his other contributions include the Photophone, a device that transmitted sound using light waves. This early work in optical communication foreshadowed fibre optic technology. He also developed an early version of the metal detector in an attempt to locate a bullet lodged in President James Garfield's body after he was shot in 1881. Although the device was not successful in that instance, it laid the foundation for modern metal detectors.

Bell had a strong interest in flight and worked on developing airplanes and hydrofoil boats. His hydrofoil, the HD-4, set a world water-speed record in 1919. Finally, he remained dedicated to improving communication for the deaf. He supported the oral method of education, which emphasised speech and lip-reading rather than sign language. Though his views on deaf education were controversial, his efforts helped shape modern approaches to hearing impairment. Alexander Graham Bell continued his scientific work until his later years. He became a founding member of the National Geographic Society in 1888 and served as its president from 1898 to 1903. His passion for innovation never waned, and he remained engaged in various experiments until his death.

Bell passed away on August 2, 1922, at his home in Baddeck, Nova Scotia, Canada. As a tribute, all telephone services in North America observed a moment of silence during his funeral. His contributions to science, technology, and communication left an indelible mark on history.

SUSTAINABLE URBAN PLANNING

Patrick Geddes. Biologist, Sociologist, and Urban Planner (1854 - 1932)

Patrick Geddes was born in Ballater, Aberdeenshire in 1854. He grew up in Perth and displayed an early interest in the natural sciences. He studied biology at the Royal College of Mines in London under the famous scientist Thomas Henry Huxley, who was a strong advocate of Darwin's theory of evolution. This education deeply influenced Geddes' thinking, particularly his approach to the relationships between environment, society, and development.

Geddes' early work as a biologist focused on botany and evolution, but he soon became interested in the application of biological principles to human societies. He believed that the way cities and societies evolved could be studied similarly to living organisms, with environmental, economic, and social factors all interacting in complex ways.

While working as a biologist, Geddes developed theories about how organisms and environments influence each other. He extended these ideas to human societies, arguing that cities and communities should be understood as living entities shaped by their surroundings. This led him to develop the 'Regional Survey' approach, in which he advocated for studying geography, history, and culture before making urban planning decisions.

Geddes developed the 'Folk-Work-Place' model, which emphasised the interdependence of people (folk), their activities (work), and their environment (place). He argued that sustainable urban development must consider all three aspects rather than focusing only on economic growth or infrastructure.

Geddes is often regarded as one of the pioneers of modern urban planning. At a time when many city planners favoured large-scale demolitions and rebuilding projects, Geddes proposed an alternative approach called 'conservative surgery'. Instead of destroying old neighbourhoods to make way for modern developments, Geddes believed in preserving and improving existing urban structures while making small, strategic interventions to enhance living conditions.

His work in Edinburgh's Old Town is a prime example of this philosophy. In the late 19th century, Edinburgh's historic Old Town had fallen into decay, with overcrowded tenements and poor sanitation. Rather than demolishing these historic areas, Geddes sought to revitalise them through careful restoration, improved public spaces, and community engagement. His approach helped preserve the character of the city while making it more liveable.

Geddes' urban planning philosophy extended beyond individual cities to entire regions. He argued that cities should be designed in harmony with their natural surroundings and that planners should consider factors such as climate, geography, and local culture when designing urban spaces. These ideas were ahead of their time and anticipated modern sustainable development principles.

Geddes' ideas on urban planning were not confined to Scotland. Between 1915 and 1919, he worked in India, where he was invited to advise on the planning of several cities. During his time there, he conducted surveys of over fifty towns and developed urban improvement plans that focused on preserving cultural heritage while addressing modern needs. His approach was particularly influential in cities like Mumbai and Indore. He also worked in the Middle East, particularly in Jerusalem, where he contributed to urban planning projects that sought to integrate historic preservation with modern infrastructure. His work in these regions demonstrated his belief that urban planning should respect local traditions and environmental conditions rather than imposing foreign architectural styles or rigid Western models.

Geddes was deeply committed to education and believed that urban planning and social development should be taught through a multidisciplinary approach. In Edinburgh, he established the Outlook Tower, which served as a centre for urban research, education, and cultural exchange. The tower contained exhibits on geography, sociology, and urban planning, allowing visitors to explore how cities and regions developed over time.

His educational philosophy emphasised experiential learning, fieldwork, and community involvement. He believed that students should not simply learn from textbooks but should engage directly with the world around them. This approach was later adopted by many urban studies and geography programs around the world.

THE WORLD ON TWO WHEELS

Mark Ian Macleod Beaumont. Cyclist and Adventurer (1983 -)

Mark Beaumont was born in 1983 in Swindon but was raised in Scotland where he was home-schooled until the age of eleven by his mother, Una. He was then educated at the High School of Dundee and grew up in the rural countryside of Perthshire. From an early age, he showed an adventurous spirit, cycling long distances around his local area. At the age of twelve, he embarked on his first major cycling adventure, riding across Scotland from John O'Groats to Land's End in England - an impressive feat for someone so young.

His passion for adventure and endurance sports continued through his teenage years. While studying politics at the University of Glasgow, where was awarded *'Graduate of the Year'* in 2009, he took on increasingly challenging expeditions, further developing the mindset and resilience that would later define his career.

Beaumont first gained international attention in 2008 when he set out to break the world record for cycling around the world. At the time, the record stood at 276 days. Beaumont meticulously planned his journey, mapping a route that would take him through 20 countries across four continents.

Setting off from Paris in August 2007, he cycled through Europe, the Middle East, India, Southeast Asia, Australia, New Zealand, North America, and finally back through Europe. Throughout the journey, he battled extreme weather, logistical challenges, and even a violent robbery in Louisiana, where he was held at gunpoint.

Despite these obstacles, Beaumont completed the journey in an astonishing 194 days and 17 hours, smashing the previous record by over two months. His feat earned him a place in the Guinness World Records and established him as one of the world's leading endurance cyclists.

After his success in cycling around the world, Beaumont sought new challenges. In 2010, he embarked on another record-breaking adventure: cycling the length of the Americas, from Alaska to Argentina. Covering over 13,000 miles, he combined this challenge with mountaineering, summiting North America's highest peak, Denali (Mount McKinley), and South America's highest peak, Aconcagua.

This expedition was as much about endurance as it was about overcoming natural obstacles. He faced extreme cold in Alaska, the heat of the Atacama Desert, and the challenges of high-altitude climbing. The journey took him just over five months and once again demonstrated his ability to push physical and mental limits.

In addition to his cycling exploits, Beaumont has taken on extreme endurance challenges in other disciplines. In 2012, he attempted to row across the Atlantic Ocean as part of a team, but disaster struck when their boat capsized in the mid-Atlantic. The crew had to be rescued after enduring days of survival in rough seas. This experience reinforced Beaumont's resilience and his ability to adapt in extreme situations.

He has also undertaken Arctic expeditions, pushing himself to the limits in some of the most challenging environments on Earth.

Never one to rest on past achievements, Beaumont set his sights on an even more ambitious goal: cycling around the world in just 80 days. Inspired by Jules Verne's famous novel Around the World in Eighty Days, he meticulously planned a new record attempt, incorporating lessons learned from his first journey.

In July 2017, he set off from Paris with the goal of riding 240 miles per day, averaging sixteen hours in the saddle. His journey took him through Europe, Russia, Mongolia, China, Australia, New Zealand, North America, and back through Europe. Despite extreme fatigue, injuries, and sleep deprivation, he completed the 18,000-mile journey in an astonishing 78 days, 14 hours, and 40 minutes—smashing his previous record and setting a new benchmark for endurance cycling. This achievement was widely celebrated in the cycling world and beyond. It was a demonstration of meticulous planning, physical endurance, and mental strength, cementing Beaumont's status as one of the greatest endurance athletes of his generation.

He is also involved in charity work and has used his expeditions to raise money for various causes.

SELECTED QUOTES

Brian Quail

"Nuclearism is the highest form of imperialism - as Lenin didn't say!"

"We are deluding ourselves if we imagine we can maintain an Independence goal and defend a nostalgia for Britishness at the same time."

James Blyth

"The wind is proverbially free and is to be had everywhere."

Andrew Carnegie

"The man who dies rich, dies disgraced".

"There is no class so pitiably wretched as that which possesses money and nothing else."

"And while the law of competition may be sometimes hard for the individual, it is best for the race, because it ensures the survival of the fittest in every department".

Alexander Graham Bell

"Mr. Watson! Come here; I want to see you." (First telephone call)

"The day will come when the man at the telephone will be able to *see* the distant person to whom he is speaking."

Professor William Cullen

"Chemistry is an art that has furnished the world with a great number of useful facts, and has thereby contributed to the improvement of many arts; but these facts lie scattered in many different books, involved in obscure terms, mixed with many falsehoods, and joined to a great deal of false philosophy; so that it is not great wonder that chemistry has not been so much studied as might have been expected with regard to so useful a branch of knowledge, and that many professors are themselves but very superficially acquainted with it".

Patrick Geddes

"Yet the leaf is the chief product and phenomenon of Life: this is a green world, with animals comparatively few and small, and all dependent on the leaves. By leaves we live. Some people have strange ideas that they live by money. They think energy is generated by the circulation of coins. Whereas the world is mainly a vast leaf colony, growing on and forming a leafy soil, not a mere mineral mass: and we live not by the jingling of our coins, but by the fullness of our harvests".

"But a city is more than a place in space, it is a drama in time".

Mark Beaumont

"Cycling is the most efficient way to travel and a great way to see the world."

"I don't want the next twenty years of my career to be the same as the first twenty."

"I was in a motel, definitely in the wrong part of town, I was literally trying to get the bike fixed and get back on the road without losing time and there was a fight happening outside my hotel room. I foolishly...well, I listened for a while thinking somebody's going to get killed, and foolishly opened the door and tried to step in".

THE PIONEER OF MODERN ROAD CONSTRUCTION

John Loudon McAdam. Roads Engineer (1756 - 1836)

John Loudon McAdam was born on September 23, 1756, in Ayr, into a well-established family. His father was a wealthy merchant, which provided young McAdam with access to education and opportunities. However, his life took a significant turn in 1770 when his family lost much of their wealth, prompting him to move to New York at the age of fourteen to live with an uncle who was a successful merchant.

In America, McAdam worked in his uncle's business, where he gained skills in trade and finance. However, during the American Revolution, he remained loyal to the British Crown and returned to Scotland in 1783 when Britain lost the war. Back home, he acquired the Sauchrie estate in Ayrshire, where he became interested in road construction while overseeing the management of his land.

During the late 18th and early 19th centuries, roads in Scotland were in terrible condition. Most roads were either muddy and impassable in wet weather or full of ruts and stones, making travel difficult and dangerous. Traditional road construction relied on large stones, which often made the roads uneven and prone to damage.

McAdam recognised the need for a more efficient, cost-effective and durable road-building method. He began experimenting with new techniques that would lead to stronger and longer-lasting roads.

McAdam's revolutionary approach to road construction involved a few key principles. First, he emphasised that roads should be slightly elevated above the surrounding ground to allow water to drain away, preventing erosion and damage. Unlike previous methods that used large stones as a base, McAdam proposed using layers of small, angular stones which would naturally compact under traffic, creating a solid, stable surface. Unlike the older techniques that required a thick stone foundation, McAdam proved that a carefully layered surface of smaller stones could provide better stability. Traditional road builders used clay or other binding materials which often became muddy. McAdam's method relied on the natural interlocking of crushed stones, which allowed for better drainage and a more durable road surface. These principles resulted in smoother, stronger, and more durable roads that required less maintenance and were cheaper to construct.

McAdam's ideas were first tested in Bristol, England, where he worked as a surveyor of roads in 1816. His method quickly proved successful, and local authorities noticed the improved durability and reduced maintenance costs.

By 1819, McAdam had been appointed Surveyor-General of Roads for Britain, allowing him to implement his system on a larger scale. Over the next few decades, many major roads in Britain, Europe, and America adopted the macadamised technique.

One of the greatest advantages of his method was that it made roads more accessible year-round, allowing for faster movement of people, goods, and military forces.

McAdam's system transformed road-building, but it also laid the foundation for later innovations. In the early 20th century, McAdam's method was further improved by John Loudon McAdam's successor, Edgar Hooley who added tar to the crushed stone surface. This "tarmac" (short for "tar-macadam") became the basis for modern asphalt roads which facilitated faster trade and travel, playing a crucial role in the expansion of industry and commerce during the Industrial Revolution.

McAdam's principles influenced road construction worldwide and many modern highways still incorporate elements of his design.

Despite his contributions, McAdam was not wealthy in his later years as he spent much of his money on research and lobbying for his method. Also, the British government was slow to compensate him for his work, though he was eventually awarded £10,000 (a significant sum at the time) in 1827. McAdam's work gained international recognition, and by the time of his death, his system had transformed road infrastructure across Europe and North America.

John Loudon McAdam died on November 26, 1836, at the age of 80. Although he did not become extraordinarily wealthy from his invention, his contribution to road-building remains one of the most important advancements in transportation history; the word "macadam" becoming a standard term in road construction. Today, nearly every paved road owes something to John Loudon McAdam's vision.

THE PIONEER OF EARLY ELECTRIC LIGHT AND WIRELESS COMMUNICATION

James Bowman Lindsay. Inventor (1799 - 1862)

James Lindsay was born in 1799 in Carmyllie, a small village in Angus. His early life was marked by a deep curiosity for learning, particularly in mathematics and science. Despite coming from a humble background, he pursued education fervently, showing a remarkable talent for electrical experiments and engineering concepts from an early age.

After working as a weaver in his youth, Lindsay's intellectual capabilities allowed him to secure a place at the University of St. Andrews in 1821. At university, he studied a variety of subjects, including astronomy, physics, and languages. His passion for both scientific research and linguistics continued throughout his life as he later worked on a universal phonetic language. However, it was his contributions to electrical experimentation that left a lasting mark.

One of Lindsay's most notable achievements was his early experimentation with electric lighting. In 1835, he demonstrated an electric lamp, one of the earliest examples of artificial electric illumination. His lamp used a constant electric current to produce light, which was revolutionary for the time.

This experiment predated Thomas Edison's more well-known work on electric lighting by several decades. However, unlike Edison, Lindsay did not commercialise or develop his invention further due to financial and resource constraints. His work, however, demonstrated that electric light could be a viable alternative to gas lamps, influencing future developments in electrical engineering.

Despite the significance of his work, Lindsay did not patent his invention. His primary focus was on experimentation and scientific discovery rather than commercial gain, a decision that may have contributed to his relative obscurity compared to other inventors of the period. Perhaps even more groundbreaking than his work in electric lighting was Lindsay's pioneering research into wireless communication. In the mid-19th century, long before Guglielmo Marconi and Nikola Tesla made their mark in radio technology, Lindsay was experimenting with transmitting messages without wires.

By 1854, he had successfully demonstrated a method of wireless telegraphy. His approach involved using water as a conductor to transmit electrical signals across distances. In one public demonstration, he transmitted signals across the River Tay in Dundee, proving that wireless communication was possible.

Lindsay envisioned his system being used for communication between ships at sea or across bodies of water where laying cables would be impractical. Unfortunately, despite the promise of his research, he lacked the necessary funding and government support to develop the technology further. Had his ideas been fully realised and refined, he might have become one of the key figures in the history of radio communication.

Beyond his scientific endeavours, Lindsay was also deeply interested in languages and literature. He dedicated much of his later life to the study of a universal phonetic language, aiming to create a system that could be understood by people across different linguistic backgrounds. Although this project never reached completion, it highlights his intellectual versatility and ambition. He also compiled extensive research on ancient languages, biblical studies, and astronomy. His work in these areas was not as groundbreaking as his electrical experiments, but it reflects the breadth of his intellectual curiosity.

Despite his impressive achievements, Lindsay struggled with financial difficulties throughout his life. Unlike contemporaries such as England's Michael Faraday, he did not receive strong institutional support or sponsorship which limited his ability fully to develop and promote his inventions. Additionally, his lack of patents meant that he did not gain financial benefits from his pioneering work in electric lighting and wireless telegraphy. His tendency to focus on pure scientific inquiry rather than commercialisation likely contributed to his historical obscurity.

He spent his later years in relative poverty, continuing his studies and experiments despite his financial struggles. His contributions went largely unrecognised during his lifetime, and he died on June 29, 1862, in Dundee. In his honour, Dundee has commemorated his achievements with plaques and exhibitions highlighting his contributions to electrical science. While he may not have gained the recognition he deserved in his lifetime, his legacy lives on in the technologies he helped pioneer.

THE LAST OF THE RED CLYDESIDERS

Harry McShane. Communist, Journalist, Trades Union Organiser. (1891 - 1988)

Harry McShane was sometimes referred to as 'the last of the Red Clydesiders' and was one of the leading activists in the British Marxist movement. Born in the working-class Gorbals district of Glasgow, he was brought up mainly by his Irish catholic grandparents before developing an interest in socialism which early on led to his complete rejection of religion. He joined the Independent Labour Party in 1909, the newly-formed British Socialist Party in 1911, and the Communist Party of Great Britain in 1922. He became a revolutionary Marxist in 1908, (and died a revolutionary Marxist aged 96 in 1988), possibly the only person in history to have been a revolutionary Marxist for eighty years. He was active in campaigns against Britain's involvement in the First World War, which included activity during a brief spell in the army. He joined so as to promulgate his anti-war and socialist views within the ranks, declaring upon entry that he would not shoot a German soldier. He refused inoculation (thereby not being permitted to go to the front) and persuaded his fellow soldiers to follow suit. Eventually he accepted inoculation in order to obtain home leave but upon his return to Glasgow, he dumped his uniform in the River Clyde, refused to return and was never pursued by the War Office.

Housing conditions and wages in Glasgow, according to McShane, were deplorable and he became involved in organising support for tenants evicted from Glasgow tenements because they could not afford their rents. "At that time," he recalled, "engineering labourers got a pound and threepence a week and engineers got thirty-two and eightpence. Very few skilled workers got more than two pounds unless they worked overtime but there was very little overtime to go round." He also worked for the Tramp Trust Unlimited, which was formed by his friend and leading Scottish socialist John Maclean to campaign for a minimum wage, a six-hour day and other socialist policies. He was the

Scottish correspondent of the Daily Worker and Scottish organiser of the National Unemployed Workers Movement. In workplaces where he was employed as a skilled engineer, he led a number of hunger marches organised by the National Unemployed Workers' Movement. In 1953 he left the Communist Party of Great Britain as members were always expected to agree with the leadership. He was disciplined for not taking part in a standing ovation for a party official and resigned although he had many other disagreements with its leadership but remained a convinced socialist for the remainder of his life. In 1954, he combined with other socialist figures such as Eric Heffer to create a new organisation, the Federation of Marxist Groups. Wary of joining another political organisation, in 1963, he nevertheless attended the first fledgling meeting of the International Socialists, forerunner of the Socialist Workers Party, in Glasgow's Horseshoe Bar near the city's Central Station and never subsequently missed a meeting.

In his book, *No Mean Fighter*, he manages to convey the complex evolution of political movements in an accessible way. McShane's analysis of the political and social climate also provides valuable historical insights as when he wrote about the Russian Revolution: 'We began to now realise what was meant by revolution. We had only known working-class revolt: now we could talk about working-class power'. He also criticised a number of his academic colleagues when he stated, 'The intellectuals are writing for one another instead of for working-class people; they seem to think that workers can't read!' McShane would never be accused of that calumny.

Arrested many times for sedition he nevertheless returned to work as an engineer aged sixty-two until his retirement at the age of sixty-nine in order to become eligible for an old age pension. Aged ninety-three he was awarded the Freedom of the City of Glasgow for his services to the Labour and Trade Union movements at a ceremony in the City Chambers. At its conclusion, the programmed British National Anthem was discretely overlooked and 'I Belong to Glasgow' sung instead. Earlier that day McShane unveiled a plaque in City Hall to his friend John Maclean whom he viewed as the most outstanding figure brought forward by the Scottish Labour Movement and as a 'world figure'.

Throughout his life, he argued that 'socialism will be possible only when the workers, those who meet the needs of society, decide that they are determined to lay the living conditions of mankind on a new foundation.

The whole future of humanity rests on the emergence of the proletariat as the creative force in society'.

He died in an old people's home, leaving a few books to his friends. He survived solely on his pension for the last twenty-eight years of his life and died aged ninety-six in 1988.

SONGS OF A SOURDOUGH

Robert William Service. Poet (1874 - 1958)

Although born in Preston in England, Robert William Service was of Scottish lineage. His father, also Robert, was a banker from Kilwinning in Ayrshire and bestowed Robert the middle name William in honour of a rich uncle but when no provision was made for young Robert in his will, he dropped the middle name.

Aged five, he was sent to live in Kilwinning with his three maiden aunts and his paternal grandfather who was the town's postmaster. On his sixth birthday he was said to have composed his first verse, a grace, and three years later rejoined his parents when aged nine when they moved to Glasgow where he attended Hillhead High School. Upon leaving, he joined the Commercial Bank of Scotland, later to become the Royal Bank of Scotland.

His sense of adventure took him, aged twenty-one, to Vancouver Island in Canada. He travelled a lot in the Western United States, Mexico and British Columbia undertaking employment as he could find it. It was there while working as a store assistant that he met Charles Gibbons, editor of the Victoria Daily Colonist who invited him to submit his work. In July 1900, six of his poems had appeared in the paper. In 1903 while short of money, Service was hired by the Canadian Branch of Commerce in British Columbia where he showed promise. The following year he was sent first to Kamloops in British Columbia before further dispatching him to Whitehorse, a frontier town, less than ten years old, in the Yukon.

During this period, Service continued writing and saving his verses (he felt sufficiently abashed by his talents that he tended to refer to his work as mere verses rather than poems). However, more than a third of the poems in his first published volume had been written before he moved to the Yukon in 1904.

While working at the bank in Whitehorse, Service began writing verses about the North. His most famous poem, '*The Shooting of Dan McGrew*', was composed in 1906 while he was out for a walk. Inspired by the characters he had met in saloons and mining camps, he penned the poem in a single night. Encouraged by its reception, he wrote another legendary ballad, '*The Cremation of Sam McGee*', based on a real-life prospector's story.

In 1907, he published *'Songs of a Sourdough'* (titled *'The Spell of the Yukon and Other Verses'* in the United States). The book was an instant success, selling thousands of copies and making Service famous. Readers were captivated by his lively storytelling, strong rhymes, and ability to capture the harsh beauty and lawlessness of the Yukon.

With the success of his first collection, Service left his banking job and devoted himself to writing full-time. Over the next few years, he published several more books, including *'Ballads of a Cheechako'* (1909) and *'Rhymes of a Rolling Stone'* (1912), further cementing his reputation as the poet of the North.

At the outbreak of World War I, Service wanted to enlist but was rejected for military service due to health reasons. Instead, he worked as an ambulance driver for the Red Cross in France, witnessing firsthand the horrors of war. He later wrote *'Rhymes of a Red Cross Man'* in 1916, a collection of war poetry that reflected his experiences.

After the war, Service continued to travel. He lived in Paris for many years, mingling with the literary elite of the time, including Ernest Hemingway and F. Scott Fitzgerald. He also spent time in Hollywood, where some of his works were adapted into films. Despite his success, he remained a private man, preferring the quiet of his travels over the limelight of literary circles. In the 1930s and 1940s, Service continued to write poetry and novels, though none achieved the same level of fame as his early Yukon works. During World War II, he lived in France but was forced to flee to California when the Nazis occupied the country. After the war, he returned to Europe and settled in Monte Carlo, where he lived comfortably until his death on September 11, 1958. Despite being dismissed by some literary critics as a mere ballad-maker, Robert Service remains one of the most widely read poets in the English language. His works have endured because of their accessibility, humour, and sense of adventure. He captured the spirit of the frontier, immortalising the wild landscapes and larger-than-life characters of the Yukon. The town of Dawson City, where he once lived, maintains his cabin as a historic site, attracting visitors who want to step into the world he so vividly described.

PIONEERING RESTAURATEUR AND PATRON OF THE ARTS

Miss Catherine Cranston, Restauranteur (1849 - 1934)

Catherine Cranston, widely known as Kate Cranston or Miss Cranston, was born into a prosperous Glasgow family. Her father, George Cranston, was a successful hotelier and tea merchant which gave her early exposure to the hospitality trade. During this period, Glasgow was a booming industrial city, and social reformers were promoting temperance movements to counteract the excessive alcohol consumption among its citizens. Tearooms emerged as a respectable alternative to public houses, offering people - especially women - a space to socialise without alcohol. Like other cities in the United Kingdom, Glasgow, due to the Temperance Movement, sought an alternative to male-centred public houses. Tea had previously been a luxury for the rich but from the 1830s it was promoted as an alternative to alcoholic drinks. Cranston was influenced by these social movements and recognised an opportunity to create elegant spaces where people from all walks of life could dine and interact. Unlike many women of her time, she pursued an independent career, choosing to manage and expand her own business rather than conform to traditional domestic roles.

Although she was known professionally as Miss Cranston, Kate married Major John Cochrane, an engineer and Provost of Barrhead, in 1892. The couple lived in a semi-detached villa in Carlibar Road in Barrhead. Some years later, they moved to a much larger mansion house called Househill in the nearby village of Nitshill. This time, Charles Rennie Mackintosh was commissioned to re-design the interior in 1904 and the completed house became known as Hous'hill.

In 1878, Miss Cranston opened her first tearoom on Argyle Street, Glasgow. It was a modest establishment compared to what would come later, but it reflected her vision; a beautifully designed, welcoming space offering high-quality tea, coffee and light meals. The success of this venture led her to open more locations in Glasgow; on Buchanan Street in 1896, Ingram Street in 1900 and Sauchiehall Street in1903.

Each of her tearooms was unique, but they shared key characteristics: attention to detail, impeccable service, and an emphasis on artistic and architectural excellence. Unlike the dark, smoky interiors of traditional dining spaces, Cranston's tearooms featured light, airy environments with carefully curated decor. She employed leading designers and artists to craft spaces that were both functional and visually stunning.

One of Cranston's most significant contributions to art and design was her collaboration with renowned Scottish architect and designer Charles Rennie Mackintosh. At a time when Mackintosh's *avant-garde* style was not widely accepted, Cranston recognised his talent and commissioned him to design interiors for her tearooms.

Mackintosh's contributions began with small projects such as furniture and decorative panels before he was given full control over the design of her famous Willow Tearooms on Sauchiehall Street in 1903. This establishment remains one of the best examples of Mackintosh's work, blending Art Nouveau and Japanese-inspired minimalism with his distinctive geometric patterns and elegant simplicity.

The Willow Tearooms were a masterpiece of holistic design. Every element, from the furniture and lighting to the wall decorations, was carefully crafted to create an immersive experience. Cranston gave Mackintosh the freedom to experiment, resulting in iconic spaces such as the White Room, a serene and ethereal environment, and the *Room de Luxe,* an opulent setting with silver accents and stained-glass details. These designs set a new standard for tearoom aesthetics, influencing interior design for years to come.

Miss Cranston's tearooms were more than just places to drink tea - they were social and cultural hubs. They provided an elegant yet accessible venue where women could meet without male chaperones which was a progressive idea at the time. Her establishments also attracted writers, artists, and intellectuals, fostering a creative and open-minded atmosphere.

Cranston retired in 1917 and lived a quiet life until her death in 1934. Despite her business closing, her impact on Glasgow's cultural landscape endured. The Willow Tearooms, in particular, became an enduring symbol of the city's architectural and artistic heritage. Efforts have been made to restore and preserve these spaces, ensuring that her legacy remains alive.

THE COLOSSUS OF ROADS

Thomas Telford. Civil Engineer (1757 - 1834)

Thomas Telford was born in 1757, in the small village of Glendinning in Dumfriesshire. His father, a shepherd, died shortly after his birth, leaving his mother to raise him in poverty. Despite these humble beginnings, Telford showed an early talent for craftsmanship and problem-solving.

He started his career as an apprentice stonemason, working on various construction projects in Scotland. His skills in masonry led him to Edinburgh and later to London, where he worked on the restoration of Somerset House under the supervision of architect Sir William Chambers. Telford's ambition and talent soon attracted attention, allowing him to transition from masonry to civil engineering.

Telford's first major breakthrough came in 1787 when he was appointed Surveyor of Public Works for Shropshire. In this role, he was responsible for the maintenance and improvement of roads, bridges, and drainage systems. He quickly gained a reputation for his innovative and durable designs, particularly in bridge construction.

One of his early successes was the Buildwas Bridge over the River Severn, completed in 1796 but now destroyed. This was one of the first bridges made entirely of cast iron, showcasing Telford's ability to incorporate new materials into his designs. His expertise in bridge building would later lead to the construction of some of Britain's most iconic bridges.

Telford revolutionised road building in Britain, earning him the nickname 'The Colossus of Roads'. He was commissioned by the government to improve the country's road network, particularly in Scotland and Wales. His roads were designed with careful attention to drainage, camber and durability. He introduced techniques such as layering stones of different sizes to create a solid foundation, which made his roads smoother and longer-lasting than those built using traditional methods.

One of his most famous projects was the London to Holyhead Road, a crucial route connecting England to Ireland via the port of Holyhead in Wales. This road included several engineering marvels, including the

Menai Suspension Bridge (completed in 1826), which remains one of his most celebrated works.

Telford built over one thousand bridges during his career, many of which were notable for their strength and innovative use of materials. Some of his most famous bridges include the Menai Suspension Bridge spanning the Menai Strait between mainland Wales and the Isle of Anglesey, the Craigellachie Bridge, an elegant cast-iron arch bridge over the River Spey in Scotland and the Conwy Suspension Bridge in Wales, another pioneering suspension bridge that remains a landmark of early 19th-century engineering.

Telford also played a significant role in the expansion of Britain's canal network, which was essential for transporting goods during the Industrial Revolution. His work on canals included the Caledonian Canal which took nineteen years to build. This massive project connected Scotland's east and west coasts, allowing ships to avoid the dangerous waters around northern Scotland. Though it faced numerous challenges, it remains one of Telford's most ambitious engineering feats. He also constructed the Ellesmere Canal including the stunning Pontcysyllte Aqueduct, a cast-iron and masonry structure that carries the canal 126 feet above the River Dee in Wales. Completed in 1805, it is now a UNESCO World Heritage Site. His expertise extended to the design and improvement of harbours, including major works at Liverpool, Holyhead, and Aberdeen. His harbour designs focused on improving access for ships, reducing silting, and increasing efficiency for trade.

Telford was known for his meticulous attention to detail and commitment to using the best available materials and construction techniques. He also placed great emphasis on proper planning and surveying before construction began, ensuring that his projects were both functional and aesthetically pleasing. Unlike many of his contemporaries, Telford also had a strong interest in training and mentoring young engineers, helping to advance the profession of civil engineering in Britain. In 1820, he became the first president of the Institution of Civil Engineers, an organisation dedicated to advancing engineering knowledge and professional standards.

Telford continued working on major projects until his death in 1834 at the age of seventy-seven. He was buried in Westminster Abbey, a fitting honour for a man who had transformed Britain's infrastructure.

THE PIONEER OF THE PNEUMATIC TYRE

John Boyd Dunlop. Veterinarian and Inventor (1840 - 1921)

John Boyd Dunlop was born in1840, in Dreghorn, Ayrshire. He pursued a career in veterinary medicine, studying at the Dick Veterinary College in Edinburgh before establishing a successful practice in Downpatrick, Ireland. His veterinary work focused primarily on treating horses and farm animals, a profession that kept him closely connected to transportation and the use of wheeled vehicles.

Although he spent most of his life working as a veterinarian, Dunlop had an inventive mind and was interested in mechanical improvements. His greatest invention was not driven by professional ambition but by a practical problem he encountered in his daily life.

The idea for the pneumatic tyre came about in 1887 when Dunlop noticed his young son, Johnny, struggling to ride his tricycle over rough, cobbled streets in Belfast. The solid rubber tyres commonly used at the time made for a rough and uncomfortable ride. To solve this problem, Dunlop experimented with rubber tubing wrapped around the wooden wheels of the tricycle. He inflated the tubes with air and secured them with fabric, effectively creating the first practical air-filled tyres.

Dunlop's innovation dramatically improved the comfort and speed of the bicycle. The air cushion reduced vibrations and made riding on rough terrain significantly smoother. Recognising the potential of his invention, he sought a patent, which was granted on December 7, 1888.

Dunlop's invention gained widespread attention when a local cyclist, Willie Hume, used the pneumatic tyres in a series of bicycle races in 1889. Hume's overwhelming success in these races demonstrated the superiority of air-filled tyres over the solid rubber alternatives, generating immense interest in Dunlop's invention.

As demand for the new tyres increased, Dunlop partnered with businessman Harvey du Cros to establish the Dunlop Pneumatic Tyre Company. This company became instrumental in promoting and manufacturing the new tires, expanding their use beyond bicycles to motorcycles and eventually, automobiles.

By the 1890s, the pneumatic tyre had become the standard in the cycling industry, and the automobile industry soon adopted it as well. The rapid expansion of the Dunlop company led to the opening of manufacturing plants across Europe and beyond, solidifying its place as a dominant force in the tyre industry.

Despite his success, Dunlop faced legal challenges regarding the originality of his invention. It was later discovered that Stonehaven-born Robert William Thomson, another Scottish inventor, had patented a similar air-filled tyre in 1845. However, Thomson's design had not been commercially successful and Dunlop had independently developed and popularised the idea decades later.

As a result of these legal disputes, Dunlop lost his patent rights in 1890. Despite this setback, his company continued to thrive as he had already helped establish the pneumatic tyre as the industry standard. Dunlop himself gradually stepped away from the business, allowing others to manage its expansion.

Although Dunlop did not become a wealthy man from his invention, his contributions to transportation were invaluable. His pneumatic tyre laid the foundation for modern tyres used in bicycles, motorcycles, and automobiles. The improved comfort, speed, and efficiency provided by air-filled tyres helped fuel the growth of cycling and motoring in the late 19th and early 20th centuries.

The Dunlop brand remained one of the most recognisable names in the tyre industry, expanding into sports equipment and various other sectors. Today, Dunlop tyres are still widely used in motorsports and commercial vehicles, a testament to the lasting impact of his invention.

John Boyd Dunlop passed away on October 23, 1921, in Dublin, Ireland. While he did not reap significant financial rewards from his invention, he is remembered as a visionary who transformed transportation and mobility. His name continues to be associated with innovation and quality in the tyre industry, ensuring that his legacy endures.

COMEDY'S MOST CONTROVERSIAL VOICE

Jerry Sadowitz. Comedian and Magician (1961 -)

Jerry Sadowitz was born in 1961, in New Jersey, USA to his Scottish mother named Roslyn and a Jewish-American father who worked as a scrap metal merchant. His parents split up when he was three and he moved with his mother back to her native Glasgow when he was seven. Sadowitz attended Calderwood Lodge Primary and then Shawlands Academy in Glasgow. He took an interest in magic at the age of nine, and by the age of eleven he decided that he wanted to become a magician, acquiring books from Tam Shepherd's Magic and Joke Shop. Growing up, he also developed an interest in comedy, two passions that would define his career. His early life was not easy—he has spoken openly about struggling with depression and feeling like an outsider; this sense of alienation perhaps contributing to the anger and cynicism that would later become hallmarks of his comedic persona.

Sadowitz started performing stand-up in the early 1980s, quickly gaining a reputation for his abrasive, no-holds-barred approach. While many comedians of the time focused on observational humour or political satire, Sadowitz was something else entirely, unfiltered, confrontational and willing to say the unsayable. His act was not for the faint-hearted, featuring a mix of brutal insults, taboo subjects and a deep misanthropy that set him apart from his peers.

He first gained wider recognition in 1987 when he performed at the Edinburgh Festival Fringe, a platform that would remain central to his career. His act was notorious for its offensiveness, but it also showcased his sharp wit, unique delivery, and refusal to pander to audiences.

One of the defining aspects of Sadowitz's career has been the controversy surrounding his material. Unlike many comedians who occasionally push boundaries, Sadowitz has built an entire persona around going too far. His performances frequently include offensive jokes about race, gender, politics, and almost every sensitive topic imaginable. He has been described as both an anti-establishment hero and a comedian whose material is indefensible.

One of the most infamous moments of his career occurred in 1991 when he performed at a show in Canada and was punched unconscious by an audience member who took offence to one of his jokes. This incident cemented Sadowitz's reputation as one of the most dangerous acts in comedy.

He has also been banned from multiple venues and television networks. In 2022, his scheduled show at the Edinburgh Fringe was cancelled after one night due to complaints about his material. While some defended his right to free expression, others argued that his act had become too extreme for modern audiences. Sadowitz responded in his usual fashion, unapologetic and dismissive of his critics.

Despite the backlash, he has always had a loyal following. His fans argue that his comedy is not meant to be taken literally and that he operates in the tradition of shock comedy; using exaggeration, irony, and provocation to highlight societal hypocrisies.

Beyond comedy, Sadowitz is also a highly respected magician. In fact, he considers himself a magician first and a comedian second. He has written books on magic, performed sleight-of-hand tricks at prestigious venues and even hosted television shows focused on magic, such as *'The Gerry Sadowitz Show'* in the early 1990s.

Unlike his stand-up, which thrives on chaos and offence, Sadowitz's magic performances demonstrate incredible skill and precision. His ability to combine both talents - sometimes using magic tricks as part of his stand-up routine - sets him apart from other comedians.

While he may be best known for his controversial humor, those who follow the world of magic regard him as one of the most technically gifted sleight-of-hand artists alive today. His ability to shift between these two vastly different forms of entertainment is a testament to his unique talent. He is an irredeemable provocateur.

Despite never achieving much in the way of mainstream success, Sadowitz has influenced generations of comedians. His confrontational style paved the way for later stand-ups who push boundaries in their own ways. Many alternative comedians admire him for his refusal to compromise, even if they wouldn't dare imitate his approach. Regardless of one's stance, there's no denying that he is one of the most distinctive voices in British comedy.

SCOTLAND'S BELOVED CARTOONIST FRAE CALTON CREEK

William (Bud) Neill (1911 - 1970)

Born as William Neill in Glasgow's Partick, Bud Neill moved with his family shortly thereafter to Troon in Ayrshire. Growing up there, the young Neill would spend his Saturdays at the local cinema and displayed an early talent for drawing and humour. Before becoming a full-time cartoonist, he worked as a commercial artist, including a stint designing advertisements. His career as a cartoonist truly began when he started contributing to Scottish newspapers, a medium that would define his legacy.

During the 1930s and 1940s, Neill's cartoons appeared in several publications, including the Glasgow Evening Times and the Daily Record. His work, often featuring ordinary Glaswegians in exaggerated yet relatable scenarios, resonated deeply with readers. Neill had a knack for capturing the humour in everyday life, poking fun at Glaswegian speech, working-class struggles, and Scottish identity in a way that felt both affectionate and satirical.

Neill's most famous creation, Lobey Dosser, debuted in the early 1940s and quickly became a beloved character. Set in the fictional Western town of Calton Creek (a play on Glasgow's Calton district), the strip followed Sheriff Lobey Dosser's adventures as he attempted to maintain law and order against his nemesis, Rank Bajin.

The world of Lobey Dosser was a surreal pastiche of American Westerns and Glasgow life. While it drew inspiration from cowboy movies, it was unmistakably Scottish in humour, language, and themes. Lobey himself was a no-nonsense, moustachioed sheriff with a heart of gold, constantly battling Rank Bajin, a scheming outlaw whose name became synonymous with troublemakers in Scotland. Another unforgettable character was Elfie, the world's only two-legged horse, a surreal invention that highlighted Neill's playful imagination.

Neill's use of Glaswegian dialect in Lobey Dosser made the strip especially endearing to local readers. Phrases like "By the beard of the

Prophet!" and "See me, see you, see him?" became part of the strip's charm, making it a true reflection of Scottish humour. The cartoons often carried subtle social and political messages, poking fun at authority figures, bureaucracy, and class struggles while remaining lighthearted and accessible.

While Lobey Dosser was Neill's most famous creation, he produced several other memorable characters and cartoons. His work extended to The Sunday Mail and The Daily Record, where he introduced figures such as G.I. Bride, a humorous take on the war brides who married American soldiers during and after World War Two. Neill's ability to find humour in cultural changes and social phenomena kept his work fresh and relevant.

Another of his notable creations was Sheriff Ned, a Western-themed character who predated Lobey Dosser and shared many of the same comedic elements. His cartoons often depicted working-class Glasgow life with exaggerated but affectionate humour, portraying local dialects, attitudes, and quirks with an insider's understanding.

Despite his popularity, Neill's career was not without its struggles. He reportedly found it difficult to secure fair financial compensation for his work, a common issue for cartoonists of his time. Nevertheless, his impact on Scottish culture was immense.

Decades after his passing in 1970, Neill's work continues to be celebrated. In 1992, a bronze statue of Lobey Dosser riding Elfie was erected on Glasgow's Woodlands Road, making it the only known statue of a two-legged horse. This tribute underscores the lasting affection Glaswegians have for Neill's work. In 2009, the West of Scotland Transport Authority in conjunction with businessman Colin Beattie, a private sponsor, commissioned a bronze statue of the G.I. Bride and her wean, for the newly renovated Partick Railway Station. In recent years, reprints of Lobey Dosser strips have been published, introducing Neill's humour to new generations. His influence can also be seen in contemporary Scottish comics, where his unique blend of surrealism, satire, and working-class humour still resonates.

William 'Bud' Neill was more than just a cartoonist - he was a storyteller who captured the essence of Scottish humour and identity. His work remains a touchstone for many Scots, a reminder of the wit, resilience, and absurdity that define Glasgow's cultural landscape. Through Lobey Dosser and his many other characters, Neill carved out a legacy that continues to inspire artists and entertain audiences to this day.

THE MISSIONARY OF NIGERIA

Mary Mitchell Slessor. Christian Missionary. (1848 - 1915)

Mary Slessor was born in 1848 in Gilcomston in Aberdeen to a poor working-class family which could not afford proper education. She was the second of seven children of Robert and Mary Slessor. Her father, Robert, originally from Buchan was an alcoholic shoemaker and her mother was born in Old Meldrum and was a deeply religious woman. The family moved to Dundee and at the age of eleven, Mary began work as a part-timer in the Baxter Brothers' Mill, meaning she spent half of her day at a school provided by the mill owners and the other half working for the company.

Despite her hardships, Mary developed a deep interest in missionary work. Inspired by the famous Scottish missionary David Livingstone, she dreamed of bringing Christianity and education to Africa. Her faith was strengthened through her involvement in local church activities, where she taught Sunday school and engaged in evangelistic work. When she learned about the work of the United Presbyterian Church's mission in Calabar, she felt called to serve there.

In consequence, in 1876, at the age of twenty-eight, Mary was accepted as a missionary and set sail for Nigeria where she would spend the next thirty-eight years of her life working tirelessly to improve the lives of the people in the region.

She arrived in Duke Town, Calabar, in September 1876. At the time, Calabar was a dangerous place for Europeans due to tropical diseases and cultural differences. Many missionaries had died of malaria, but Mary was determined to adapt to the environment. She quickly learned the Nigerian *Efik* language, which helped her communicate directly with the local people.

One of the most horrific practices she encountered was the killing of twin babies. Many in the *Efik* and *Ibibio* tribes believed that twins were cursed and that one of them was the offspring of an evil spirit. As a result, twin babies were often abandoned in the forest or killed. Mary was deeply disturbed by this practice and made it her mission to rescue these abandoned infants. She took many of them into her home and raised them as her own, challenging local superstitions and working to change cultural perceptions.

Her bravery extended beyond rescuing twins. She also worked to end tribal wars, promote peace and fight against the mistreatment of women. In many parts of Calabar, women had little to no rights and were often subjected to extreme violence, including being forced to drink poison to prove their innocence in disputes. Mary intervened in these cases, offering protection to women and advocating for fairer treatment.

Mary was also known for her unconventional lifestyle. Unlike many missionaries of her time, she did not insist on European customs or dress. Instead, she adopted local clothing, lived among the people and even went barefoot. This endeared her to the local tribes, who saw her as one of their own rather than an outsider trying to impose foreign ways.

Over time, Mary Slessor became a respected figure among the people of Calabar. She gained the trust of local chiefs and was often called upon to mediate disputes. The British colonial authorities even recognised her influence and appointed her as a vice-consul in *Okoyong*, giving her the power to enforce British law in the region. However, she remained dedicated to her humanitarian mission rather than colonial administration.

Her work had a lasting impact on education, health, and social reforms in Nigeria. She established schools, promoted Christian teachings and improved medical care in the region. She also continued to adopt and care for children, raising many as her own.

Despite her influence, Mary lived simply, refusing material wealth or comfort. She devoted herself entirely to the people she served often working under extreme conditions and enduring frequent illnesses.In her later years, her health deteriorated due to repeated bouts of malaria and the harsh conditions she endured. Still, she refused to leave her mission. Even when she was physically weak, she continued working, traveling to villages, and advocating for social reforms.

Mary Slessor passed away on January 13, 1915, at the age of 66. She was buried in Calabar, where she had spent most of her life. The people of Nigeria deeply mourned her loss and she was given a state funeral, an extraordinary honour for a missionary. In Scotland she is honoured through various memorials, including a statue in Dundee.

A CONTENTIOUS BUT FORENSIC INTERVIEWER

Andrew Ferguson Neil (1949 -)

Neil was born in 1949, in Paisley, Renfrewshire to Mary and James Neil. His mother worked in cotton mills during World War Two and his father ran the wartime Cairo fire brigade, worked as an electrician and was a major in the Territorial Army in Renfrewshire. Neil grew up in the council-housed Glenburn area of Paisley area and attended the local Langcraigs Primary School. At age eleven, he passed the qualifying examination and obtained entrance to the selective Paisley Grammar School before securing a place at the University of Glasgow where he studied political economy and served as editor of the student newspaper, The Glasgow University Guardian and was chairman of the Federation of Conservative Students. He graduated in 1971 with an MA with honours in political economy and political science. His early involvement in journalism and politics laid the groundwork for what would become a notable career in the media industry.

Neil's professional journey began at The Economist in the 1970s, where he served as a correspondent in the United States. His time there gave him an understanding of American politics and economics which he would draw on frequently throughout his career. His work at The Economist eventually led to his appointment as Editor of The Sunday Times in 1983, aged only thirty-four, by media mogul Rupert Murdoch. This move was controversial at the time, especially considering Neil's relatively young age and his lack of traditional Fleet Street credentials. However, it proved to be a pivotal decision.

During his tenure at The Sunday Times, Neil revitalised the paper, steering it through a time of transformation in British journalism. He was instrumental in modernising the publication, introducing new sections and expanding investigative journalism. His editorial leadership often courted controversy, particularly in his handling of sensitive issues such as the coverage of the AIDS crisis and contentious foreign policy topics.

Nevertheless, he remained a central figure in shaping public discourse in the UK during the 1980s and early 1990s. According to Neil, he was replaced as *Sunday Times* editor in 1994 because Murdoch had become envious of his celebrity.

In addition to his print journalism, Neil has also made a significant impact in broadcasting. He became a familiar face on British television, known for his incisive political interviews. His BBC shows, including This Week, Daily Politics and The Andrew Neil Show, showcased his talent for forensic questioning. Neil earned a reputation for being a tough interviewer, capable of challenging guests across the political spectrum. His interviewing style was marked by meticulous preparation which made him both respected and feared among political figures.

Neil's political stance has often been shown to be right-leaning and libertarian. He has supported free market economics, criticised the European Union and advocated a smaller state. However, he has also expressed skepticism about some of the more extreme positions within conservative politics. His ability to balance sharp critique with journalistic integrity has helped him maintain credibility across a broad audience, even as political divisions in the UK have become increasingly pronounced.

In 2020, Neil left the BBC, citing the corporation's changing direction and cutbacks to political programming. Soon after, he became the founding chairman of GB News, a right-leaning news channel intended to offer an alternative to what Neil and others viewed as a metropolitan bias in British media. The launch of GB News was widely anticipated, with Neil taking a central role in promoting the channel. However, his time there was short-lived. He left the network just a few months after its launch, citing differences over the channel's editorial direction.

Beyond journalism, Neil has also had a hand in business and publishing. He served as chairman of Press Holdings which owns The Spectator and has overseen its expansion as a significant platform for conservative commentary. He has also made frequent appearances as a public speaker and has been a commentator on issues related to politics, economics and the media industry.

Andrew Neil's legacy in journalism is defined by his commitment to rigorous reporting and his ability to adapt across multiple formats - print, broadcast, and digital. Whether admired or criticised, his presence in the British media landscape has been impossible to ignore. A combination of intellect and tenacity has ensured that Neil remains a major voice in political journalism, with a reputation built on decades of work at the intersection of media and power. He viewed Alex Salmond, whom he interviewed frequently, as the most accomplished and significant Scottish politician of modern times.

SELECTED QUOTES

Harry McShane

"A number of us thought a few of us should join the army and do our propaganda in the Army. In September 1914 I joined the Royal Engineers but I told them straight out that I wouldn't shoot any Germans. I refused to be inoculated so they couldn't send me to the front. They even offered me stripes but I refused. I then took the jag so I could go home on leave and when I did I threw my uniform in the bin and never heard from them again!"

Robert Service

"Be master of your petty annoyances and conserve your energies for the big, worthwhile things. It isn't the mountain ahead that wears you out - it's the grain of sand in your shoe."

"The clock is always slow; it's later than you think."

"It's a different song when everything's wrong, when you're feeling infernally mortal; when it's ten against one and hope there is none, buck up, little soldier and chortle!"

Kate Cranston

"What happened in Glasgow was rather tardily copied in London; other large cities following suit, and the movement spread over the length and the breath of land, was taken up on the continent, and spread to every civilised spot on earth".

Jerry Sadowitz

"I used to think I was great in bed until I discovered that all my girlfriends suffered from asthma."

"Terry Waite? Bastard. I dunno, you lend some people a fiver, you never see them again."

"I probably wouldn't like to admit it so much but there's an element that I've nothing to lose. I sometimes describe my stand up as the longest suicide note ever written."

"You can't be that kid standing at the top of the water slide overthinking it. You have to go down the chute."

Bud Neill

"Ony o' youse blokes goin' the length o' Pertick?" (A GI Bride thumbing a lift home in Arizona)

"It's his teeth, aye. Awfy crabbit. Like a bear wi' nae fags." (A mother about her crying child)

Mary Slessor

"Oh Lord, I thank Thee that I can bring these people Thy Word. But Lord, there are other villages back in the jungle where no white man has gone. They need Jesus, too. Help me reach them"!

Andrew Neil

"It is actually getting much harder for someone from an ordinary background to break through the ranks. In the period from 1964 to 1997, every single Prime Minister - from Harold Wilson to John Major - was the product of a state school".

THE MAN BEHIND SCOTLAND'S ICONIC PEAKS

Sir Hugh Thomas Munro, 4th Baronet. Mountaineer (1856 - 1919)

Hugh Munro was born in 1856, in London but his family had deep Scottish roots. He grew up on the Munro family estate at Lindertis in Angus, Scotland, where he developed a deep love for the mountains and wild landscapes. This passion was further fuelled by his extensive travels in the Alps, where he climbed several notable peaks. Munro became a member of the Alpine Club, a prestigious organisation for mountaineers, and his experiences abroad helped shape his approach to cataloging Scotland's mountains.

Despite his enthusiasm for climbing abroad, Munro remained fascinated by his homeland. At the time, no official record existed of Scotland's highest mountains, and many believed there were only a few peaks over 3,000 feet. Munro set out to change that, using maps, measurements, and personal exploration to create the most comprehensive list of Scottish mountains ever compiled.

In 1891, Munro published his groundbreaking list, known as the 'Munro Tables', in the Journal of the Scottish Mountaineering Club. His work identified 283 mountains in Scotland that exceeded 3,000 feet in elevation. These peaks, now called 'Munros', were further divided into main summits and subsidiary tops with an additional 255 tops recorded.

Munro's meticulous research and classification revolutionised Scottish mountaineering. His tables provided a definitive guide for climbers and hillwalkers, offering a new challenge - climbing all of the Munros. Over time, this pursuit became known as 'Munro-bagging', an endeavour that has since become one of the most famous outdoor challenges in the UK.

Today, there are officially 282 Munros (some peaks have been reclassified over the years). The highest, Ben Nevis (4412 feet), is also the tallest mountain in the UK, while the smallest, Ben Vane (3005 feet), just barely qualifies for the list. Munro's work not only changed the way people viewed Scotland's mountains but also helped foster a deep appreciation for the country's rugged and remote landscapes.

Although Munro dedicated much of his life to mountaineering, he never managed to complete his own challenge. He is believed to have climbed most of the peaks on his list, but passed away before finishing all of them. Ironically, one peak he never reached was *Carn Cloich-mhuilinn,* a relatively modest mountain in the Cairngorms.

Beyond Scotland, Munro was an accomplished climber who tackled peaks in the Alps and beyond. His international experiences provided him with the expertise necessary to accurately measure and classify mountains. However, his passion remained firmly rooted in Scotland, and his work there ultimately defined his legacy.

Today, climbing all 282 Munros is a respected and sought-after achievement. Those who complete the feat are known as 'Munroists' and as of recent years, thousands of people have officially finished the challenge. Some take decades to complete all the peaks, while others attempt speed records, completing the entire list in a matter of weeks. The appeal of Munro-bagging lies not just in the physical challenge but also in the beauty and diversity of Scotland's mountains. From the dramatic ridges of the Cuillins on Skye to the remote wilderness of Knoydart, Munros offer climbers a chance to experience some of the most breathtaking scenery in the world. Hugh Munro's contribution to Scottish mountaineering extends beyond just his tables. He helped popularise hillwalking in Scotland and inspired the creation of national parks and conservation efforts to protect the country's mountain landscapes. The Scottish Mountaineering Club continues to update and maintain his original list, ensuring that his legacy lives on.

Munro-bagging remains one of the most iconic and beloved pastimes in Scotland. Thanks to Hugh Munro, Scotland's mountains are not just landmarks but a lifelong challenge and an enduring source of inspiration.

Sir Hugh Munro died in 1919 at the age of sixty-three from pneumonia, possibly exacerbated by the Spanish flu pandemic. Despite his passing, his influence only grew stronger. The first recorded person to complete all the Munros was Rev. A.E. Robertson in 1901, a milestone that marked the beginning of a lifelong challenge for many climbers.

Hugh Munro's impact on Scottish mountaineering is immeasurable. His dedication to cataloging the country's highest peaks transformed the way people engage with the mountains, creating a challenge that continues to inspire thousands.

A SALVO FOR SCOTLAND

Sara Margaret Salyers. Educationalist and Activist. (1957 -)

Salyers began her professional journey in the media industry, managing two independent television production companies. In this capacity, she served as the investigator and producer for several noteworthy documentaries, including two that were shortlisted by Channel 4 and the BBC and one that received an award from the BBC. These projects often focused on Scottish history and culture, reflecting her deep-seated passion for her nation's heritage.

In 2010, Salyers relocated to the United States, where she joined a community college near Knoxville, Tennessee, as an adjunct faculty member in the Transitional Studies Department. Her role involved assisting 'remedial' students in achieving the academic standards required for college entry, a task she approached with innovative teaching methods. Rejecting the prevailing notion that these students were inherently 'not academic,' Salyers developed a new curriculum designed to dismantle mental blocks and empower students to realise their potential. Her success in this endeavour earned her an 'Outstanding Adjunct' award, highlighting her ability to inspire and educate.

Upon returning to Scotland, Salyers continued her work in education, teaching communications at Fife College from 2015 to 2017. However, her focus increasingly shifted toward activism, particularly concerning Scotland's constitutional status and the sovereignty of its people. She became a key figure in the Scottish Sovereignty Research Group, collaborating with other researchers and writers to challenge the imposition of UK parliamentary sovereignty over Scotland. This work aims to restore the sovereignty of the Scottish people, as outlined in the historic Claim of Right.

Salyers is also actively involved with Salvo, an organisation committed to reinstating Scotland's constitutional integrity and promoting 'the common good.' Through Salvo, she has authored numerous articles and essays dissecting the historical and legal aspects of Scotland's union with the United Kingdom, advocating for a reevaluation of this relationship based on principles of self-determination and popular sovereignty.

In July 2023, Salyers made the decision to resign from the Alba Party, a political organisation in Scotland. In her resignation letter, she cited concerns over the party's stance on sovereignty, particularly the notion that elected representatives could assume custody of the people's sovereignty. Salyers argued that, according to Scottish constitutional tradition, sovereignty is an inalienable right of the people and cannot be transferred to any parliament or representative body. This principled stand underscored her unwavering commitment to genuine popular sovereignty and her belief in the necessity of an indigenous Scottish political establishment.

Beyond her organisational affiliations, Salyers continues to engage in public discourse through various platforms. She maintains an active presence on social media, using it as a tool to educate and mobilise support for Scottish constitutional restoration. Her efforts are not only focused on political sovereignty but also on addressing the cultural and psychological impacts of historical colonisation. Drawing from her teaching experiences in the United States, Salyers has written extensively about the concept of 'internal colonisation,' where imposed foreign values and systems lead to a sense of inferiority and helplessness among the colonised population. She emphasises the importance of reclaiming Scotland's cultural narrative to overcome these deeply ingrained psychological barriers.

Salyers' multifaceted approach combines scholarly research, grassroots activism, and public education to advocate for a Scotland that is both politically autonomous and culturally self-assured. Her work continues to inspire many within the Scottish independence movement, highlighting the interconnectedness of constitutional rights and cultural identity in the pursuit of national self-determination.

THE SAGE OF ECCLEFECHAN

Thomas Carlyle. Historian and Philosopher. (1795 - 1881)

Thomas Carlyle was born in 1795 to James and Margaret Aitken Carlyle in the village of Ecclefechan in Dumfriesshire where his parents were members of the Presbyterian Church. His father, James was a stonemason, later a farmer, who built the Arched House wherein his son was born.

A gifted student, Carlyle initially attended Annan Academy before enrolling at the University of Edinburgh in 1809. Initially studying mathematics with the intention of becoming a minister, he soon abandoned theology in favour of literature and philosophy. His exposure to Enlightenment thought, particularly the works of German idealist philosophers such as Immanuel Kant and Johann Gottlieb Fichte, shaped his intellectual development. Carlyle mastered German and became one of the first English-speaking writers to introduce German philosophy and literature, particularly the works of Johann Wolfgang von Goethe, to a British audience.

After leaving Edinburgh, Carlyle worked briefly as a schoolteacher before dedicating himself to writing. His early works included translations of German literature, notably Goethe's '*Wilhelm Meister's Apprenticeship*' and essays introducing British readers to figures like Schiller and Jean Paul. These efforts helped establish his reputation as a serious scholar of German thought.

However, it was '*Sartor Resartus*', a novel written in 1833 that purports to be a commentary on the thought and early life of a German philosopher called Diogenes Teufelsdröckh (which surname translates as 'God-born Devil's-dung') that first showcased Carlyle's distinctive style and philosophical depth. The book explores themes of existential crisis, faith, and the search for meaning in a rapidly changing world. '*Sartor Resartus*' was initially met with confusion but later gained recognition as a groundbreaking work that anticipated existentialist thought. However, his breakthrough came with '*The French Revolution: A History*' in 1837, a dramatic and impassioned retelling of the tumultuous events that reshaped France. Unlike conventional historical narratives, Carlyle's French

Revolution was written in a vivid, almost poetic style, emphasising the emotional and psychological dimensions of historical events. His portrayal of figures like Louis XVI, Marie Antoinette and Robespierre was marked by a sense of moral urgency, reinforcing his belief that history was driven by great individuals rather than abstract forces.

The book's publication was nearly derailed when Carlyle's manuscript was accidentally burned by a friend's servant, forcing him to rewrite the entire work from scratch. Despite this setback, The French Revolution cemented his reputation as one of the era's foremost historians and literary figures.

Carlyle's fascination with individual greatness culminated in '*On Heroes', 'Hero-Worship',* and the *'Heroic in History'* in 1841, a series of lectures arguing that history is shaped by extraordinary individuals. He classified heroes into different types such as prophets (Muhammad), poets (Dante and Shakespeare) and rulers (Napoleon) asserting that societies thrive under strong, virtuous leadership. This emphasis on heroism reflected Carlyle's broader critique of modernity. He was deeply skeptical of democracy and the increasing mechanisation of society, fearing that materialism and bureaucracy were eroding moral and spiritual values. His belief in the necessity of strong, enlightened leadership resonated with many but also drew criticism, particularly for its authoritarian implications.

However, Carlyle's views became increasingly controversial, particularly his essay '*Occasional Discourse on the Negro Question'* in 1849 in which he argued against the abolitionist movement. His racial views, which defended forced labour in the colonies, damaged his reputation and alienated many of his former admirers. Nevertheless, his call for moral leadership and his critique of materialism inspired figures as diverse as John Ruskin, Mahatma Gandhi and even Friedrich Nietzsche. Carlyle married Jane Welsh Carlyle in 1826, a marriage marked by deep intellectual companionship but also frequent tension. Jane, an accomplished writer in her own right, often struggled with Carlyle's intense personality and long bouts of introspection. Their correspondence remains one of the richest sources of insight into their turbulent relationship and Victorian intellectual life.

In his later years, Carlyle withdrew from public life following Jane's death in 1866. He continued writing but became increasingly bitter and melancholic. He died on February 5, 1881 and was buried in his hometown of Ecclefechan, declining the offer of burial in Westminster Abbey.

THE FIERY VOICE OF SCOTTISH PROTESTANTISM

John Thomas Atkinson (Pastor Jack) Glass. Clergyman (1936 - 2004)

Jack Glass was born in 1936 in Glasgow, into a working-class family. Growing up in the post-war period, he witnessed a Scotland grappling with social and economic change, as well as shifts within its religious landscape. From an early age, Glass was deeply influenced by the strong Protestant ethos that shaped many Scottish communities. He felt a profound spiritual calling during his youth, which led him to pursue theological studies.

Glass attended the Free Church of Scotland College in Edinburgh, where he was trained in reformed theology. However, even during his academic years, it was clear that he was not destined to be a conventional preacher. His zealous personality and fierce independence set him apart. He soon broke away from mainstream denominations, believing they were compromising with Roman Catholicism and liberal theology. This conviction led him to establish the Zion Sovereign Grace Baptist Church in 1965, where he preached until his death in 2004.

Jack Glass's theology was rooted in Calvinism, emphasising the sovereignty of God, the total depravity of man, and salvation by grace alone through faith. He was a staunch believer in the inerrancy of Scripture, viewing the Bible as the ultimate authority on all matters of faith and life. His sermons were characterised by passionate oratory, vivid imagery, and an unwavering commitment to biblical literalism.

Glass's preaching style was fiery, confrontational, and unapologetically direct. He did not shy away from addressing controversial topics, often condemning what he saw as the moral decay of modern society. Issues like abortion, homosexuality and the influence of the Roman Catholic Church were frequent targets of his sermons. His boldness drew large crowds, both supporters who admired his courage and detractors who criticised his harsh tone.

Perhaps the most defining aspect of Pastor Jack Glass's ministry was his militant Protestantism and fierce opposition to ecumenism. He viewed the ecumenical movement which sought to promote unity among different Christian denominations as a dangerous compromise that diluted the truth of the Gospel. To Glass, any alliance with the Roman Catholic Church was tantamount to betrayal.

His opposition to Catholicism was not merely theological but also political. In the context of Scottish history, with its long-standing sectarian tensions between Protestants and Catholics, Glass's views resonated with certain segments of society while alienating others. He famously protested against the visits of Pope John Paul II to the United Kingdom, organising public demonstrations and delivering scathing critiques. During the Pope's 1982 visit to Britain, Glass led protests that attracted media attention, holding banners that declared, 'No Pope Here!'

While many saw his actions as divisive and inflammatory, Glass believed he was standing firm in defence of biblical truth. He often cited the Protestant Reformation and figures like Martin Luther and John Knox as inspirations for his confrontational stance. To him, silence in the face of what he perceived as spiritual error was not an option.

Jack Glass's influence extended beyond the pulpit. He was a political activist who believed that Christianity should play an active role in shaping public policy. In the 1970s and 1980s, he ran for political office several times, though he was never elected. His campaigns were often platforms to voice his views on moral and religious issues rather than genuine attempts to secure political power.

Public demonstrations were a hallmark of his ministry. Whether protesting against abortion clinics, gay rights marches or ecumenical gatherings, Glass was a visible and vocal presence. His protests were often theatrical, designed to attract attention and provoke debate. He would frequently quote Scripture in his public appearances, framing his activism as a divine mandate.

Pastor Jack Glass died in 2004 after a battle with lung cancer, but his legacy remains a subject of debate. To his supporters, he was a fearless defender of the faith, a modern-day prophet who stood against the tide of compromise and moral relativism. They admired his courage, conviction, and unwavering dedication to what he believed was the truth of God's Word. To his critics, however, Glass was a divisive figure whose rhetoric fuelled sectarian tensions and intolerance.

ALMOST KILLED BUT TRIUMPHANT

Sir Matthew (Matt) Busby Footballer and Manager. (1909 - 1994).

Matthew Busby was born in 1909 in the mining village of Orbiston near Bellshill, Lanarkshire. Raised in a working-class family, Busby experienced hardship early in life. His father was killed during World War I when Matt was just six years old.

Football became a passion for young Matt, his talent as a footballer soon becoming apparent, and in 1928, he signed for Manchester City where he played as a right-half; a position that required both defensive acumen and creative playmaking. His intelligence on the pitch, precise passing and calm demeanour made him part of the Manchester City team that won the FA Cup in 1934.

In 1936, Busby moved to Liverpool, continuing to impress with his performances. However, his playing career was interrupted by the outbreak of World War Two during which time he served in the British Army and played in wartime football matches. Busby signed up for the King's Liverpool Regiment but was able to continue with football through his role as a coach in the Amy's Physical Training Corps. He also played football throughout the war for teams including Middlesbrough, Chelsea and Edinburgh's Hibernian.

It was during this period that Busby began to develop an interest in coaching, laying the foundation for his managerial career.

After the war, Manchester United was a club struggling both on and off the field. They had not won a major trophy in decades and their facilities had been damaged during wartime bombings. In 1945, Busby was appointed as Manchester United's manager. His appointment marked the beginning of a new era, as he negotiated unprecedented control over football matters, including team selection, training and transfers, an unusual arrangement at the time. His football philosophy was both simple and revolutionary: he believed in attacking football, nurturing young talent and fostering a strong sense of team spirit. This approach would soon redefine Manchester United's future identity and set the club on a path to greatness.

Busby's approach led to the creation of the legendary '*Busby Babes'*, a group of exceptionally talented young players including Duncan Edwards, Bobby Charlton, Roger Byrne, Tommy Taylor, and Eddie Colman. Under Busby's guidance, the team won the First Division title in 1952 ending a forty-one year league drought. They went on to win back-to-back league titles in 1956 and 1957 with an average squad age of just twenty-two.

Manchester United became the first *English* team to compete in the European Cup, reaching the semi-finals in 1957, signalling Busby's ambition to make United a force on the continental stage.

On February 6, 1958, tragedy struck when the plane carrying Manchester United's players, staff and journalists crashed on takeoff from Munich, Germany, following a European Cup match in Belgrade. The disaster claimed 23 lives including eight first-team players: Roger Byrne, Eddie Colman, Mark Jones, Duncan Edwards (who died later from his injuries), Tommy Taylor, David Pegg, Liam Whelan and Geoff Bent.

Busby himself was critically injured, suffering severe chest injuries and spending weeks in a hospital where he was twice read his last rites. The emotional toll was immense as he lost not just players but friends and protégés he had mentored since their youth.

Despite his grief, his resilience shone through. Encouraged by his wife, Jean, who urged him to continue for the sake of the club, he returned to management. With the help of Jimmy Murphy, who had stayed behind during the ill-fated trip, Busby began the painstaking process of rebuilding Manchester United.

After Munich, Busby faced the enormous challenge of rebuilding both the team and the spirit of Manchester United. He signed key players like Denis Law and nurtured emerging talents such as George Best alongside the resilient Bobby Charlton. He was knighted in 1969, passing away on January 20, 1994. Busby inspired future generations of managers, including Sir Alex Ferguson, who often cited Busby as a role model. His spirit lives on at United's Old Trafford stadium. The Sir Matt Busby Way, leading to the stadium and his statue standing proudly outside, are lasting tributes to the man who built Manchester United into a global footballing powerhouse.

AN ACTOR WITH A POLITICAL VOICE

Peter Mullan. Actor and Activist (1959 -)

Born in Peterhead and raised in Glasgow in a large Catholic family, Mullan experienced poverty, violence, and the effects of alcoholism first-hand, elements that would later inform his creative and political worldview. His father, an alcoholic and abusive man, died of lung cancer when Mullan was seventeen just as he started university. This turbulent upbringing in 1970s Glasgow, against the backdrop of Thatcherism and deindustrialization, left a lasting impression on him. Mullan often cites this period as key to his political awakening.

He attended the University of Glasgow, where he studied economic history and drama. The intellectual climate of university life, combined with his personal experiences, pushed Mullan toward left-wing politics. Over the years, he has become one of the UK film industry's most outspoken socialist voices.

Throughout his career, Mullan has remained committed to exploring issues of social injustice, poverty, class struggle and institutional abuse - both in the characters he plays and the films he directs. His breakthrough role in *'My Name is Joe'* in 1998, directed by Ken Loach (a fellow leftist filmmaker) saw him portray a recovering alcoholic in working-class Glasgow. The film was raw, compassionate, and politically charged. Mullan won Best Actor at the Cannes Film Festival for the performance.

Loach and Mullan would later collaborate again on other socially driven projects, as both shared similar ideological leanings: anti-capitalist, pro-labour, and strongly critical of neoliberalism and austerity.

Mullan's most significant directorial work, *'The Magdalene Sisters'*, was a searing indictment of the Catholic Church and its abuse of women in Ireland's Magdalene laundries. It wasn't just a film, it was a political statement and tackled the intersection of religion, patriarchy and institutional cruelty. Despite its critical acclaim, including the Golden Lion at Venice, the film stirred controversy in religious circles. But Mullan remained unapologetic, describing the film as a necessary exposure of a long-suppressed truth.

He followed up with *'Neds'*, a semi-autobiographical film that explored gang culture and youth violence in 1970s Glasgow. Again, Mullan's background and political beliefs were on full display, highlighting the ways in which systemic inequality and toxic masculinity shape the lives of working-class boys.

Mullan has never been shy about voicing his political opinions publicly. An avowed socialist and self-described Marxist, he has consistently criticised the UK government for its treatment of the working class. He's called out what he sees as the hypocrisy and corruption of mainstream politics, and he's not afraid to speak out against powerful institutions.

In 2010, he was highly critical of the Labour Party under Tony Blair, particularly for Blair's role in the Iraq War. He's also taken aim at the Scottish Labour Party, calling it a "shadow of its former self," and has supported more radical political movements in Scotland.

Mullan was a vocal supporter of Scottish independence during the 2014 referendum. He saw independence not as a nationalist project but as an opportunity for Scotland to pursue a more progressive and egalitarian political path. He believed that breaking away from Westminster rule could allow Scotland to build a society that better reflected its values, including more investment in public services and a rejection of austerity policies.

Unlike some figures in the independence movement, Mullan brought a distinctly left-wing flavour to his support. He emphasised class politics, redistribution of wealth, and community empowerment, often in contrast to the more centrist or business-friendly elements within the Scottish National Party.

Over the years, Mullan has become something of folk hero for many on the Scottish left; articulate, angry, intelligent and unafraid. He's one of the few prominent actors willing to publicly challenge not just governments but also the film industry itself. He's criticised Hollywood's obsession with profit and celebrity and he's been open about rejecting roles or projects that don't align with his values. In a world where celebrity often comes at the cost of conviction, Mullan stands out as a rare and powerful exception.

FAITH, FOOTBALL AND FEEDING THE POOR

Brother Walfrid. Priest. (1840 - 1915)

Brother Walfrid, born Andrew Kerins in Ballymote, County Sligo, Ireland in 1840, was a Marist Brother, educator, and social reformer best remembered as the founder of Celtic Football Club in Glasgow. His life was one of quiet but determined service, shaped by faith and the harsh realities of immigrant life in Victorian Britain. Through his work, he left a legacy that transcends sport, touching on issues of poverty, identity, and community.

Born during the final years of the Great Famine in Ireland, Kerins' early life was marked by hardship. His family, like many others, was deeply affected by famine, colonialism, and forced migration. These experiences shaped his later concern for the poor and dispossessed. In 1864, he joined the Marist Brothers, a Catholic religious order dedicated to education and youth work, taking the name Brother Walfrid after a seventh-century French bishop.

In the 1870s, he was sent to Glasgow, where a large Irish Catholic community had settled. The influx of Irish immigrants into industrial cities like Glasgow was met with discrimination, sectarianism and widespread poverty. Catholics, particularly those of Irish origin, were frequently excluded from economic opportunities and often lived in overcrowded, unsanitary slums.

Brother Walfrid began teaching at Sacred Heart School in the East End of Glasgow, in the heart of this impoverished community. He saw firsthand the devastating effects of poverty on children and families. But he was not content with teaching alone; he believed education had to be accompanied by action. He took the Marist mission of service seriously and began organising charitable activities aimed at alleviating poverty.

In 1887, a hand-written circular was passed around the needy of the area. It stated simply: 'A football club will be formed for the maintenance of dinner tables for the children and the unemployed', although there is controversy over the inclusion of the unemployed as scholars insist that children were only ever included.

A year later, in 1888, in response to widespread hunger and unemployment among the Irish Catholic community in Glasgow, Brother Walfrid founded Celtic Football Club. The club's primary aim was not sporting glory, but social relief. The idea was to use the proceeds from football matches to fund the 'Poor Children's Dinner Tables' – a charity that provided meals for hungry children attending Catholic schools. In this sense, Celtic was not merely a football club but a social project, rooted in compassion and Catholic values. The choice of football was strategic. The sport was growing rapidly in popularity in Scotland, and Brother Walfrid saw it as a way to raise funds and galvanise community spirit. Celtic was also a way for the marginalised Irish Catholic population to assert a positive identity in a city where they were often viewed as outsiders. The club quickly attracted support, both for its charitable aims and its on-field success. The founding of Celtic also had a broader cultural significance. At a time when Irish Catholics were often vilified and segregated, the club offered a source of pride and solidarity. It provided a space where a maligned community could come together, celebrate its heritage, and find a voice in public life. That Celtic's identity has remained closely tied to its Irish and Catholic roots is a testament to Walfrid's original vision.

Despite his pivotal role in establishing the club, Brother Walfrid did not stay in Glasgow indefinitely. In the 1890s, he was transferred to London, where he continued his work as a teacher and religious brother. There, too, he worked among poor immigrant communities, dedicating his life to service until his death in 1915. Today, Brother Walfrid is remembered not just as a founder of one of Scotland's most iconic football clubs, but as a man of principle and compassion. His statue stands outside Celtic Park, a symbol of the club's origins in social justice and community solidarity. For many fans, Celtic remains more than a club—it is a living expression of the values that Walfrid stood for: charity, dignity, and identity.

In a time when football is often associated with vast wealth and corporate interests, Brother Walfrid's legacy serves as a reminder of what sport can be at its best—a means of bringing people together, supporting the vulnerable, and giving voice to the voiceless. His life is a powerful example of faith in action, and his work remains relevant today, not just for Celtic fans but for anyone interested in the intersection of community, culture, and justice. Brother Walfrid is buried in Mount St. St. Michael Cemetery in Dumfries next to St. Joseph's College, where he played an important role in its development.

RED CLYDESIDER AND SUFFRAGIST

Helen Crawfurd. Suffragist (1887 - 1954)

Born Helen Jack, later Anderson, at 175 Cumberland Street in the Gorbals area of Glasgow, her parents were Helen Kyle and William Jack. Her mother worked a steam-loom before she wed. Helen's family moved to Ipswich while she was young. Crawfurd later went to school in London and Ipswich before moving back to Glasgow as a teenager where she was raised in a conservative and religious household. Her early life was steeped in the traditions of the Free Church of Scotland, and she initially followed a path of conventional faith. At the age of twenty-one, she married Alexander Crawfurd, a much older Church of Scotland minister. This marriage initially kept her in a more traditional role, but her growing awareness of social injustices soon pushed her toward activism. The poverty and inequality she witnessed in Glasgow's working-class neighbourhoods were instrumental in shifting her political views.

Crawfurd's political awakening began in earnest through her involvement with the women's suffrage movement. Unlike many middle-class suffragists, who advocated more moderate strategies, Crawfurd joined the more militant Women's Social and Political Union (WSPU), founded by Emmeline Pankhurst. The WSPU adopted direct action and civil disobedience to press for the vote, including protests, property damage, and hunger strikes. Crawfurd was imprisoned multiple times for her activism, and her time in jail only deepened her resolve. She later distanced herself from the Pankhursts due to their support of World War One, a position that contradicted her growing pacifist convictions.

During the First World War, Crawfurd emerged as a leading voice in the anti-war movement. She was a co-founder of the Women's Peace Crusade in 1916, which organised protests and public meetings across the country against the war. She believed that the war served capitalist and imperialist interests at the expense of working-class people. Through her speeches and organising, she helped mobilise thousands of women to speak out against conscription and the human costs of war. Her activism often put her at odds with the authorities and even with more conservative elements within the women's movement.

Crawfurd's political beliefs were firmly rooted in socialism, and her activism increasingly aligned with class struggle. She joined the Independent Labour Party and later the Communist Party of Great Britain in 1921, becoming one of its most prominent female members. Her political trajectory shows a deepening commitment to not only gender equality but also economic and social justice. She was part of the Red Clydeside movement, a period of intense labor unrest and socialist activity in Glasgow and surrounding areas. Alongside figures like John Maclean and James Maxton, Crawfurd fought for better housing, fair wages, and the rights of workers.

One of her most significant contributions was her involvement in the rent strikes of 1915, which erupted in response to exploitative rent hikes during the war. Working-class women, already burdened by low wages and poor living conditions, led the resistance. Crawfurd was among the leaders who organised tenants, held mass meetings, and confronted landlords. The movement succeeded in pressuring the government to pass the Rent Restriction Act, freezing rents at pre-war levels. This was a landmark victory, achieved through grassroots activism led primarily by women.

Crawfurd also engaged in international politics. She traveled to the Soviet Union and was inspired by the Bolshevik revolution, seeing it as a model of working-class empowerment. Her admiration for the Soviet experiment informed her work with the CPGB and her critiques of Western capitalism and imperialism.

Despite her radical politics, or perhaps because of them, Crawfurd was never elected to public office, although she stood as a candidate multiple times. However, her influence extended far beyond electoral politics. She edited the '*Worker's Dreadnought*', a socialist newspaper, and wrote extensively on feminist and socialist issues. Her work laid the groundwork for later generations of activists who sought to unite struggles across class and gender lines. Helen Crawfurd's legacy is that of a trailblazer who defied the expectations of her time. She combined a fierce commitment to women's suffrage with a broader vision of social transformation.

THE HEROINE OF THE JACOBITE REBELLION

Flora MacDonald. The Embodiment of Highland Honour (1722 - 1790)

Born in 1722 on Milton on the Isle of South Uist in the Outer Hebrides, Flora Macdonald remains one of the most romantic and enduring figures in Scottish history. She is best remembered for her courageous role in aiding the escape of Charles Edward Stuart - better known as Bonnie Prince Charlie - after the failure of the Jacobite uprising of 1745. Her act of bravery, carried out at great personal risk, cemented her legacy as a symbol of loyalty, compassion, and Scottish resilience.

Flora came from a family with a complex set of loyalties. Though the Highlands were known for their Jacobite sympathies, the MacDonalds of Sleat, with whom she was associated, were not active supporters of the Stuart cause. This nuance in her background only adds to the intrigue of her story. Educated partly in Edinburgh and raised in a devout Presbyterian family, she was a poised and intelligent young woman, fluent in both English and Gaelic - a trait that helped her navigate the differing social worlds of her time.

The defining moment of Flora's life occurred in the aftermath of the Battle of Culloden in April 1746. The Jacobite forces, led by Bonnie Prince Charlie, were decisively defeated by the British army under the Duke of Cumberland. In the weeks that followed, the prince became a fugitive, hunted across the Highlands with a bounty of £30,000 on his head. It was during this desperate time that Flora MacDonald became involved in his escape.

Despite her family's neutral stance, Flora agreed to help the prince flee to the Isle of Skye, where he might find safe passage out of the country. With the help of her stepfather, Hugh MacDonald, she secured permission to travel with two servants and an Irish spinning maid - who, in fact, was the disguised Charles Edward Stuart. Flora's courage and discretion were critical throughout the journey. Disguised as 'Betty Burke', a maid, the prince boarded a boat with Flora and a small crew and set off under cover of night from Benbecula.

After a perilous sea voyage, they landed on Skye on June 29, 1746. From there, the prince continued his escape and eventually made it to France in September. Flora's involvement, however, did not go unnoticed. She was arrested and taken to the Tower of London where she was imprisoned for a short time. Unlike many others involved in the Jacobite cause, she was treated with a degree of leniency - likely due to her youth, gender, and the widespread public sympathy she attracted. In 1747, after an act of indemnity was passed, Flora was released.

Flora returned to Scotland and married Allan MacDonald of Kingsburgh in 1750. The couple later emigrated to North Carolina in 1774 seeking a better life. However, their involvement in the American Revolutionary War on the side of the British forced them to return to Scotland in 1779. By this time, Flora had endured considerable hardship, including imprisonment and financial losses. Yet, she remained dignified and resilient in the face of adversity.

She lived out the rest of her life on the Isle of Skye, where she died in 1790 at the age of 68. Flora was buried in Kilmuir Cemetery on Skye, and her grave is marked with a simple monument that reads, *'Flora MacDonald - Her name will be mentioned in history, and if courage and fidelity be virtues, mentioned with honour'*.

Flora's legacy lives on in Scottish folklore, literature and popular culture. She has been celebrated in songs, poems and biographies, often depicted as the embodiment of Highland honour and self-sacrifice. Sir Walter Scott, the famed Scottish novelist, was one of many who admired her. Even Queen Victoria is said to have visited her grave and paid tribute. A bronze statue was erected at Inverness Castle in 1896 with her dog Flossie by her side. *'The Skye Boat Song'* is a late 19th-century Scottish song adaptation of a Gaelic song composed in 1782 by William Ross entitled *'Cuachag nan Craobh'* and commemorates Flora's assistance to the Prince.

What makes Flora MacDonald so remarkable is not just her bravery, but her humanity. She was not a soldier or a political agitator, but a young woman who took a moral stand in a time of great danger. Her choice to aid Bonnie Prince Charlie was not rooted in fanaticism, but in empathy and loyalty to another human being in need. In the grand tapestry of Scottish history, Flora MacDonald shines as a poignant reminder of how individual courage can shape the course of events. Her story endures not only because of the drama and romance surrounding it but because of the timeless values she represents - compassion, courage and quiet defiance in the face of overwhelming odds.

SELECTED QUOTES

Pastor Jack Glass

"We do not believe that time is an illusion! Rather, we believe that time only existed for thirty-three years, when God himself fell into the temporal element. Time ended when he ascended to heaven."

"No Surrender...Down with the Pope of Rome!"

"Through the power of prayer I have beaten the cancer the devil had given me." (He died a few weeks later)

Peter Mullan

"What point is there to all the wealth and power that America may have if they can't look after its own?"

"I was on the set of 'Braveheart' and my mate says to me, 'Do you think this film will be any good?' And I really meant this, too, I told him 'Let me put it this way - It won't win any awards.' Cut to: five Oscars."

"I've got nothing against the English but I don't want Westminster ruling my country. I want neighbours not masters".

Sir Matt Busby

"I hope we shall never sacrifice our sporting principles on the altar of big business. We must prevent a football club ever being run like a supermarket with profit the only real motive. The fear is that the big business of soccer will dwarf the sport."

On George Best. "We had our problems with the wee fellah, but I prefer to remember his genius."

Hugh Munro

“Compared with the Alps, our Scottish hills are but small, but they have all the characteristics of mountains, and when seen in winter and early spring it is difficult to realise that the ordnance surveyors have not been mistaken by some few thousands of feet.”

“We don’t conquer mountains. They allow us the privilege to climb them. We treat them with respect.”

Thomas Carlyle

“It is a mathematical fact that the casting of this stone from my hand alters the centre of gravity of the universe”.

“The times are very bad. Very well, you are there to make them better”.

“A great man shows his greatness by the way he treats little men”.

Brother Walfrid

‘A football club will be formed for the maintenance of dinner tables for the children and the unemployed’

THE AUTHOR...NOT A RADICAL!

Ronald (Ron) Culley. Author (1950 -)

Ron Culley was born in Glasgow but lived in a miner's cottage in Kirkintilloch where he spent the first few years of his life with father Ronnie and mother Mary McTavish McLeod. He was soon joined by his two younger brothers, Alastair and Campbell. Returning to Glasgow aged six, he joined his family in a council tenement in Pollok where the lavatory was inside the house rather than on the landing. His father was killed in an accident when Culley was aged nine. Attending Gowanbank and Craigbank schools, he excelled at sport but little else. He was required to repeat third year due to a prolonged year-long bout of truancy, eventually being expelled in fifth year for being *a rank bajin* according to Mr. Alan Mills, the Deputy Headmaster. A confused young man, he fell out (impetuously and ungraciously) with his mother and left home to spend the rest of his adolescence with his grandparents, Madge and Hector McLeod, in another tenement just down the road.

A job as a youth worker when he was only a couple of years older than his charges saw him subsequently being offered a place in Jordanhill College of Education to undertake a Certificate in Community Studies followed almost immediately by yet further education where he qualified as a Social Worker in Edinburgh's Moray House College of Education thereafter taking a job as a Social Worker in Ferguslie Park in Paisley. Married to childhood sweetheart Margaret Ferguson, also a Social Worker, they settled in Paisley and Culley was subsequently promoted to Senior Social Worker for the east end of Paisley.

Aged twenty-eight he was appointed as an Education Advisor to Strathclyde Regional Council in Ayrshire where he and Margaret moved and where their sons Ron and Campbell were born. Still not the emotional full shilling, he left the marital home and took a job dealing with Social Policy in the Chief Executive's Department in Strathclyde Regional Council. A Master's Degree was undertaken successfully at the

University of Strathclyde. Shortly thereafter, Culley was appointed Chief Executive of Govan Initiative Ltd, the largest local economic development company in Scotland. He stayed for thirteen years, the company coming second in the All-Europe private sector Quality Awards in Brussels. While in Govan, in 1994, he married Jean Pollock who bore him two sons, Conor and Ciaran. In 2000 he was appointed Chief Executive of Scottish Enterprise in Glasgow, Leader of the Upper Clyde Shipyards Task Force and was a Member of the Police Advisory Board for Scotland, became a Governor of the Scottish Police College and a Board Member of British Transport Police where he was given responsibility for overseeing Counter-terrorism and was a member of the Police Complaints' Committee. Six years later he was appointed Chief Executive of the West of Scotland Transport Authority where he had responsibility *inter alia* for Glasgow's Subway - where his grandfather, Hector McLeod had driven its trains subterraneously some fifty years previously. After four years in post, he retired aged sixty.

Culley has written sixteen books covering travel, biography, historical fiction and humour; his two books dealing with the suspicious shooting of SNP Vice-Chairman Willie McRae receiving particular acclaim. He is also a multi-instrumentalist, producing a CD in 2019 entitled '*Strings Mostly*' which featured a range of Scottish and Irish jigs and reels. He is also a popular and humorous public speaker on his books, Robert Burns and on the city of Glasgow. He has travelled widely; the foothills of Mount Everest, walked the ramparts of the Great Wall of China, travelled two time zones up the River Amazon from Rio de Janeiro, travelled in India, the Arctic Circle twice, Hiroshima in Japan, visited the Kremlin, the safe house used by Stalin and Lenin in St. Petersburg (an opportunity denied to Russian citizens), climbed the Pyramids and entered the Pharoes' Tombs in the Valley of the Kings in Luxor, Egypt, driven Route 66, visited Washington DC and shook the hand of President Bill Clinton, swam in Iceland, driven through Israel and Palestine and made many other more mundane trips across Europe. Politically, Culley was a Labour Supporter, standing for them in the first 1999 elections to the newly established Scottish Parliament, resigning due to the illegal 2003 invasion of Iraq and joining the SNP which he left following their contemplation of an erection of a statue to the late Queen Elizabeth. He joined Alba and the Scottish Socialist Party but is most comfortable under the wing of the pro-independence Scottish Republican and Socialist Movement. He is a member of Alba, Republic, Scottish CND, Scottish Humanists, SRSM and the Dogs Trust.

His ambition remains to die young at a very old age and still insists that he is the nicest guy he's ever met. His greatest achievement has been the success of his four boys.

www.ingramcontent.com/pod-product-compliance
Lightning Source LLC
Chambersburg PA
CBHW021210090426
42740CB00006B/181
* 9 7 8 1 8 3 6 1 5 4 9 3 8 *